Policing in an Age of Aust

C000102673

Policing in an Age of Austerity uniquely examines the effects on one key public service: the state police of England and Wales. Focusing on the major cutbacks in its resources, both in material and in labour, it details the extent and effects of that drastic reduction in provision together with related matters in Scotland and Northern Ireland. This book also investigates the knock-on effect on other public agencies of diminished police contribution to public well-being.

The book argues that such a dramatic reduction in police services has occurred in an almost totally uncoordinated way, both between provincial police services, and also with regard to other public agencies. While there may have been marginal improvements in effectiveness in certain contexts, the British police have dramatically failed to seize the opportunity to modernize a police service that has never been reformed to suit modern exigencies since its date of origin in 1829. British policing remains a relic of the past despite the mythology by which it increasingly exports its practices and officers to (especially) transitional societies.

Operating at both historical and contemporary levels, this book furnishes a mine of current information. Critically, it also emphasizes the extent to which British policing has traditionally concentrated on the lowest socio-economic stratum of society, to the neglect of the policing of the more powerful. *Policing in an Age of Austerity* will be of interest to academics and professionals working in the fields of criminal justice, development studies, and transitional and conflicted societies, as well as those with an interest in the social schisms caused by the current financial crisis.

Mike Brogden is Honorary Professor in the Department of Applied Social Sciences at the University of Lancaster. He has served as an advisor to several governments on policing matters, and inter alia, served as EU Security Advisor for the first democratic election of 1994 in South Africa.

Graham Ellison is Senior Lecturer in Criminology, School of Law, Queen's University, Belfast. He has been a Senior International Expert to the United Nations Development Programme (UNDP) in Turkey in respect of the civilian oversight of the police there.

Policing in an Age of Austerity

A postcolonial perspective

Mike Brogden and Graham Ellison

Routledge
Taylor & Francis Group

LONDON AND NEW YORK

First published 2013 by Routledge
2 Park Square, Milton Park, Abingdon, Oxon, OX14 4RN

Simultaneously published in the USA and Canada
by Routledge
711 Third Avenue, New York, NY 10017

Routledge is an imprint of the Taylor & Francis Group, an informa business

British Library Cataloguing in Publication Data
A catalogue record for this book is available from the British Library

Library of Congress Cataloging in Publication Data
Brogden, Michael.
    Policing in an age of austerity : a postcolonial perspective / Mike Brogden
    and Graham Ellison.
        p. cm.
    1. Police – Great Britain. 2. Police – Great Britain – Costs. 3. Criminal
    justice, Administration of – Great Britain – Costs. 4. Downsizing of
    organizations – Great Britain. 5. Public safety – Great Britain. 6. Crime
    prevention – Great Britain. I. Ellison, Graham. II. Title.
    Hv8195.A2b75 2012
    363.20941 – dc23
                                                2012006762

ISBN: 978-0-415-69189-5 hbk
ISBN: 978-0-415-69192-5 pbk
ISBN: 978-0-203-10560-3 ebk

Typeset in Times New Roman
by Keystroke, Station Road, Codsall, Wolverhampton

Printed and bound by CPI Group (UK) Ltd, Croydon, CR0 4YY

Mike Brogden would like to dedicate the book to a deceased colleague and friend, Sergeant Paul Perks, whose integrity was too much for his job in the Merseyside Police. Graham Ellison would like to dedicate the book to his parents and to Caitlyn, Ethan, Lauren and Ben.

Contents

Illustrations

Tables

Boxes

Acknowledgements

Thanking individuals for their contribution could logically run into a cast of thousands – many of whom we owe debts to because of their preceding work in the generic world of policing and of crime. Instead, we have restrained ourselves to three groups – those whose scholarship has directly paved the way for this text; those who have contributed directly; and those many others whose ideas we have absorbed. Robert Reiner has been a distant colleague of ours for some 40 years. His work is known to numerous students. But his most recent work has been the most critically useful, especially in the development of the concept of 'social ordering'. We wish him well in his retirement. Another academic of émigré extraction (the postcolonial world does strike back!) is Stan Cohen. His work infuses our own and we wish well him well and admire his past, and continuing, strength and vision. He has inspired many. A final émigré (whilst he may reject the term, although not that of the postcolonial) has pioneered the world of postcolonial studies in Britain. Without Peter Fitzpatrick, the concept of the postcolonial would never have crossed our lips. The long-standing work of another academic colleague, Jock Young, is filtered liberally throughout this text. His work on social exclusion and the Other (in *The Vertigo of Late Modernity*) resonates well with our arguments. More recently, his devastating critique of pseudo-science in criminology and policing studies has gone some considerable way to exposing the emperor's new clothes. We guess we should include an 'honorary Brit', Peter Manning, probably the most perceptive policing scholar of his generation, who has fought the good fight in a relatively antipathetic location for many years – and is good to disagree with! John Lea likewise deserves a mention. His eclectic work also percolates many aspects of this text.

A second layer of tributes goes to those who have, in various ways in the writing of this text, conducted a variety of necessary tasks – from editing to offering suggestions and contributing ideas to collating many sundry and often detailed materials. A few are not mentioned by name – as serving senior police officers they may be, possibly, subject to official sanction. But the following are directly aware of their individual contribution, and will not be subject to police 'incivilities' – Marcus Brogden, Conor O'Reilly, Julie Ford, Nathan Pino, Keith Humphrys, Preet Nijhar, Kieron Reid, Sophy Krajewska, Michael Livingstone, Ruth Jamieson, and Georgina Sinclair. Graham Ellison would also like to thank and acknowledge the support of his colleagues in the School of Law at Queen's over the years. Tom Sutton and Nicola Hartley at Routledge and Julia Willan (who has moved on to pastures new) also warrant special mention for their patience and guidance in seeing the book through to eventual publication.

Finally, there is an emerging cohort of younger international scholars whose ideas – and sometimes naked courage – percolate throughout this work. Until recently, as sociologists, we had never been aware of many brilliant younger academics, who 'talk the same talk' as ourselves but are ahead of us with their ideas and fieldwork, from development studies and from critical social anthropology. This listing does not of course exclude the work of many critical (and some not so critical!) historians and critical legal theorists. Again there are too many people to name. The recent 'phone-hacking' scandal in relation to News International has rightly given a number of journalists and their editors (who should know better) a bad name. Nevertheless, there is another calibre of journalist whose tenacity and perseverance against the odds has uncovered a number of scandals discussed in this book. Again there are too many to mention, but a special word of thanks goes to those journalists working for *The Times*, the *Guardian*, the BBC, and the *Telegraph*.

1 Introduction

Turning over the pebble

U.K. policing has an enviably high worldwide reputation. . . . Our policing is regarded as ethical, professional and overwhelmingly free of corruption.

(Police Superintendents Association Submission to the Winsor Report, 2011, Part 1)

Introduction: crisis and opportunism

In Naomi Klein's *The Shock Doctrine*, the author focuses on the 'fallout' from natural catastrophes, from earthquakes to tsunamis (Klein, 2007). She argues that in every recent case, while the population is traumatized (following Gramsci, 1971), conservative and free-market cadres emerge as entrepreneurs. Through their lobbies, political organizations, and private corporations, they seize the chance to construct profit-making programmes for social change. Ideologies of neoliberalism are legitimized as fabricators of transformative recovery programmes. Conservative 'think-tanks' lead the way under just such conditions, to mount an ascendancy of market intervention in the public sector.

Narratives of crisis have been an especially important weapon in what has in part been a neoliberal offensive in the UK. It is in times and places of crisis that new and conservative responses can gain traction. Desensitized, neoliberal economics 'seizes the day' to expand its doctrine of deregulation, of privatization (and the forked tongue discourse of 'outsourcing') of state utilities and partisan technological innovations. Natural disasters furnish the opportunity for the expansion of free market practices. 'Shock doctrine' uses that public disorientation to impose control by the use of economic shock therapy – physically manifest by the 'Taser on the Street'.

However, a caveat from Mike Davis in *Late Victorian Holocausts* challenges the assumption that many disasters are actually 'natural'. Davis explores the impact of colonialism and the introduction of capitalism and their relationship to disasters such as famines. Davis argues that 'Millions died not outside the "modern world system", but in the very process of being forcibly incorporated into its economic and political structures. They died in the golden age of Liberal Capitalism' (2002 p. 9).

Box 1.1   Thatcher's shock doctrine

Thatcher's shock doctrine was applied in the form of drastic cuts in benefits for the unemployed, the sick, and the elderly. Public services were slashed and the privatization of many services followed . . . Many in the workforce lost hope. Economic and social turmoil ensued. There were street riots in deprived inner-city areas suffering the brunt of Thatcherite policies, the most infamous in the south London neighbourhood of Brixton in 1981 . . . The experiment has failed, and it has failed repeatedly. It has generated deeper poverty and inequalities. It has led to high unemployment, low wages, and even lower benefits that are designed to force citizens to work. It is called competition and it is trumpeted because, in truth, it is good for company profits. The old mantra that corporate profits filter down to the lower rungs of society and benefit the poor remains as dubious today as it was thirty years ago.

Deepak Tripathi (2011)

The hurricanes of recent years may, for example, not be a supposedly natural phenomenon, but result from industrial commitment to fossil fuels and consequent global warming. History may repeat itself, but not always as farce. Crises frequently have human agency.

Both authors contribute to our understanding of seismic events: Klein seeks to explain the opportunism furnished by disasters while Davis furnishes an agency analysis of causation.

It is a major leap from man-made famines to man-made crises in Western societies, but the metaphor and its implications are clear: from catastrophes to financial crises, agency, and especially neoliberal economics, frequently plays a key part, both in causation and in subsequent opportunism, as in the continuing capital crisis of 2008. In the police services of England, Wales, Scotland, and Northern Ireland, the latter had many elements, most obvious during a short period of the summer of 2011 (especially with the reappearance of 'the Other' – the legendary criminal class of Britain and its empire). The background canvas was the major and unique impact of the Western financial crisis on British policing. As detailed in Chapter 3, the coalition government determined on a 20 per cent reduction in state policing resources over a 4-year period (as it had, to differing degrees, on other public services). This determination was unique in Britain. There have been few precedents in the use of that guillotine in the transformation of policing (inter alia, the forced redundancy of many police officers in New York during the financial crisis of the mid-1970s).

This policing crisis was included with various other manifestations of serious malaise, including the culmination of a longstanding mobile phone 'hacking' case against the British press and Rupert Murdoch's News International empire, that reached a crescendo when it revealed the 'cosy' relationship between media tycoons and an emerging elite of politicians and senior police officers at Scotland Yard (with the two most senior officers of the latter resigning). It involved practices of corruption of 'bottom feeders' amongst junior officers 'selling' prurient information to journalists. Coincidentally, the consumerist riots of a new 'dangerous class' in August 2011 revealed major failures in the system of British policing and serious disputes between senior police officers and Conservative governing politicians, a crack in the historical facade of unity between the police and the former party of law-and-order. This was typified by the populist attempt by the Conservative prime minster to impose the colourful American police officer, William Bratton, as an advisor on gang violence to the police in England and Wales. Bratton's tenure was short-lived and he quickly resigned under a cloud of impropriety; and in any case his misjudged pronouncements about 'gang violence' in the UK context were both wrong and embarrassing. Aside from anything else, the UK does not have the fundamental problem with gang related violence that the US does (Churcher and Verkaik, 2011). Other problems illustrated the depth of that financial crisis impacting on the police. For the first time in 60 years, command officers (in Cleveland) were arrested, over allegations of fraud. The investigation conducted by Warwickshire Police cost £100,000 per month. Four similar command officers, formerly of Staffordshire, are under investigation. Among many other such incidents, six elite police officers of the Merseyside Police Matrix Serious Crime Squad were summarily dismissed over self-videoed property theft from 'raid' houses and the subsequent sale of such material on eBay, an incident made even more curious by the appointment of the chief officer who had founded that (alleged) career-boosting squad as the new commissioner of the Metropolitan Police. Furthermore, a new media transparency inquiry revealed, apparently typically, that the Metropolitan Police had only investigated one out of every nine reported burglaries in the previous year (although the new commissioner has declared himself in favour of more transparency).[1] Symbolically, from July 2011 the police have committed to the new single issue of publishing all traffic speeding prosecutions (see Chapter 5). Elsewhere, other manifestations included the death by unilateral police fire of Mark Duggan that precipitated the Tottenham riots in August 2011, after which three other males died in separate incidents over that month in police custody – with 'nonlethal' pepper and CS gas sprays used in the arrests.

There have been 333 such deaths over the previous 12 years in England and Wales, with no police convictions (Davies, 2010) – 'one' subsequent interpretation being that the police frequently arrest dying or self-harming people. Radical hyperbole – that instead of renaming police cells in managerial-speak as 'custody suites', they should instead be called 'death chambers' – should of course be arbitrarily dismissed as the vast majority of those arrested survive well, given the imprimatur of the Independent Police Complaints Commission (IPCC).[2] The revelation that a gamekeeper-turned-poacher, an undercover police officer, had spent seven years as infiltrator, as resourcer, agent provocateur and apparent seducer of female activists (the function has a long lineage – see

Sergeant Popay of the Metropolitan Police in 1833) of a nonviolent protest organization, did not help (Evans and Lewis, 2011). The dismissal by the head of the Metropolitan Police's Antiterrorism Squad of the claim that the ultra-right-wing English Defence League was not a threat to social order and consequent police attention,[3] in the context of the anniversary of the Cable Street protest of 1936, was curious. Nor was the case assisted by further information that the most recent undercover agent and his colleagues had been supervised by a private non-accountable commercial organization, the Association of Chief Police Officers (ACPO).

The coalition government had earlier stoked latent combustibles with its proposal to legislate for a new breed of local crime and policing commissioners (see Chapter 6) at a cost, in the middle of policing cuts, of some £100 million. Conversely, a new breed of policing entrepreneurs has challenged certain shibboleths of British policing from within, and there are currently plans to disband the National Policing Improvement Agency (NPIA) that provides training to police in the UK.[4]

The crisis in British policing is hardly the fault of individual police officers (though the impoverished showing of senior Metropolitan officers before a Parliamentary Select Committee in the News International revelations hardly avoids some responsibility), or of individual politicians. The Police Federation frequently indulges in personalized rhetoric (such as bizarrely accusing the Conservative home secretary of 'revenge' against the police, see Reiner, 2011), and it occasionally touches the keystone in accusing the coalition government of having a hidden agenda in using the crisis to deregulate the state and its public service employees in the interest of market economics. According to the chair of the Police Federation:

> They have and will continue to spew out that much-abused *mantra* that we have to be more effective and efficient, but don't be fooled by this insincere, nihilist, smoke and mirrors, slash and burn policy, for it is in large parts economics and in greater part ideology.
>
> (BBC News, 2011b)

Critically, the crisis has two relevant if disparate components. Western police institutions are one of the major public services threatened by the turmoil in Western capitalism. But police scholars had, however indadvertently, laid the way for such downsizing by providing the justification in varied texts of a process of pluralist policing (e.g. Johnston and Shearing, 2003) in which the state police would increasingly be complemented by profit-making institutions and (optimistically, in practice) voluntary agencies. In the name of more theoretically profound police reform, scholars imbued with a curious sense of history were beneficiaries of a market economy ideology that was about to collapse around the financial citadels of Western societies. Academic theorizing encountered a welcoming economic climate, through the curious rubric of the police extended family.

Box 1.2 An anonymous Metropolitan Police officer's view of the process of police reform

We spend so much time reinventing the wheel – or in this case the truncheon. We used to have Bobbies on the beat, close to communities, who would 'cuff' the odd ragamuffin to stop, what would now be called, antisocial behaviour. Police came from the community they policed and knew who was up to what and when, now called 'intelligence'. Then came the Sweeney and police corruption. Tough hard-boiled coppers chasing dangerous and violent criminals. Stereotypes no doubt, but it feels as if we have been trying to reinvent the Dixon of Dock Green model of policing ever since. And it is still what most people who live in my area want to see. Along came zero-tolerance policing from NY where equal priority was given to small and big crime. There has been success. Police were slaves to nationally set targets, based on good research but focused on the serious and violent end of the crime spectrum. I remember endless conversations trying to get police time spent investigating crime outside the national crime indicators. Yes, they understood that graffiti etc was important to local people, but their success was not judged by catching what, when they want. No more ignoring antisocial behaviour. It works. Local communities re-engage with the police because they are doing something about low-level crime and known troublemakers. This, in turn, leads to better community intelligence on more serious crime and is a deterrent to a culture of 'anything goes'. Cuts in police numbers have not helped, but the Met in London is still following zero-tolerance policing regardless of resource levels. So, do we know what popular policing looks like? Apparently not. Nick Herbert is off to Rotterdam where the community is allocated 20 hours of police time to spend [on tackling problems on their behalf].

(Letter from anonymous police officer (*Local Government Chronicle*, 2012)

Police reform

This text is not the first to focus on crises as a source of change in policing. Several highly competent texts (e.g. McLaughlin, 2007; Morgan and Newburn, 1997; Savage, 2007) similarly direct attention to such events – from the Brixton riots to the racist murder of Stephen Lawrence – as sources of major reform in policing in the UK (including the proposals of the Independent Commission on Policing in Northern Ireland, see Mulcahy, 2006).[5] Generally, the message of those scholars has been that those policing conjunctures produce positive results. For example, the collapse of neo-Keynesian economics in the late 1970s and early 1980s contributed to the events that resulted in the inner-city anti-police riots of the 1980s. Out of the ashes of Brixton and Toxteth arose the Scarman Report (1982) and (later) the Macpherson Report (1999), resulting in institutional changes in the policing of diversity. Specific events such as the (lesser-recalled) Roger Graef television documentary on police interviews of rape victims impacted on the male police approach to such victims.[6] Such scholars, like the new policing pluralists, recognized that crises created opportunities for reform – as in the Stephen Lawrence case and the resultant Macpherson Report on institutionalized police racism.

We view that recent history differently. Scholars have correctly dispelled the traditional perception of the current structure of British policing as the product of a natural untroubled quasi-Reithian evolution (see Emsley, 1996). But many regard policy innovation events as leading inexorably to desirable administrative reform (for example, in the spurious prioritizing of that curious euphemism of incivilities).[7] Out of conflict comes policing progress. Conversely, this text challenges that fundamental assumption. The Scarman Report eventually led (assisted by North American imports) to the elevation of the false dawn of community policing and latterly Neighbourhood Policing as the way forward (Brogden and Nijhar, 2005). That venture in turn led to infinite resource demand and intensive mission creep in policing, based upon an historical misreading of relations between the state police and local 'communities'. Community policing and its affiliates constituted an idiosyncratic waste of resources on varied useless practices, such as Neighbourhood Watch.[8] Innovations from a more conservative perspective – as by the Broken Windows and Zero Tolerance researchers – have much to answer for in lowering the threshold at which young people embark on inevitable criminal careers.[9]

Second, another strand in the research literature assumes that crises such as the current financial imbroglio necessarily lead to positive developments through the technological fix. The oxymoron of 'police science' and the application of a business model and market discipline to state policing[10] reflected in the main both technically incorrect and ideologically perverse assumptions about the public sector. As in Klein (above), police crises may also lead to the promotion of opportunistic snake-oil doctors (there are many examples – Brogden and Nijhar, 1998) with their promise of panaceas for structural deep-rooted problems arising from social and economic inequalities, transparently evident to the residents of the 'mean streets' surrounding grotesque displays of never-to-be attained gross consumerism. Such false prophets take as given that the primary prophylactic against major social schisms resulting in disorder (on the street but not curiously in the banks) problems is the intervention of an opportunistic policing research agenda. The latter frequently offers a kind of pseudoscience, lacking any of the impartiality of reliance on objective historical and comparative data (see Young, 2011, for a trenchant critique of so-called 'scientific' methodologies in crimi-nology).[11] In the words of an unknown IT technician, 'if you feed s— in, you get s— out', as in the core of the natural sciences (reassurance in such matters has not been helped by recent police proposals to count incivilities!). In academic terms, it operates within a paradigm of police sociology rather than sociology of the police. It takes policing goals and functions as a given.[12] Inter alia, such proponents rarely recognize the vacuity of police duties. The latter, in Anglo-American common law societies, were inherited from the Metropolitan Police Act of 1829, which emphasized discretion over practice and purpose for the foot-soldiers of the hierarchical New Police militaristic model without specifying police objectives. That contradiction was bolstered by an array of vaguely determined common law powers, still largely based on the character of the 'Other' on streets (the Town Police Clauses Act of 1848 mirrored the Bloody Code in the extent of its new police offences if not in its severity) as reinforced by a system of lay magistrates who invented an enabling criminal law 'on the trot', especially in the continuity of their frequent use of status rather than action as an offence. Police practice led criminal development, not statute (Dubber, 2005; Chapter 6).

Such administrative reformers, however, do not problematize the police 'role'. Traditional police procedures are rightly questioned, but not police functions (whatever they are). In Manning's words (2010; see also Emsley, 1996), weighed down by the sacrosanct mythology of the Office of Constable, consequent fixations on a quaint motion of locality and vagueness over the weasel social historical concept of democratic accountability constitute the major impediments to a more rational and equable police structure and function. The lack of a statutory determination of police function meant that Sir Robert Peel and his juniors were misread by many, contributing to what Michael Ignatieff (1996) has termed 'ideology as history'. This has constituted a miasma that has impeded the modernization of British policing, a situation that is further compounded by the current financial crisis.

Third, the fiscal crisis in Western societies was a man-made event and provided opportunities for a more insidious agenda. Chaos in social and financial order frequently leads to exploitation by private and state elements with a quite different agenda, most typified by one that turns promotion of the public good into a commitment to the expansion of private profit. Initiated mainly in the Labour–Conservative consensus over law-and-order in the early 1990s, profit-making policing has been the major gainer in the age of austerity. While the primary cause of the 2011 crisis lies within the freebooting neoliberalism of Western banking, one major feature of the response to the resultant fiscal crisis has been the drive to privatize aspects of British public services. An ideological subtext permeates the coalition government's response. Relocating the previously sacrosanct services committed to the public good – from the National Health Service to the fifty-two territorial police forces of Great Britain and Northern Ireland – to the arena of private profit constitutes one major thread throughout this text. Questions of the policing of inequality, of transparency, of training, and of accountability permeate the later discussion of these matters (Reiner, 2012; McLaughlin, 2007).

Fourth, sudden ruptures in the social and economic fabric – such as in the catastrophic consequence of promotion of neoliberal economics in the Western world and the virtual collapse of national economies from Ireland to Greece – expose the way the conflictual history and ad hoc development of modern social institutions has been sanitized (Young, 1999). Accustomed normality and institutional growth are suddenly revealed as a facade over a crumbling, fractious edifice. Conjunctures and crises reveal the conflicting interests in the apparent stable institutions as they are threatened with meltdown. The old criminal class (conceived in this text as a component of the 'Other') rears its head. What have previously been regarded as cases of evolutionary tranquillity – a model for so-called transitional and post-conflict societies (see Chapter 4) – are now perceived as a medley of internal and external contradictions as each agency fights for a share of a diminished cake. A dialectical relation is revealed: an equation in which 'thesis' conflicts with 'antithesis'. A temporary synthesis emerges before dividing again into a thesis and antithesis – the state police and the periodically estranged 'Other'. The 'Other' and the state police are two sides of the same coin: the harmonious facade, such as the mythology of policing by consent, and the natural history of state institutions such as the state police is revealed as totemic, without substance.[13] The institution is, and always has been, driven by a power-play between the more resourceful parties whose interests are primarily affected. In the words of Jefferson and Grimshaw (1984) 'the history of the police (is) the successive outcome of struggles between classes, parties and groups, struggles which are necessarily constrained by the context within which they take place, even in the process of transforming that context' (p. 24). *Shock Doctrine* demonstrates how material changes can be conducted when the vox pop is so traumatized that it can passively accept changes that would otherwise have been inconceivable. The contradictory cuts in British policing turn the spotlight on socially illegitimate coalitions of powerful forces, like the close relationship between senior police officers and News International in delaying an inquiry on the latter's freebooting criminality. State policing has always been subject to (and sometimes succumbs to) pressures over practice and function, internal as well as external. Crisis opens the door to opportunism and unholy alliances between institutional and state interests on one side, and formerly critical scholars of policing, now bemused by conceptions of police governance and of 'private' nodes of security and risk.

Finally, in considering the state of the British police, we are aware of a fundamental theoretical void. It would be opportunistic and wrong, for example, to simply focus on isolated serious policing malpractices without reference to context. This, although a study of an institution, is not an institutional study. Events and trajectories, divorced from a context of political economy, have little meaning and can be reduced to isolated anecdotes. Context, structure and on occasion the acts of individual agents, are the key to analysis of British policing practice. Dramatic police failings do not, of themselves, demonstrate instability and serious limitations in the policing institution. The deaths of Jean Charles de Menezes, Ian Tomlinson and Mark Duggan as a result of police malpractice rightly make good newspaper copy and raise public concern. But Duggan's death is especially important not because of what it tells us of the characteristics of individual officers and their competence, but because it epitomizes a process of widening the gap between the priorities of the police and of the policed. Unless such events can be demonstrated to be part of a systemic process of police inefficiency at best, and casual brutality at worst (unlike the Stephen Lawrence case, which revealed institutionalized racism), they indicate relatively little about policing as a structural problem. Such a division is subjective. Cases like the extraordinary experience of an undercover officer stretch credulity. The officer was a member of a dedicated unit administered (at the time) by the private fiefdom of the ACPO. He operated on the verge of legality for seven years against nonviolent 'green' activists before inevitably 'going native'.[14] In Maurice Punch's felicitous terms (2009), how do you distinguish between 'bad apples' and 'rotten orchards'? Nevertheless, however qualified, our primary concern is with structure rather than agency.

The narrative: postcolonial theory and policing

Academic studies of policing are bedevilled by different theoretical approaches. Some reach back to the past[15] to reinvent a quaint notion of police science. A house divided – like Caesar's Gaul – into three parts. Left realism was committed to praxis and included, amongst many other themes, the recognition that working-class people were the primary victims of crime, and often the offenders (especially with regard to minor crime) came from cognizant social strata. A second theme was developed within the Home Office and later in universities, as its practitioners spread into relatively flexible academic positions. Its primary motif, via the instrument of crime surveys, was to concentrate both on unrecorded crime and the disjunction between the 'actuality' of crime and the 'fear' of crime. Beyond these two comparators were the Ultras, still fighting the state and especially its apparatchiks the 'zookeepers of deviance'. But there was also a growing influence within academic studies of policing – as in the early 1960s from the US of a new police science[16] – that sought via a resurgent positivism into applying scientific methods and principles, bereft of policing objectives and structural inequalities, to enhance techniques of apprehension and crime stabilization.

It is therefore with reluctance that this text seeks to subsume many of the excellent critical UK texts (see above) with an alternative approach. Many current academics (within the interdisciplinary of literature, politics, critical social history, critical legal studies, and psychology) have contributed to the development of postcolonial theory, but few scholars (Agozino et al., 2009; Cain, 2000; Cunneen, 2011) have appreciated the insights of postcolonial theory in focusing on an institution that was a product of a period of both external (Brogden, 1987a, b; R. Williams, 2003) and internal (Storch, 1975, 1976) relationships between the rulers and the ruled.[17] This text is committed to both placing state policing as an institution – counter-intuitively – within the realms of political economy (Neocleous, 2000) and especially of globalizing neoliberalism (Aas, 2007; Mosley, 2007) and of postcolonial theory (Ghandi, 1998; Nijhar, 2009). The latter approach (as in Chapter 6) is central to understanding the key proposition of this text.

We propose, first of all, that state policing has always been committed to maintaining a divisive social order. Targeting of 'police property' has been a perennial problem (Reiner, 2012). As Loader and Mulcahy suggest:

Policing, of course has long been directed mainly at the poor, the powerless, the dispossessed. Police contacts tend to be most frequent and adversarial with social groups that make routine use of social space: those who lack the resources needed to shield their activities from the public gaze.

(Loader and Mulcahy, 2003, p. 12)

Second, that most state police forces have been designed within a colonial experience with regard to the indigenous (imperial and provincial). As Emsley (2009) notes, the transfer of colonial and provincial personnel lubricated the way common standards and notions of the Other still reflect that structural embrace, purpose and practice. The Other of colonial imaginative construction[18] was both an external and internal construct that determined, and continues to determine, the object of police practice. As in Said (1979), the Occident (for that read the metropolis) constructed the Other. For example, the 'criminal tribes' of India were legally proscribed though appropriate discourse as the 'habitual criminals' of Victorian Britain (Nijhar, 2009). Empire created the Orient in its own image. However, there are several criticisms that can be levelled at Said's (1979) heuristic approach.

First, he assumed that the Orient accepted as passive subordinates the construction applied to them by Westminster. Second, he applied categories of Orient to those geographically/ethnically distinct from that of the European colonialists. Third, Said did not appreciate that the concept of the Other was not just applicable to the colonies of the Empire but should equally be applied to the lower strata of an increasingly heterogeneous Occident.[19] The 'Other' was a concept that could be applied not just to the Orient but also to ethnically similar (on a Darwinian scale) lower-class members of the Occident – as in the 'criminal'/'dangerous' classes (see Hay and Craven, 2004).[20] Fourth, Said did not credit social formations within the Orient as having the capacity to respond: in this context, to construct countervailing images of the state policing system of the Occidental within what Loader and Mulcahy (2003) call a 'residual memory'. The Other has the capacity to fight back and construct the oppressor in its own terms – a process of desubordination (Loader and Mulcahy, 2003). The relevance of this theme to the current text is threefold.

State policing was designed both locally and imperially to deal with the Other (though as Reiner notes, one model of the 'Bobby' was sold to the local and another, the Irish, to the Orient, though in practice the two were not that different – Brogden, 1987a, b). From the 'criminal classes' in the early nineteenth century to more recent 2011 English rioters, policing the Other, local and imperial, was especially important in legislative replication. The domestic missionary (Storch, 1976 – the example is from the Salvation Army) spread the secular gospel of civilization to natives in the Empire and to the provinces. Second, race/ethnicity per se was relatively unimportant. The policing target, which embraced both the criminal classes and the criminal tribes in its tutelage mandated then as now, was the Other. At the time of the Metropolitan Police Act (1829), the Other was mainly white (although including stranded Lascar seafarers and migrant Irish – see Nijhar, 2009). By the early twenty-first century it had come to encompass a range of disparate and overlapping ethnicities. Reiner (2010a) is empirically wrong to claim that its incorporation into the industrial working class is a viable explanation of the apparent decrease in the level of recorded crime in the 1890s.[21] What the latter had, and have, in common is their continuing contestation of public space with the state (and indeed latterly with the private police, especially in the new shopping malls and other sites of mass private property) (Shearing and Stenning, 1987). Space, especially the public streets, was the arena of contest between state police and the Other. As many histories confirm (see Chapter 5), since their formation the state police forces of England and Wales have maintained continuity in this role. From the use of an array (the Bobby symbolized 'the state on the street' – see Brogden, 1991) of adversarial street powers,[22] 'normal' police work has been committed to the beat, most intensively on the streets inhabited by the Other. The continuity of this role is exemplified in both the events leading up to the urban riots in England of 2011, such as that symbolized by the continuity of discriminatory use of stop-and-search powers (Newburn, 2011), to the subsequent uneven contest by the Other engaged in the mayhem of mass property theft that August and the reaction of the state police.

In the latter context, police racism was one critical issue; a product of both an extraordinary police killing and incompetent police reaction against a backdrop of the traditional policing of the Other in public space. Recent – let alone past – history had not been learnt. But the convergence of black, Asian, and white rioters in conflict with the police suggests that racism itself was a subcategory in both opposition to the police and in the unified pillaging by the Other. The latter concept exists over and above the single issue of race or ethnicity. Place, unemployment, and residential location were the key links between the practices of the New Police in 1829 and the riots of 2011. Social ordering against the Other was central, not limited to the hybridity of race and ethnicity.

In more traditional critical accounts the state police have been portrayed primarily as the apparatus committed to the defeat of the industrial working class. However, while that continues to occur (as most evidenced during the miners' strike of 1983–84), the primary police role in class relations has been one of disciplining (some would say 'regulating' or 'sanitizing') the urban 'Other'. In that conflict, the state police still receive majority support from the general public. As every opinion poll demonstrates (whatever the qualms regarding such methodology in recounting the view of the disenfranchised Other), the majority support a policing style that has changed little: from the solitary beat patrol of the period between the 1830s and 1950s to the unit beat of the 1960s and Neighbourhood Policing strategies of the present day.

The various opinion polls and surveys demonstrating support for that police action have a curious twist. While generically, the majority support such action, the minority Other appearing in such polls as oppositional (they are after all the most likely to meet the police in adversarial contact) demonstrates the continuity of such divisive state policing. The Other, whatever its heterogeneous composition, is the main target of police ordering powers (street regulation). In the process of street policing, the Other is deemed to consist of non-citizens (Balbus, 1977).

This thesis of the structural underpinning of the British police in pursuing the control of the 'Other' is the central theme of this text. In organization, in generic training (despite the growth of more specialist state police agencies), this is what police do with majority consent. Arguments about the rhetorical police commitment to the so-called frontline[23] are essentially debates about the policing of the Other, irrespective of the degree of threat to state institutions by the latter. The Other becomes most visible in the context of crisis – both a general neoliberal economic crisis which impinges on the Other the most, and the crisis of a police institution whose policing of the Other in public space has become more transparent and visible due to commercial media developments. The view of it as being incompetent and partisan contrasts with the positive residual memory of a mythical police that contributed to local harmony in the post-war years (see Loader and Mulcahy, 2003).

This introductory chapter sets the scene of an *Alice in Wonderland* world, by considering critically the current state of play in the British police system with the advent of the criminal justice guillotine cuts, especially with regard to the process of modernization. The text generally concentrates, for ease of compression, on the English and Welsh forces, though drawing also upon materials from the different jurisdictions of Scotland (especially prosecution procedures) and Northern Ireland (in the context of the peace process and policing transition). Lessons are drawn across the board. Inevitably, the material selected for analysis is selective and partisan. We make no apologies for the latter. Official sources present a particular, partial image (Brogden and Nijhar, 2005). Impression management (Manning, 1992) is crucial to the official presentation of state policing, especially since a police elite has been able to command such a powerful voice in the post-war years (Loader and Mulcahy, 2003). Some of those practices are both more ludicrous and politically cynical than others (such as the requirement for local forces to publish website postcode crime rates, with no caveats regarding the tenuous nature of such data, bolstered by including a medley of subjective Anti-Social Behaviour Orders (ASBOs).[24]

Policing in an Age of Austerity is not a crusade to redress the balance. That would be impossible. However, there is a different story to tell. It is one that recognizes that many of the basic premises and data on which British policing are founded are fundamentally flawed: especially the role of policing in relation to crime prevention and resolution, and the curious way Peel's key recommendation for an impartial prosecution system has been exorcised from history.

One controversial claim to be dissected is that British policing is not just unique – with many 'bastard' progeny overseas – but qualitatively better. Being unique does not make it ideal despite the institutional histories. In the wake of the recent trial in Perugia of Amanda Knox and Raffaele Sollecito, it is both easy and xenophobic to scorn other juridical and policing systems. In the UK, this mythology also exudes a notion of Britishness (Hall et al., 1978) of the natural evolution of policing from the days of Sir Robert Peel; in their role as 'domestic missionaries' (Storch, 1976); and in the importance of the 'Bobby' in post-war mythology amongst certain social strata (Loader and Mulcahy, 2003; McLaughlin, 2007;

Reiner, 2012). As a cursory reading of many Home Office reports shows, this evolutionary history justifies legitimacy. It exudes a portrait of policing as a dramatic and dangerous task with the emblematic signifying of the police as embodying the moral high ground in the fight against evil. Crime control and the hubris of public consent are the primary (flawed) signifiers of the evolving role of the police.

The view within the text is that a different reading of the materials presents British policing itself as the result of disputed development, not the outcome of an evolutionary social Darwinian process.[25] As Manning (2010 p. vii) phrases it: 'Democratic police systems are usually seen as natural developments, the result of a salutary yet unexplicated process'. In reality, the present state of Anglo-American policing more generally – and the policing of England and Wales in particular – represents an uneasy compromise between unequal partisans, not a naturally evolved product: the impartial congruence within a society in supposed social harmony. The text draws insights from the political economy that directs neoliberal intervention in the so-called modernization project: succinctly, as with other public services, increasing privatization. Policing-for-profit is to be increased and even the full-scale privatization of the Probation Agency has been mooted in a coalition proposal. Finally, in disentangling the woollen skeins of past and present, it emphasizes the continuing discord between the local nexus of policing and the polar opposite of increasing centralization.

The state police is an antiquated early nineteenth-century idea that was born in the crucible of urbanization and of empire-building, and in the rise of the industrial working classes (Brogden, 1982; Palmer, 1988). It may have become a complex multilayered bureaucracy, with specialist units (Reiner, 2012); but practices have changed little since then (Manning, 2010), with its primary commitment to challenging the 'Other' and their use of public space via the beat system. But myths perpetuated during late modernity are liable to gradually disappear as memories and diverse accounts emerge, principally from the multi-textured social formations of migrants and younger people.

Policing in an Age of Austerity uses the vehicle of the Western financial crisis, with its resultant major cutbacks in essential state-funded services, to deconstruct one such institution – the supposedly evolutionary history of an agency epitomized by that fantasy creature the British 'Bobby' (Emsley, 2009; Reiner, 1992) and, more importantly, the institution in which he/she is a lowly foot-soldier: 'The traditional myth of the British policeman includes concepts of friendliness, reassurance, solidity, non-aggressiveness, lack of firearms . . . the cliché of a corpulent jolly bobby patting a little girl on the head!' (Fiske, 1990 p. 88; see also Morton, 1994). The holder of the Office of Constable is the taken-for-granted symbol, like the London bus, of an insular history (Loader, 1999; Loader and Mulcahy, 2003), of colonial experience of ruling the Other (Sinclair, 2006), and of contemporary cultural and media reproduction (McLaughlin, 2007).

Together with the empirically flawed assumption of local policing, it is this myth of the sacrosanct beat and the Bobby with original powers that is at the centre of the key problems of modernizing policing in England and Wales. It represents the conflict between the local and the national, the centre and the periphery. This mythology is reinforced by the Office of Constable status whereby a police officer has an original and not a delegated jurisdiction, and is directly answerable to the law for their actions. The image of the constable is tightly intertwined with a notion of locality. Localism and the constable are symbiotic. Centrifugal forces may pull policing towards the core, the central state and beyond. However, as Savage (2007 p. 203) phrases it,

> British policing, as well as being pushed 'upwards' by centrally driven forces towards greater standardization and consistency, which the National Policing Plan and the Police Standards Unit would help deliver, was also being pulled 'downwards' to become more responsive to local needs and priorities, more accountable to local communities and more engaged with those communities.

Similar myths continue of popular 'local' law enforcement, a major impediment in the modernization process. Local 'mission creep' continues: the infinite expansion of neighbourhood British state policing, in a variety of tasks and presences, emphasizes locality. Local police authority supervision and Local Crime Partnerships, together with the new Police commissioners, pull British policing in one direction. Other exigencies: technology; efficiency; terrorism; globalization; economic processes; cross-border crime; migration; political centralization; policing intervention overseas through aid missions; the cost-benefits of central purchasing and coordination; the merger of regional policing infrastructures, drive towards the centre (see Box 1.3). You can rarely stop structural forces in their tracks. The continuing myth of the Bobby and of the Local attempts to do exactly that. This theme is highlighted inter alia in the Winsor Report (2011).[26] Winsor praises the discretionary role of the constable but fails to recognize that it would take a highly determined officer to exercise that discretion against the advice of his superiors. It is very difficult to understand how, as the Winsor Report assumes, such an odd status for a state office holder can be coupled with concerns for efficiency, transferability and efficacy in the twenty-first century, given further the realization by many senior officers of that pointless, local, adversarial policing of the Other as its key practice.

Box 1.3   A people's police force

There are problems in holding people to account for their responsibility for dealing with problems of crime and disorder at the local level . . . the lack of clarity about the purposes of the criminal justice system as a whole . . . not least because conflicts can arise between police commanders, police authorities, and local councils when there is confusion over the purpose of police work.

(Blunkett, 2009 p. 8)

What is policing? A debate without resolution

In recounting our alternative perspective of the British Bobby and of the traditional beat, we are conscious of limitations of both theory and practice. Theory in policing, as elsewhere, is convoluted. Many accounts draw on the accumulated work of Egon Bittner that the primary focus of the police is essentially to regulate and protect the social order backed by legitimate force (Bittner, 1994). Unfortunately, Bittner's discursive work, while critical in emphasizing the social ordering coercive role of the state police, contains many problems. The police are unifying and organic in their use of not just legitimate but also legitimized coercion. But Bittner does not ask by whom or on whose behalf. It is a street-level phenomenological view (see the discussion in Manning, 2010 pp. 31–7) that serves little purpose in the exercise, and with no questioning of its social value. It takes the world as it is (or rather appears): the 'view-from-the-street' (but only the perspective of the state police). It assumes that policing is a unifying function rather than structurally divisive, especially in the policing of the 'Other'.

Further, as Manning, amongst others, points out (e.g. Johnston and Shearing, 2003) we are in an age of questionable plural policing institutions (Reiner, 2012) which are not acknowledged in Bittner's analysis. The establishment based around the sworn constable forms the basis of policing in the UK and generically across common law jurisdictions. 'Police fetishism' (Reiner, 2007 p. 276) characterizes state police as the necessary prerequisite of modernism. However, there are many other institutions. 'Policing' in the current literature is an oxymoron of a concept and confusing – mainly because few have ever grappled with what exactly is the police function. The term is open to many differing interpretations. Does it simply mean the uniformed sworn officer on Anglo-American streets? But what about the European 'high' police of the Napoleonic Code, the state security police of many dictatorial societies, informal policing by vigilantes, and the extraordinary expansion of commercial (private) police? As early as the 1980s, in Britain non-sworn social ordering agencies had become increasingly apparent, making a substantial contribution to social ordering in public services. Questions were raised such as 'Was it necessary for the police to undertake all the tasks that they performed? Might some tasks not be contracted out? Might they not be performed by other agencies?' This recognition of other potential contributions to social ordering included a push to utilize more civilians in the police service, both in policing-for-profit, the civilianization of certain policing tasks, as well as increased reliance on volunteers such as special constables (Morgan and Newburn, 1997).

The continuation of informal justice

Informalism is the study of normative practices of social ordering in civil society. A wider definition of policing as social ordering (Shearing, 2001; 1992; Shearing and Wood, 2006), rather than of the conventional state institution, would recognize the extent to which social ordering problems are frequently conducted outside formal state mechanisms. In early societies – pastoral and hunter-gathering – most conflicts, disputes and injuries to others were resolved according to traditional values and local pragmatics. In a dispute between two parties, a third agent would act as intermediary or dispute solver in that process. In colonial societies, pluralistic systems of dispute resolution acted in parallel – the social order of colonialism at one level, and the traditional structures of mediation of indigenous people. In the modern state, many such practices continue: teachers mediate in disputes between pupils; referees rule over football games; and Citizen's Advice Bureaus seek to intervene between clients and organs of the state. Informal justice has historically always played a major part in social ordering. Nevertheless, increasingly state dispute mechanisms have dominated social relations, as highlighted by the juridical reform of the Benthamite era and the rise of the New Police. The informal sector diminished and the formal systems expanded as essentially civil disputes became subject to state determination. However, there is no natural decline in informal social order policing processes: they 'wax and wane'. In particular, they tend to reappear, and indeed become defensive strategies in societies during a period of crisis. Thus under the latter years of apartheid, the People's Courts of the black townships in South Africa become the dominant structures of justice for the majority, denying the legitimacy of the state system (Brogden and Shearing, 1993). With the advent of democracy, such informal structures have largely disappeared. Fiscal crisis may see their resurrection. There are three key features of such informal justice processes under modernism. First, as the largely mythical rural *Gemeinschaft* is replaced by the functional complexity and schisms of the *Gesellschaft*, the formal justice processes were increasingly displaced by the encroachment of the state. In the UK, amongst other Western societies, informalism and bottom-up security governance initiatives have been colonized and crowded out by formal practices (Ellison, 2007). This can be seen for instance in the ways that the police institution inexorably expands its mandate, assuming responsibility for resolving many minor civil disputes as in the concept of police action against incivilities (McLaughlin, 2007). New structures sponsored by the state attempt to resurrect and incorporate past forms of dispute resolution (such as civil justice), as in the development of Dispute Resolution Centres (Lea, 1992; Matthews, 1988) but specifically in the last decade by the adoption of Restorative Justice schemes and initiatives in many jurisdictions (Lea, 1992).

More pertinently, sworn police functions have increasingly been usurped or bypassed, as in Western military interventions overseas, by private contractors committed to policing as a profit-making exercise on behalf of the few against the interests of the non-profiting majority.[27] Different functions from community safety to state security and counter-terrorism, to commercial security of property and profit motivation suggest that the label 'police' is used to describe a maze of functions, practice, and rewards. Private companies, within the ideology of neoliberal economic dogma, increasingly conduct traditional state police functions (often carefully cultivating and employing present and former state police personnel). We are witnessing an increasing state–corporate symbiosis in the sphere of policing and security (O'Reilly and Ellison, 2006). As we discuss in Chapters 3 and 4, senior police personnel flit effortlessly and seamlessly between the state and the corporate security sector via a revolving door (see O'Reilly, 2010). In addition, a back door process of rehiring has allowed hundreds of recently retired officers from the Royal Ulster Constabulary (RUC) in Northern Ireland to embark on alternative careers within the new Police Service of Northern Ireland (PSNI) and other UK forces as civilian police/security advisors.[28] Many such officers play a key role in the promotion of what has been termed the UK Police plc brand internationally (discussed in Chapter 4). Local council initiatives may pay private security companies to conduct patrol duties on housing estates and elsewhere, and commercial agencies pay for the private policing of major private property assets like shopping malls and airports. Increasingly, guard-type duties are contracted, as in escort duties for judicial requirements, the transport of cash deposits, and the controversial forced expulsion of illegal migrants. The state police appeared to be conducting many other tasks than those easily located under the rubric of private enterprise. Amongst many other examples, eight seaports in England (and two in Northern Ireland) have their own independent police forces (although the numbers of officers overall is small). The UK Border Agency furnishes many social ordering functions. What has been termed the UK's FBI (Federal Bureau of Investigations), the Serious Organised Crime Agency (SOCA), includes police officers, private security contractors, international police personnel, government officials, statutory agencies and civilian employees assuming a variety of formerly excluded roles. SOCA works as a policing agency, specializing in covert operations and intelligence-gathering, but its staff now combines civilians with sworn officers, both enjoying many delegated powers (Jones and Van Sluis, 2009 pp. 201–5). SOCA is answerable to the Home Secretary, not to a police authority. Nor should one neglect the expansion of technological policing via devices such as CCTV.[29]

Increasingly, civilians contribute to both direct and indirect functions for the different police forces. The significant drive to civilianization began during the 1980s (Newburn et al., 1994) supposedly dealing with non-core police duties. Home Watch schemes may have faded as a transitional gimmick, but Police Community Support Officers (PCSOs), under a variety of labels with limited policing powers, operate in the limbo land of central state and local authority interstices. The Home Office has encouraged and sponsored civilian social ordering through any number of similarly transitory gimmicks: for example, developing ad hoc schemes such as Shopwatch, Busbeat, Hospital Watch and many others. This litany leaves out all those other agencies that may conduct police functions informally, if the definition of policing is widened to encompass simple 'order maintenance' in many localities. The concept of accountability is blurred in this convergence of private and state ideological interests. Much policing has become commodified (Loader, 1999). While the variations are germane to an analysis of policing as opposed to that of 'the police', bodies of sworn constables with (mainly) common law citizens' powers have complex relations with civil society, in order maintenance, crime prevention and investigation (Crawford, 2006a).

The discourse of policing needs clarifying (see Table 1.1). Recent Western scholarship in policing has come to distinguish between the state police (curiously

Table 1.1 A typology of policing

	State police	*Commercial security*	*Civil police*
Primary objective	Maintaining traditional social order	Profit making for shareholders	Maintaining local social order
Secondary objective	Preventing crime: determined by paymasters	Enforcing particularistic rules	Reacting to local moral panics
Legitimacy	Based on office of constable delegated powers and delegated authority	Vague: mix of specific and delegated authority	Based entirely on local vox pop
Priorities	Targeting 'crimes' as determined by political and organizational elites Public order	Various: from static and mobile guard duties to national security and counter-terrorism	Specific local problems
Practices	Notional beat duties; intelligence work; 24-hour social work	Guard duties; corporate security activities such as intelligence work	Various: night patrols; potential for vigilantism

referred to as the 'public police' in recent texts, implying a uniformed police beholden and acting on behalf of a democratic state for the public good) and policing-for-profit (the 'private' police, equally confusing given its primary goal one of maximizing the profits of company shareholders). The problem is not just one of semantics in defining policing. Many studies, following Shearing and Stenning (1987) and consensual North American studies, refer to the neutral-sounding 'public police'. This distinction is important but inadequate. The notional public police implies a commitment to the common good as well as giving priority to the equally notional consensual citizenry. In an unequal society, the idea that such police continually balance out competing interests for the citizenry in their practices is a long way from reality. Ultimately, state policing is committed to the defence of the socially and economically unequal political order of the state and to particular forms of local social order (Reiner, 2012; Neocleous, 2000). State police are only required where there is no such consensus. Public police are paid from the public purse to enforce order against social dissidents. We refer instead to the 'police of the state' or to 'state police' (essentially, 'sworn constables') since to our mind this is a far more accurate characterization. The concept of private police is also peculiar. The term again is a North American import that conflates two different systems – corporate profit-making with voluntary policing (as in informal justice practices). Private police in this text is a synonym for 'policing-for-profit'. Civil police refers to social ordering conducted by non-sworn, non-commercial civilians (see Crawford, 1997).

However, this volume is specifically concerned with the construction and practice of the state police in Great Britain and Northern Ireland, as mythologized and reified under the rubric of the New Police of Sir Robert Peel vintage – one rendered under common law as conducted by sworn constables. However, even that limitation has to recognize that the late RUC had the primary function of national security and the defence of the state and that Scottish police forces have a legal mandate derived from Roman, not common law. That formation means that Scotland has had rather different systems in place with regard to investigation and prosecution (the office of the Procurator Fiscal for example) compared to the situation in England & Wales and Northern Ireland.

Social ordering is the key, with crime control as a primary function in that process. However, that crime control assumes neutrality in both legislation and in practice. Police studies scholars tend to treat both as neutral. Apart from the major topic of accountability, they have rarely questioned the legal context of policing. Law and policing are inseparable.[30] There is no disjunction between legal function and police process and practice. In an obvious example, there is minimal legislation and few state interventions with regard to high level deviance in the financial sector responsible for the current fiscal crisis. The only rules are those of neoliberalism. The market requires minimal intervention. Policing, indeed, regulation, in that sector is notable only by its absence. In the US, only one person has been criminalized, Bernie Madoff, despite widespread corporate criminality. (In the UK, such major deviance may simply result in the loss of an honorific knighthood!) Most legislation in modern society, especially the conferment on the police of summary powers, is directed towards the policing of the street and its population, the Other. The current coalition government has reputedly refused to develop and enforce legal codes against the major social and economic deviance of the City. This is hardly a revelation. One is partly dependent on the other and ideologically symmetrical. Criminal law guides police officers to the regulation of the lower classes. Historically-derived organizational traditions and structure mediate. Police officers direct their attention to the imperatives of law. There is no disjunction between legal objectives and policing practice. Policing is about conducting the maintenance of a conservative social order which takes as given the normality of inequality. Even where the law is unequally structured, there is little critique by the judiciary when the state police emphasizes the social ordering and regulation of problem populations. Thus where legislation may be explicit, as in the criminalization of fox-hunting, prosecutions are rare (BBC News, 2011d) – despite the continuing weekend pursuits of some 200 hunts in England and Wales (chief constables appear to have forgotten the limits on their discretion set in the Blackburn accountability case of 1968).[31] This latter is especially curious given the legal mandate of police discretion. As in Lord Denning's judgement in the Blackburn case, while police officers are required to be selective in law enforcement (i.e. exercise their discretion) they must nevertheless enforce *all* criminal laws at some point in time. They cannot, in effect, by dint of their discretion arbitrarily decriminalize[32] certain illegal criminal activities (see Box 1.4).

In the fox-hunting controversy, the police – together with the Crown Prosecution Service (CPS) – have done exactly that, under the spurious rationale that that legislation is too complex and controversial under which to commit scarce resources. Conversely, in spite of the reclassification of cannabis from a class B to class C[33] drug there were 30,000 arrests for relatively minor victimless cannabis possession in four police districts studied by May et al. (2007) in 2004–5. As the authors point out, from an examination of custody records only in less than 1 per cent of cases did 'simple posession arrests open the door to the discovery of other more serious offences' (p. ix). Such work is occupationally easy and focuses on those who have little political power or means of articulation. The example is crude. But it could be replicated many times. State policing is primarily a practice of enforcing unequal laws within an unequal social order mandate against unequal peoples. Some essentially regulatory practices escape that net, such as traffic offences. But state policing in neoliberal society cannot escape, even if police discretion allows, from its primary function of maintaining the current social order. Structure, an inherently unequal legal system, determines police functions and process. Agency, patterned systems of discretion in policing, contributes. Where an institution is defined by its opposite, the other, marginal reforms are irrelevant.

Our focus is initially on the state police of Britain today (though principally England and Wales) and its directly associated civil society contribution. That focus is a means to an end. Our major concern is to utilize that vehicle to analyse the recent and continuing cuts on the state police, as part of larger complex of public service agencies, in the context of a fiscal crisis that hits the poor much more than others. We refer to this as the 'crisis in policing'. That perspective informs a major question to which the book is mainly directed. In a crisis, conflicts occur between the different affected agencies, which aim to bolster their own interests. There is no natural continuum after such an event through which a new consensus or equilibrium naturally emerges. What constitutes the state police is the result in the UK of a history of conflicting interests, led by chief police officers, rank-and-file associations of officers, taxpayers, interest groups such as 'think tanks', and central and local government concerns (Brogden, 1982; Loader and Mulcahy, 2003; McLaughlin, 2007). This is the way the social and political history of state policing has unravelled.

Crises expose fractures in institutions, past and present. Cleavages and conjunctures reveal internal and external contradictions. Contradictions make conflicts

---

Box 1.4   One view on the *News of the World* 'hacking' case

On police discretion (in relation to the News International 'hacking' case), Ian Hislop of Private Eye stated sardonically to the Leveson Inquiry that no new laws were required in relation to 'phone-hacking'. As he suggested, 'Most of the heinous crimes that came up and that have made such a spread of this inquiry are already illegal . . . Contempt of court is illegal, phone tapping is illegal, policemen taking money is illegal . . . We already have laws for them. The fact that these laws were not rigorously enforced is again due to the failure of the police, the interaction of the police with News International . . . [and] our politicians'.

(*Metro*, 17 January 2012)

visible between internal and external agencies, their compromises and relative power. If one had a blank sheet of paper and the opportunity to construct British policing from scratch, what would one construct? Would we construct it again around the principles and precepts rooted in the nineteenth century and earlier?[34] The text uses the cracks in the effigy of British policing revealed by the financial crisis to expose the reality of the 'English Bobby'. It uses the methodological vehicle of the fiscal crisis in the financing of the British police to depict the development of policing in Britain as the product of a convoluted and continuing conflictual history, personified by a functionary who is unsuited to the twenty-first century. Differences in power – between state, local, organizational, professional, and interest groups – become transparent during a period of crisis.

The British police are the primary concern of this book: their supposedly evolutionary, social Darwinian history; their spread as an imperative for the 'natives' in the former Empire, and currently offering (insular) 'best practice' to transitional societies. Chapter 2 exposes the underbelly of British policing, the procedural, aberrant, and systemic reality at the present day, as highlighted by the impact of the Western economic crisis on the UK: problems of history structure the contribution of willing agents to deform a supposedly democratic police. Chapter 3 recounts and examines some of the current myths about the effects of the cuts. Bluntly, very few state police officer posts are being lost. The myth of the frontline (code for beat policing and the policing of the Other) is being maintained as a key practice, regardless of function. The weight falls both tactically and expediently elsewhere. Privatization and increasing resort to technological innovations have been controversially postulated as solutions. Chapter 4 explores the reified historical and international myths that have given rise to the present hugger-mugger of a police establishment – from the oxymoronic citizen-in-uniform (the Office of Constable) to the xenophobic export of the 'Metropolitan' model (and especially its militarized offspring, contrarily, its Peelite predecessor, the Irish Constabulary) to a colonial and postcolonial empire. We consider the emergence of what has been termed the UK Police plc brand as a superlative model for export, but point to its manifest contradictions. What is being exported owes less to London and more to Belfast. Deconstructing the 'brand' exposes a number of myths about its nature, origin and export and its role in an expanded 'policing-for-profit' enterprise as well as cultivating and containing an international 'Other'. In many ways transitional and post-conflict societies have become refuse tips for discarded goods. Chapter 5 focuses on the critical contribution of common and criminal law to policing practices. Deconstruction involves shattering myths, especially in detailing the conflict between locality and the central state in determining state policing needs, however much they have been warped through interest group politics in official discourse. Few studies of policing have directly related police practice to criminal law, customary and statutory. Nor have they questioned the curious degree to which the English and Welsh police, unlike other Western police forces, continue to have direct and indirect influence over the prosecution process despite the establishment of the CPS in 1986. The question posed by George Bernard Shaw in a 1919 address to the Police Prosecution

Society – 'If there is a police for the prosecution, why is there not a police for the defence?' (cited in Brogden, 1982) – has not been answered.

In Chapter 6, we argue, using both historical and contemporary materials, that the major reason why the British police is largely ineffective both normatively and especially in a time of economic crisis, lies in its imperial and postcolonial context. Postcolonial theory offers insights into the peculiar nature of that institution. The New Police (and indeed its immediate predecessors) were constructed during the latter days of colonialism (Brogden, 1987a, b; R.Williams, 2003). Few other Western countries, apart perhaps from Portugal[35] (to a lesser extent) went through that process. It is not just that the British tried, in reacting to the presumed centralism of the Napoleonic Code, to construct a policing system that would fit both the provinces (internal colonies) and externally (the Empire). Ireland, arguably Britain's first colony, was one testing ground for the variants of the new policing model (the term 'Peelers' is still the currency in working-class districts of Belfast). Policing in England and Wales, as elsewhere, is principally the social ordering of the Other. The adage adopted by colonial administrators – 'Knowing the country' – was in many ways a euphemism for knowing the Other (Bayley, 1993). That final chapter furnishes a discourse on the role of the historical Other, utilizing the example of one relevant complex social formation, the Travellers, in determining the peculiarity and function in maintaining inequality of the emblematic totem of British policing.

2   The state of the police of the state

... the last great unreformed public service.

(*Guardian*, editorial, 13 May 2011)

The Government plans to change the structure of the police, for a long time the least modern of all public services. The police will resist but change cannot come a moment too soon.

(*The Times*, editorial, 6 May 2011)

Introduction

State policing has been unique amongst public services in never having experienced considered redirection and reform. The last three major inquiries into policing which have been implemented concentrated mainly on police remuneration.[1] Only the relatively small number of provincial police mergers in the 1960s and 1970s have disturbed the overall tranquillity of the police organization. Most recently, in 2006, the then home secretary – in the interest of efficiency – tried to reduce the number of forces in England and Wales to twenty from the current forty-three. He was forced to abandon this attempt at rationalization when faced with opposition from a range of sources, some of which related to the myth of locality and community. Arbitrary, ad hoc changes carry their own social and economic cost. Even in Northern Ireland, the largely successful change process (for example, in reducing the 13,000-strong RUC to the current 7,500 in the PSNI) was extraordinarily expensive.[2] Such a luxury is not possible in the present recession – change should have reflected modernization, internal 'best practice' guidelines, coordination with other criminal justice agencies, and clearer vision of the police role. Instead, it has been directed by pragmatism and opportunism.

In the following section, we discuss the key areas – personnel, organization, police objectives, and the contribution of quasi-policing agencies – in which police reform has been pursued. Practice, in the policing of England and Wales, is not an exact or a demanding science.

Policing as a labour-intensive, multilayered institution

Policing, as presently practised, is a labour-intensive activity with some four-fifths of expenditure on staffing costs. Nearly half of officers work in the so-called frontline of public space, neighbourhood and instant response roles. Even though the pay of officers has, like that of other public servants, been frozen from 2011 to 2013, incremental salary increases continue. Like other major public institutions, the beat constable is only the tip of a largely submerged iceberg within a highly complex and diffuse organization. According to the Winsor Report (2011 Part 1), the nature of policing has changed since the Edmund-Davies report (Committee of Inquiry, 1978), with the police service becoming increasingly specialized in terms of roles and skills. For example, the Kent Police has 529 different police officer roles and 752 specialized police staff roles. Policing is constituted of varied specialist units: from 'frontline' policing (see below for clarification); foot and vehicle patrols and traffic regulation at one extreme, to the infrastructure of administration and of technological expertise at the other. There is also a key distinction between sworn constables and an array of varyingly-skilled civilian staff. Integral to that organization are several specialist civilian agencies intimately involved in policing, as in forensic science, private agencies substituting for sworn police in varied 'guard' duties (such as court service), crime scene investigation, and the introduction in 2002 of approximately 16,000 PCSOs, who patrol alongside, or in support of, dedicated Neighbourhood Policing officers. Finally, it is also a complex feudal (insofar as the term may reflect hybridity with a military) form of organization with a clear hierarchy in depth, complicated by the unique position of sworn officers not being formal employees (they are 'employed' by dint of their common law status). Structurally, England and Wales' division into forty-three relatively autonomous police forces conceals increasing central direction and the growth of relatively autonomous regional and national policing agencies (McLaughlin, 2007). That division also complicates both the analysis of police procedures in England and Wales and the quality of any resulting data.

Differentiation has also occurred, primarily in the lower ranks. In 1978, over 93 per cent of police officers were men, drawn mainly from a working-class background (policing was an important avenue of social mobility), few having undertaken higher education (Emsley, 2009). By 2010, 31 per cent of new recruits were women (with a clutch of female chief constables) and 27 per cent were university graduates.[3] Black and minority ethnic officers, clustered in the lower ranks, now account for 4.6 per cent of the police service, as compared with 7 per cent in the general population. Progress in diversity will, of course, be hit by the current freeze in recruitment. Policing, as a public service, has made great strides in social integration – a subject that has traditionally been subject to impression management. But there is a curious addendum in relation to black police, unlike the female experience. There are presently no black chief police officers. The ranks of the superintendents from which they would normally be drawn are finite. All existing relevant candidates for a chief's post will have retired by 2012. There has been no evidence of increased black recruitment over the decade since the Macpherson Report. In other words, there is no possibility of the appointment of a new black command officer for many years. Further, given that entry qualifications for police officers exclude reference to academic qualifications ('the way a working-class man could better himself'), lack of black recruitment and of retention remains a major problem. Civilian staff were insignificant in number in the 1970s but today constitute some 36 per cent of all police personnel (Winsor Report, 2011 Part 1). As noted above, the introduction in 2002 of approximately 16,000 PCSOs who patrol alongside or in support of beat officers has also greatly expanded patrol work.

The cost of the police

British sworn police are expensive. International comparisons are difficult because of varying police functions in different countries. Nevertheless, generally, the British police are well remunerated. If one recognizes starting salaries (relative to formal qualifications), the advantages are increased by the low age of retirement and subsequent pensions, security of employment, and the bizarre (if recently curtailed) range of unchecked benefits (especially for senior officers). Police pay has traditionally been increased in relatively arbitrary 'fits and starts'. Typically, in response to the police strike of 1919, there was a substantial increase (Brogden, 1991). After World War II, the Oaksey Report (Oaksey, 1949) responded to a combination of manpower shortages and internal police complaints about workload with a 15 per cent increase in personnel.[4] Over the next half century, there was little difference between the police and other public sector employees. By the early 1950s, class and economic composition were similar. But dramatic change was to come.

In 1979, in the first week of the new Conservative government of Margaret Thatcher, symbolically, police pay (like that of the military) was substantially increased. It was, she said, 'an earnest of our intention to back the police in the war against crime. We must have a strong and experienced police force' (Thatcher, 1979). The result was a huge boost in pay (45 per cent in some cases) and a (presumably) consequent sizeable increase in recruitment. (Indeed, many of the officers who joined at that time have recently retired, compounding the cost of police pensions.) There may, of course, have been ulterior motives here: 'Thatcher recognised that their goodwill would be needed when they were required to conduct political controversially actions as in the miners' strike just a few years later' (Johnston, 2007).

Currently, police pay scale rates are typically 10 per cent to 15 per cent higher than most other public sector workers, and in some regions of England and Wales, police officers are paid approximately 60 per cent more than median local earnings (Winsor Report, 2011 Part 1). The average weekly wage of a sergeant or constable – around £743 a week – exceeds that of paramedics by around £30 a week, of nurses by around £160 per week, of fire-fighters (who also have early retirement benefits) by around £190 per week and of prison officers by around £210 per week.

They earn up to £6,000 a year more than their equivalent ranks in the armed forces. Together with the unique 'perks', benefits, and pensions (detailed below), policing in the UK, insofar as one can compare it with public service occupations of similar levels of qualification, is exceedingly well paid. Police officers are now, in relative terms, paid perhaps the best they have ever been (Winsor Report, 2011 Part 1). Policing the Other has major financial benefits.

Discretionary payments: a culture of legal 'perks'

'Gifts' from the public – sometimes for favours, sometimes not – have been common throughout police history. In a late Victorian city, payments for 'knocking-up' and sundry services were common (Brogden, 1991). A bottle of beer might have been given to an Edwardian constable, but frankly, in lower-class districts (apart from bookmakers), there was little surplus to offer. At the other end of the scale, in 2010, Wiltshire senior officers recorded bottles of champagne, tickets for rugby matches, and pheasants (Crooks, 2011). There is a grey area covering such practices. Legally, discretionary payments were formally introduced by the 2003 pay negotiations (although existing in ad hoc form amongst different forces for a century and a half). Performance-related pay for the police was first mooted (then abruptly shelved) following the Posen Inquiry (HMSO, 1995) into 'Police Core and Ancillary Tasks', and again in the 2001 White Paper, 'Policing a New Century: A Blueprint for Reform' (Home Office, 2001). While falling short of offering the scale of private-sector inducements, the White Paper did propose financial incentives to attract officers to those posts deemed 'unrewarding' within the organization, as well as to officers who could demonstrate professional competence in line with agreed national performance standards and targets (Tonge et al., n.d.). For instance, provision was made for the payment of bonuses of up to 15 per cent of chief police officers' pensionable pay. Superintendents could move up their pay scales more quickly if their performance was considered to warrant it. Similarly, constables who have been at the top of their pay scale for at least a year, and who can demonstrate higher professional competence, can be paid an additional £1,212 per annum (Competence Related Threshold Payment – CRTP). It was expected that 75 per cent of those eligible would receive the latter. As the Winsor Report notes, in the case of some 98 per cent of constables who have applied for CRTP, they have been successful, normally without any formal submissions or justifications (Winsor called for the abolition of the system[5]). The introduction of a bonus scheme is a discretionary part of the overall pay and conditions package agreed as part of the 2002 Police Negotiating Board. The chief constable may award bonuses of between £50 and £500 per person for occasional work of an outstandingly demanding, unpleasant or important nature. Typically, in 2010/11, officers in the Merseyside Police, across the whole spectrum of the force, received a total of £4.5 million in bonus payments (Siddle, 2011).

There is of course a history to police salaries. The Winsor Report had detailed the relative fall in police pay until the Thatcher rewards. The Sheehy Report (Sheehy, 1993) and the earlier Edmund-Davies Report (Committee of Inquiry,

1978) proposed higher rewards for sworn officers. However, while Edmund-Davies qualified his proposals with a concern for effectiveness and productivity, his report failed (unlike, in part, the Winsor Report) to recognize other incentives for becoming a police officer: historically, the attraction of a guaranteed state pension was a key factor for many working-class males (Brogden, 1991; Emsley, 2009). Winsor also claims that independent of pay, policing, because of the nature of the work, rates highly in terms of job satisfaction. Nevertheless, he claims, somewhat arbitrarily, that police officers are apparently not motivated by financial reward, whereas, by contrast, so-called backroom staff have low job satisfaction.

Police officers receive other financial rewards. Winsor notes that many police officers work unsocial hours and consequently receive a 9 per cent shift allowance for that disruption. In reality, however, just over half of officers actually work unsocial hours, but they still receive the shift allowance. Bizarrely, 15 minutes 'overtime' officially transmutes into 4 hours extra pay – the minimum overtime payment is £100! Overtime rates for uniformed staff are traditional. For example, the Sussex Police saw its overtime bill increase by 25 per cent over 3 years despite major increases in staff. For England and Wales, the overall cost of over-time is some £400 million a year. Officers in some of the country's rural forces earned upwards of £25,000 in overtime alone in 2009. Nearly 500 received more than £15,000 on top of their salaries. One London-based PC earned more than £90,000 – an increase of at least £50,000 on his salary (Hughes, 2009). Differences between different police forces in the rules governing the payment of overtime are sizeable and incomprehensible (Brasnett et al., 2010). Much overtime is linked to the processing of prisoners and related court duties, practices that are outside the control, indeed, coordination, of local police authorities (LPAs). Among the constants, CID officers in some forces work 5-day weeks, treating weekend work as overtime. Uniformed officers have no such rights. Some officers arrive for shifts early and claim overtime for that period. Other officers make no such claim. An average police officer in the Metropolitan Police received just over £4,000 in overtime payments in 2010/11. According to Boyd et al. (2011) 'Paying police officers overtime can make sense in some cases, but police forces have allowed these payments to spiral out of control, with a huge amount spent over the last decade even while officer numbers have increased'. Currently, some officers are paid overtime if they take a work phone call while off duty, others not. Police minister David Hanson said there was a 'culture' within the police service that such a level of overtime was 'acceptable' (cited in Whitehead, 2010). Police who take a 'short phone call requiring a decision' while they are off duty can claim their hourly pay rate plus one-third. The minimum overtime pay rate is (as above) for 4 hours.

There are several other additional extra salary payments to police officers, typically to compensate officers and police staff for particular expenses and to retain scarce skills. These range from the housing replacement allowance (between £1,777.66 per officer in Northumbria and £5,126.70 in the Metropolitan Police) to minor payments such as allowances for meals taken at unusual times (Winsor Report, 2011, Part 1). Since 2003, Special Priority Payments have been available, primarily directed to frontline operational posts, up to a maximum of £5,000 per annum for a police officer. These discretionary payments were intended to target between 20 per cent and 40 per cent of police officer posts, where the officer has significantly more responsibility than normal for the rank, where retention of particular skills is important, and where the officer works in demanding working conditions. These discretionary payments (costing approximately £84 million in England and Wales for 2009/10) have been criticized by ACPO and the Police Federation as divisive (and subject to non-accountable determination by senior officers) given the proportion of officers excluded from those payments (all figures from Winsor Report, 2011).

There are many incremental payments in policing – legal and extra-legal – that may accrue to individual officers by virtue of their particular guard duties. Royal protection duties are typical. Prince William, Duke of Cambridge and heir to the British throne, has cost North Wales Police (and taxpayers) £1.4 million per annum for living 'off base' in a country cottage on Ynys Mon (Anglesey), in addition to the costs of his own state-financed royal protection officers (RPOs) and the Royal Air Force Police. Such expenditure is covered by the euphemism of 'security matters'. This information appeared at a time when the North Wales Police was threatened with a cut of around £30 million from its budget over the next 4 years (BBC News, 2010a). Two of his more distant relatives have recently been stripped of their half a million pounds per annum police protection costs. A more senior progeny of the extended Windsor family incurred the Metropolitan Police £1.5 million per year. Such exhaustive duties did not prevent RPOs in their spare time developing a gambling syndicate – 'Dozens of royal protection officers have run up serious losses after investing in a spread betting syndicate that was operated secretly from inside the royal palaces' (Laville, 2009). Scotland Yard investigated an officer at the centre of the syndicate, which gambled millions of pounds of officers' money on the currency and commodity markets. Documents showed that the syndicate lost more than £1.1 million in just one of the spread betting firms they used (Laville, 2009) in between 'collecting golf balls' on behalf of the royal golfer William Windsor, trading pornography, and using police cars for their own domestic purposes, and entertaining on the British monarch's throne.[6] The RPO organizer was subsequently found guilty of a £3 million pound 'scam'.

More evident in the media has been the revelation that chief officers can, in effect, determine bonuses on reaching self-determined targets without apparent question from the LPA, targets such as crime clear-up successes or decreases in the artificial recorded crime rate (especially controversial because of the way such targets can be internally manipulated). LPAs act as eunuchs in such matters. Perhaps atypically, Chief Constable Richard Brunstrom of the relatively small North Wales Police paid himself £17,000 extra through that device in the year of his retirement (with £25,000 shared amongst other senior officers of the force).[7] In the Metropolitan Police, 136 of the highest paid officers shared £567,000 in bonuses, a 70 per cent increase over 2 years. In Northumbria, five chief officers divided up £115,000 between them. In Northumbria, Temporary Chief Constable Sue Sim received but subsequently turned down a £47,000 bonus for 18 months' work while she was assistant and later deputy chief constable.[8] In addition, many chief constables will have other job-related benefits, such as private health care, chauffeured cars, and occasionally provision of free accommodation. Such extravagances have been much criticized by the majority of senior officers in recent years and only a handful continue the practice. Nevertheless, chief officers in eleven forces received bonuses in 2010/11. The chief constable of Avon and Somerset police, Colin Port, received £17,341 on top of his £151,000 salary even though his force is faced with £40 million of cuts – with around 200 staff set to lose their jobs.[9] Lincolnshire deputy chief constable Neil Rhodes received £13,271 on top of his £112,000 salary (the force is making cuts of £20 million over the next 4 years).[10]

Chief officers may also retire early to well-funded civilian occupations. Thus the BBC reported that a company chaired by the former Metropolitan commissioner, Lord Stevens, was due to receive a proportionate profit from a £4 million contract with Huddersfield University, in a project to train 100 Libyan police officers and civilian scientists in forensic science techniques.[11] Norman Bettison retired from successive chief constable posts in January 2005 to become chief executive of Centrex.[12] Sir Ronnie Flanagan, previously chief constable of the RUC and Her Majesty's Chief Inspector of Constabulary, has landed a highly lucrative position as strategic advisor to the Minister of Interior of the United Arab Emirates (McAdam, 2008). Sir Ronnie has brought his own team of mainly ex-RUC/PSNI personnel with him (discussed in Chapter 4).

Typical of such retirees is one who has legitimately exploited legal rules over state pensions. Deputy Assistant Commissioner Alf Hitchcock retired from the Metropolitan Police aged 49, gaining an £80,000 pension, then immediately commenced duties as deputy chief constable of the NPIA at an estimated £120,000-a-year salary (*Daily Mail*, 20 January, 2009). In that post, he mentors potential chief constables. The senior officer's package, which will entitle him to another pension when he retires, will far exceed the pay of the officers he is mentoring. Officers can stay in the police and qualify to collect pay and pension if they retire from one of the Home Office forces and join a force or agency that falls under a different department. Critics (including senior officers such as Sir Hugh Orde) have labelled the practice of officers simultaneously collecting large pensions and salaries as the 'gravy beat', which gave a 'bad impression' of the police. Other officers who have retired and immediately gone into other policing roles include the chief constable of the British Transport Police (BTP), Ian Johnston, and his deputy Andy Trotter. They left Scotland Yard and joined the BTP, which is not under Home Office control, entitling them to the 'double hat' windfall.[13]

Prior to his arrest and suspension for alleged misconduct in public office, the chief constable of Cleveland, Sean Price, was one of the highest paid chief constables in the country. Cleveland Police Authority recruited him from Nottinghamshire where he was deputy in 2003. In 2009/10 he received £4,176 in benefits in kind, £24,000 in bonuses and £54,000 in 'other payments' on top of his £130,000 basic salary.[14] Secondary jobs furnish additional benefits. Data obtained by the *Independent* newspaper under Freedom of Information legislation suggests that from a voluntary registration survey, at least 8,618 police officers have second jobs or outside business interests (Shields, 2010). These include very senior officers (on six-figure salaries) including three Metropolitan Police commanders and Strathclyde's chief constable. Scotland Yard, the UK's largest force, had the highest number of officers with outside registered business interests – 3,957 in 2010. The number of new business interests registered in that force rose from 333 in 2005 to 496 in 2009. West Yorkshire saw officers registered more than triple from 104 in 2005 to 335 in 2009. Strathclyde, Scotland's largest force, witnessed a sixfold increase, from 25 to 154 over the same period – including Chief Constable Stephen House, who registered a buy-to-let property (again such data is grossly understated by the voluntary character of the registration of such interests).

Minor perks accrue to less prominent junior staff. The Police Federation, like many other organizations in the private and public sector, has legitimately negotiated discounts for its members from commercial sales organizations. Such discounts (as below) are far more relevant to associates of ACPO. Because many officers began their police service in their late teens, they could retire and draw their pension before their fiftieth birthday. This was historically dated because it enabled a relatively healthy cohort of workers to be released into the job market and assume new remunerated posts with prospective occupations for retirees advertised weekly in the *Police Oracle*. Skills can be transferred to other occupations. For example, a civilian investigator employed by the *News of the World* had followed some eighty target citizens in 12 months. A former police officer, he had been trained in surveillance techniques by the domestic intelligence service, MI5. Many senior officers are able to undertake new paid employment – for example in the burgeoning security industry, in international advisory posts,[15] and/or to be newly employed as consultants on fixed contracts with their former police force.[16] Given changes in life expectancy and the increase in retiree numbers, this has become an extraordinarily expensive problem for both state and LPAs, and an embarrassment to the Home Office.

Perks also include the occasional jollies abroad.[17] But it did not help the Police's case for police saving when the new chief constable of Merseyside was caught on camera enjoying sunbathing, snorkelling, and boating, while formally on a joint expedition to advise on 'gang busting' (there are not many relevant Merseyside precedents for the utilization of such expertise) in the Cayman Islands – a venture paid for by the latter's government (Sky News, 8 October 2011).

The pension

Historically, the evidence shows (Brogden, 1991; Emsley, 2009) that a primary motivation for joining the state police was the 'pension'. For the previous century and a half, few other public service posts could offer a guaranteed half-pay pension after 30 years' service. For working-class men, the pension was a major incentive. Young men joined the force because it uniquely guaranteed a house (if vetted by

CID in earlier years) and financial support for retirees. Until 2003, when the scheme was modified for new entrants, under the Police Pension Scheme (1987) officers were ensured a target pension of two-thirds of their final salary. Alternatively, an officer could elect to take a lump sum in exchange for a lower pension; thus leaving the officer with a pension of half the final salary. Officers under that scheme currently pay contributions of 11 per cent of their pensionable pay – a point that the Police Federation suggests is more than other public service employees and therefore justifies the size of their pension. LPAs pay the employer contribution of 24.2 per cent (the average pension of a police officer after 30 years in 2011 was some £16,500, compared to a teacher's £10,500 at the age of sixty). This scheme was closed to new recruits under the Police Pensions Regulations 2006. Under the latter, officers will receive a pension equal to one-seventieth of the final salary for each year's service, over 35 years. Again, it provides a target pension of half the final salary. Officers would also receive four-seventieths of the final salary for each year's service over 35 years (obviously increasing the length of service), to provide a target lump sum of twice the final salary. These officers pay a slightly lower direct contribution than their predecessors (9.5 per cent of their pensionable pay) while the Police Authority contribution remains the same.[18]

Calculations by the Independent Public Sector Pensions Commission (IPSPC) in 2010 estimated that taxpayers will have to fund a £770-billion black hole to deliver pensions already promised to public sector workers (Cowie, 2010). The costs of public sector final salary schemes range from 19.5 per cent of salary for teachers to 37 per cent for police officers (Cowie, 2010). The police final salary scheme also provides a range of benefits, including survivor pensions for nominated unmarried partners. Rent and housing allowances were replaced with a substantial fixed sum, placing a police officer who provided his own accommodation in broadly the same position as one who was provided with free accommodation (available only to officers who were already in the service in 1994). Remarkably, when the coalition government raised the age of pension entitlement to 68 years from 2020, it exempted police officers and fire fighters from this requirement, presumably justified by the claim that policing was a hazardous occupation requiring a particular physique; an argument that seems contradictory in the face of the acknowledgement of equal rights for female fire officers.

The Pay Tribunal and the Winsor Report

The major hurdle in a radical overhaul of police pay and conditions has been cleared after an independent tribunal backed proposals to save between and £160 million and £177 million a year on their pay bill by streamlining overtime and allowances (later ratified by the coalition government) (see ACAS, 2012). The bulk of the savings will come from the abolition of so-called 'special priority payments' and a 2-year freeze on officers automatically moving up pay scales. However, the tribunal ruled that there should be more generous treatment of police officers who are deployed to deal with disturbances outside their force area with a new 'away from home overnight allowance' of £50 a night to be paid to those involved in 'mutual aid' operations (Travis, 2012b).

Officers also faced a 2-year pay freeze and increases in their pension contributions along with the rest of the public sector. The tribunal[19] recommended that the pay progression freeze should apply to all officers, except new probationers, to produce savings on the annual pay bill (ACAS, 2012). The proposal instead backed scrapping special priority payments, that were supposed to reward high priority frontline roles but had become commonplace and would save a further £86 million a year (all data from Travis, 2012a). The competence-related threshold payments (of around £1,000 per annum) are also to be scaled back with a 2-year freeze on new applications. The tribunal package also recommends £10 million savings in overtime and a further £2 million in chief officers' and superintendents' bonus payments. The package includes extra payments for some police officers who work unsocial hours with improvement in maternity pay from 13 to 18 weeks. The tribunal report has estimated that the savings to be made are in the region of £163 million a year – just £5 million short of Winsor's original proposals (Travis, 2012a).

Diversity

It is curious that a government that has recently raised the future pensionable age for both male and female public servants to the age of 68 years has exempted both police and fire services from that edict. Having overcome the gender bias with regard to police service, it is odd that (the assumptions of relative gender capacity to 'do' policing as an occupation that requires physical stature), policing is still implicitly a physique-driven occupation. Rare female construction workers (where the highest rates of physical injury occur) may not appreciate that paradox.

The police services of the UK have a recent progressive record with regard to gender and issues of sexuality. They are ahead of the private sector in ensuring that the non-police partner in a same-sex relationship receives identical benefits to a heterosexual couple, and in allowing police officers to dress in uniform in gay parades.[20] Ethnicity is certainly not the barrier to entry that it was some years ago when bizarrely the Cumbria Police declared that it did not require a black quota of officers because the ethnic minority of the police area was minute. But 'old' stereotypes remain, in different ways. While the UK appointed its first black police officer (to the Kent Constabulary) in 2003, there are no longer any black chief officers following the resignation of Michael Fuller to take up his new role as chief inspector for the CPS (BBC News, 2008). As above, the higher ranks are about to lose the three black chief superintendents on the promotion ladder. Entry of black and Asian officers has stalled at a non-proportionate level. Black officers have a higher turnover than white officers. The effect of cuts in probationer training will decrease black and Asian representation in the state police. In some respects the police organization has made remarkable headway in its attempts to recruit black and minority ethnic officers. Nevertheless, the pernicious effects of the police occupational culture continues to hinder progress. This is evidenced in the occasional institutional forays against the 'Other'[21] and the overuse of stop-and-search powers (Newburn, 2011), but also in the position of black and minority ethnic officers within the organization (Cashmore, 2002). In his resignation announcement from Kent Constabulary, Chief Constable Mike Fuller made the point that black officers 'have to work twice as hard to compete' in promotion terms, and find it tremendously difficult to break into specialist teams (BBC News, 2008). The police organization may not be the racist bastion it was, but there is certainly room for improvement.

Police discipline and corruption

> See how yon justice rail upon yon thief? Change places and handy, dandy, which is the justice, which the thief?'
>
> (William Shakespeare, *King Lear*)

Disciplinary procedures in policing are interesting in this context because of both their cost and their practice. Cases involving alleged criminality by police officers are noteworthy for their low conviction rates, despite objective preparations by the IPCC and the CPS. In August 2011 the IPCC released the results of a study into deaths in police custody between 1998 and 2010, which revealed that although a total of 333 people have died in or following police custody over the past 11 years, no officer has ever been successfully prosecuted (IPCC, 2011b). Out of the total number of deaths, eighty-seven people had been restrained; generally by being physically held down by officers (IPCC, 2011b). In sixteen of those cases, restraint was linked directly to the death and four deaths were classed as 'positional asphyxia' (see Box 2.1). Overall the trend is downwards, with a 14 per cent drop in all such deaths over a decade. But there has been a curious recent 'blip' – if that is the right word. In 2010, three black detainees died. Between January and August 2011, there were eight such deaths. 'It is quite clear that juries often do not want to convict police officers', the Winsor Report clamed. Prosecutions were recommended against thirteen officers based on 'relatively strong evidence of misconduct or neglect', but none resulted in a guilty verdict. Their findings illustrate that in only one case was a civilian member of police staff found guilty of misconduct, and sentenced to six months' imprisonment (IPCC, 2011b). This situation is not peculiar to the UK. Data for other jurisdictions cite similar rates of police acquittal.

Over 200 police officers were suspended in England and Wales on full pay at the beginning of 2011 (Edwards, 2010). Suspensions on full pay can drag on for a considerable period – in a small minority of cases over several years. Between 2005 and 2010, suspensions cost the police forces of England and Wales £53 million (Edwards, 2010). Following a Freedom of Information request, *The Times* newspaper reported that the cost of placing accused officers on either full pay or on restricted duties, pending the hearing of cases in 2010/11 was £2.7 million (*The Times*, 4 December 2010). Conventionally, hearings in such cases are held in private. What is also striking about such cases, as *The Times* points out, is the

---

Box 2.1   Deaths in custody unrecorded

The number of people who have died after being forcibly restrained in police custody is higher than officially stated, an investigation by The Bureau of Investigative Journalism and *The Independent* reveals today. The investigation has identified a number of cases not included in the official tally of 16 'restraint-related' deaths in the decade to 2009 – including a landmark case that changed the way that officers carry out arrests. Some cases were omitted because the person had not been officially arrested or detained. The omission raises questions about the statistics used by the Independent Police Complaints Commission (IPCC) to inform the debate over the use of restraint by police in the sensitive area of deaths in custody, campaigners said yesterday. Analysis of the figures reveals the omission of eight high-profile cases from the list, including that of Roger Sylvester, who died after being handcuffed and held down by up to six officers for 20 minutes. The case led to changes about how police arrested suspects and detained the mentally ill. The Sylvester case led to a review of techniques by the Metropolitan Police that resulted in changes in training. Any force used by police must be 'lawful, proportionate and necessary', according to guidelines by the Association of Chief Police Officers. Deborah Coles, the chief executive of Inquest, which takes up cases of deaths in custody, said it was 'absolutely astonishing' that some of the cases were not described as 'restraint-related' deaths. 'I think there are some very serious concerns about the IPCC and I don't think it's fulfilling its purpose as a robust independent watchdog for the public and indeed bereaved families to have confidence in', she said. The IPCC's research found that 333 people died in police custody between 1998–99 and 2008–9, including 86 who died after being restrained. That figure included 16 of the most controversial cases which were classed as restraint-related. However, only those who have been formally arrested or detained are included in the figures.

(*The Independent*, 31 January 2012)

---

variation between different police forces. The South Yorkshire Police, with 1,400 officers, recorded only three misconduct hearings over 3 years, while the City of London force, with 800 officers, produced twelve cases. Offences that attract a fine in one police area are dealt with by dismissal in another two forces. In the years 2008–11 in England and Wales, 1,303 officers faced disciplinary proceedings and almost 90 per cent were found guilty – with about a third dismissed or required to resign. One officer spent more than two years suspended on full pay, and then a further year on limited office duties before being dismissed for criminal offences. Another paid a fine of less than 1 per cent of his year's suspended salary. Punishments vary wildly between police areas. Six per cent of offenders were

---

Box 2.2   The criminal records of police officers

More than 900 serving police officers and community support officers have a criminal record, official figures show. Officers in England and Wales have convictions for burglary, causing death by dangerous driving, robbery, supplying drugs, domestic violence, forgery, and perverting the course of justice. Among those with criminal records are two detective chief inspectors and one chief inspector . . . according to figures released by 33 of the 43 forces in England and Wales in response to freedom of information request.

(*Guardian*, 2 January 2012)

---

fined in Tayside while the Metropolitan Police has only fined one officer in 150 cases over the 3 years (*The Times*, 4 December 2010).

Police complaints run at approximately one complaint for every four officers per annum[22] (IPCC, 2011c) a figure that is some 30 per cent higher than a decade earlier. In 2009/10, the most common complaints were for neglect or failure in duty (26 per cent), incivility, impoliteness and intolerance (20 per cent), and excessive force (13 per cent). However, complaints, as a measure of effectiveness, are subject to many caveats. For example, as Nick Hardwick, former chair of the IPCC, suggests,

> If you think the police are all bastards, you don't bother to complain because you think it will get you victimized. If you are Mr. and Mrs. Suburban, who have a good view of the police and think that they do a good job, and they stop and swear at you, you are shocked and then you complain.[23]

Historically, what appears evident (bearing in mind the major methodological problems in enumerating such material) is that the prosecution and subsequent conviction of officers on corruption/misconduct charges is relatively rare. This has been true of the vice enrichment practices of commanders Virgo and Drury in Soho in the 1960s and 1970s;[24] the notorious half-brick case involving Detective Sergeant Challenor at West End Central in 1963;[25] through to the antics of the West Midlands Organised Crime Squad in the 1980s. Things have of course improved immeasurably since then with the adoption of Professional Standards Units in current police forces. Nevertheless, at least 489 officers from 47 forces facing misconduct action were allowed to discreetly leave through the 'back door' between 2008 and 2010 (BBC News, 31 October 2011). There were 1,915 guilty findings against officers for misconduct over the same period. Lack of substantive evidence of police corruption has always been the case, partly by policy and partly due to the lack of convictions. Juries invariably find police officers innocent of any offence (the 'Birmingham Six' apparently beat themselves up at both Morecambe and Birmingham police stations and at Winson Green Prison).

Police corruption is a many-faceted phenomenon, not one simply reducible to financial gain. Punch (2009) develops a typology of *meat eaters* (who proactively seek out opportunities for corruption), *grass eaters* (who might accept low level gifts in order to maintain the staus quo) and *birds* (who actively avoid corrupt or potentially corrupt activity). In Punch's study *grass eaters* formed the majority. However, as he acknowledges, even this typology can blur more than it can reveal: corruption can range from the normative acceptance of free meals from an Indian restaurant or take-away (a tradition going back to shopkeepers' Christmas boxes for police officers) to the conspiracy to prosecute suspected IRA bombers without any hard evidence (the 'Guildford Four' case also occurred under the old regime before the days of the CPS) to payments received in 'regulating' the illegal drugs market (Punch, 2009). Corruption traditionally was simply regarded as a legal matter in which a police officer used his/her authority for financial gain. A more contemporary sociological usage adds a whole gamut of police misuse of authority as above. The latter is the concept now followed. Newburn (1999) cites as examples of the current usage: bribery, violence and brutality, fabrication and destruction of evidence, racism, and favouritism or nepotism. The new conception is reinforced by ethical concerns raised by Kleinig (1996), arguing that the boundaries of police corruption are inevitably going to be indistinct and unclear, despite the guidelines of the Police and Criminal Evidence Act 1984. As Transparency International (2011), has pointed out, details of how many officers in the UK have been jailed for corruption and misconduct are notoriously difficult to access. However, their report notes a trend towards invividual corruption rather than systemic corruption (as was the case in the 1970s and 1980s). Of course, whatever temptations might come an officer's way have to some extent been assuaged in England and Wales by the legacy of the constable's discretionary inheritance. The latter simply extends the constable's powers in making decisions. A typical example is where an officer, or specialized squad, in effect, 'regulates' the abundant market in illegal drugs (Newburn, 1999).

There have been some curious rationales for allowing officers to retire from the force and thus avoid prosecution. For example, according to Chief Constable Peter Fahy of the Greater Manchester Police: 'If such an officer remains suspended on full pay for a protracted period, it may have a damaging impact on public confidence' (cited in Fallon, 2011). Clearly there is a judgement call to be made here about whether officers should be taken off the payroll and retired out of the force or whether they should be subject to a long drawn out and potentially unwinnable legal process, given a jury's traditional reticence to convict and the vigour with which the Police Federation defends such officers in the legal arena. Nevertheless, chief constables have a long tradition of such odd rationales for not dealing with corruption by judicial process. Over a decade earlier, Sir Paul Condon had claimed that any such police corruption was due to the relative poverty of police pay, not an argument that could be readily accepted today as a legitimate view of preventing corruption by City bankers. Other public service workers and many similar functionaries might claim the same bizarre justification for not appearing in the criminal courts.

But there are several key points about present-day corruption. If it occurs amongst the rank-and-file, the cases are relatively clear-cut under the legal definition of corruption. A sociological definition might raise alarming questions about the pervasive relationship between the senior members of the Metropolitan Police and key media figures in the 'phone-hacking' case of 2011. Regular convivial contact with senior members of the Murdoch press, exchange of (and dual) employment during the hacking case, and a bizarre delay and lack of prioritization in investigating simultaneous allegations of phone-tapping have not been regarded as corruption. A senior member of the Metropolitan Police's media staff was in joint employment with the *News of the World* during the eventual investigation (some 5,000 cases have been noted to date).[26] Seven years earlier, the responsible senior officer of the Metropolitan Police had dismissed proposals for a sustained investigation, partly because it might require the commitment of significant resources. That decision now looks peculiar in the light of 3,000 arrests to date in relation to the riots of August 2011 (and the extraordinary commitment of resources), within a short period of time. The existence of such close relationships between senior police officers and media personnel is perhaps unsurprising given that the police organization increasingly depends on presentational strategies and senior officers being media savvy in order to get their message across (McLaughlin, 2007). However, the *News of the World* phone-hacking scandal appears to have taken this to a new level. It also casts doubt on the 'slippery slope' argument, that corruption starts at the bottom and slowly works its way up the officer's career to the top. There is no suggestion that the senior Metropolitan Police officers had been involved in corruption as juniors. Equally, it squashes the claim that police corruption is due to a few unrepresentative police officers (see Punch, 2009). Indeed, Punch has pointed out that one problem of police corruption is the commitment not to investigate the 'orchard', but rather directing attention at the 'bad apples' (Punch, 2009). Although we should remember Sir Robert Mark's unfortunate claim that the police are simply representative of the public they serve. It was Sir Robert Mark after all, who admitted that he had casually broken a suspect's leg as a junior officer in order to obtain a confession. If corruption and criminal behaviour is common in the public, then *ipso facto*, it is also common in the police.

The Police Federation has an extraordinary success rate in defending its own. Prosecutions for police corruption are decisions that CPS officers take with trepidation, in the face of Police Federation legal adversaries. 'Grasses' have a habit of recanting their evidence when officers are charged (see Box 2.3). The relative separation of powers between the Crown Prosecution Service and police forces (though the former's remit is proposed to be reduced by the coalition government) has had evidently some success in preventing the older-style 'fitting-up' process.

Official views on the extent of police corruption point mainly to the 'bad apple' thesis, and while, for example, the IPCC recognizes that corruption is present in all forces, it nevertheless does not regard this as endemic (IPCC, 2011). A similar view is shared by the chair of ACPO, Sir Hugh Orde (Evans, 2011a). Similarly, a report by Her Majesty's Inspectorate of Constabulary (HMIC, 2011a) found that while serious corruption was infrequent, the police did not escape with a clean bill

Box 2.3   Supergrasses and police corruption

One of the most significant police anti-corruption cases in modern times collapsed on Wednesday after two former detectives, who had both served lengthy jail sentences, were cleared at a retrial. Robert Clark and Christopher Drury were drummed out of the force in disgrace after being convicted in 2000 of robbing drug dealers and recycling their narcotics. Their convictions were among the highest profile and most significant obtained by Scotland Yard in its long-running battle against corruption. They walked free after a supergrass witness recanted her evidence, leaving Scotland Yard facing a potential bill for the former officers' back wages and compensation running into hundreds of thousands of pounds. Mr. Clark and Mr. Drury's original convictions were quashed and a retrial ordered in 2010 by the appeal court, after it emerged the Crown Prosecution Service had failed to disclose material to defence lawyers at the original trial. [. . .] [T]he second attempt to prosecute Mr. Clark and Mr. Drury collapsed after the main witness against them, Evelyn Fleckney, said she had no recollection of any criminality involving the two former detectives. She had testified against them at the original trial and was a former lover of Mr. Clark. The pair had allegedly signed into hotels using the name 'Bart Simpson'. Both Mr. Clark and Mr. Drury denied conspiracy to supply class-B drugs and perverting the course of justice. The two men were among five officers convicted in 2000 of corruption who had served at the south-east regional crime squad at Dulwich, south London, which was meant to tackle major drug traffickers. Corrupt officers based at the now disbanded unit were known as the 'groovy gang'. Mr. Clark, the alleged ringleader of the group, served 10 years of his 12-year sentence. Mr. Drury received 11 years and served eight. The sentences were some of the longest ever handed down to allegedly corrupt police officers. The investigation against them was codenamed Operation Russia and helped launch the career of John Yates, who in July this year resigned as an assistant commissioner over the phone-hacking scandal. The first trial heard that Fleckney, a drug dealer known as 'the chairman of the board', passed Mr. Clark information about drug shipments. Part of any shipment seized by the squad was stolen by Mr. Clark and recycled by Fleckney through her network of dealers, the court was told, with profits allegedly shared among corrupt officers. Fleckney turned supergrass after she was convicted in March 1998 of conspiracy to supply ecstasy, cocaine and cannabis and jailed for 15 years. A statement from the men's solicitors said: 'Mr. Clark and Mr. Drury have had their careers ruined by these allegations. They will now be looking for appropriate compensation and damages . . . ' The former detectives are now working as bus drivers in the north of England, their solicitor said. Fleckney claimed her evidence followed pressure put upon her by detectives from the anti-corruption 'ghost squad', called CIB3. Fleckney told the court that anti-corruption officers had threatened her with a long prison sentence unless she co-operated. 'Sometimes they would be nice and sometimes horrible ...' The CPS said: 'Evelyn Fleckney ... demonstrated a clear hostility to the prosecution: making new allegations of misconduct against the investigators who debriefed her; claiming to have no recollection at all of any criminality by the defendants that she previously described; and expressed a determination not to give evidence at any retrial, even to the extent of moving abroad to avoid doing so. 'We consider that without Evelyn Fleckney's willing evidence in this case there is no longer a realistic prospect of conviction ...' The MPS accepts this finding but is disappointed by the outcome and will continue to take allegations of corruption extremely seriously and deal robustly with any officers who do not uphold the high standards expected.

(Dodd, *Guardian*, October 2011)

of health. It found extreme geographical inconsistencies between what is judged acceptable up and down the country in 'grey areas' like the use of corporate credit cards, gifts, hospitality, second jobs and business interests. According to HMIC's Roger Baker: 'This inconsistency made little sense to us and nor do we believe would it to the general public'.[27]

In England and Wales complaints against the police are the responsibility of the IPCC, which was established in the aftermath of the Police Reform Act (2002) and became operational on 1 April 2004.[28] While not without its problems, the IPCC is a significant improvement over its predecessor the Police Complaints Authority. The IPCC will automatically investigate all cases involving a death in police custody or police corruption, even where no complaint has been made. The highest levels of investigation are independent investigations where the IPCC uses its own staff (who have police powers), or managed investigations where the IPCC directs the Professional Standards Department within the police. Minor complaints, such as those involving incivilities and impoliteness, are dealt with by a process of informal resolution. Where a complaint has been found to have been upheld, the IPCC can direct the chief constable to take action against a particular officer. The IPCC's independence, however, came under scrutiny with the death of Ian Tomlinson, who had been hit by a police baton following the G20 summit protests in 2009. The IPCC initially appeared to believe the police version of events (i.e. that Tomlinson fell), and it was only after the *Guardian* published a video on its website showing Tomlinson being struck by a police baton that the IPCC was forced to reopen the investigation. It subsequently emerged that a number of police officers had witnessed the assault on Tomlinson but this information was not passed to the IPCC. Concerns were raised about the degree of independence of the IPCC from the police (Lewis, 2011).

Aside from the recent Tomlinson case (above), police conduct has arguably changed for the better for several reasons. Whether this is normative or expedient is, of course, another matter entirely. Some reasons are: better qualified staff, changes in the oversight procedures both internally (professional standards) and (partly) externally (the role played by the IPCC), and potential – though rare – investigations by HMIC and Parliament's own Home Affairs Select Committee. Greater press and public scrutiny has created a sea-change in police practices, as has the emergence of new technologies such as the incorporation of video recording capabilities within mobile telephones and other portable devices. The watched are increasingly watching the watchers – or at least capturing their activities on video and posting them on You Tube. This 'sousveillance' or inverse surveillance (Mann et al., 2003) has made policing more 'visible' and for some commentators has fundamentally transformed the terrain of police governance and accountability (e.g. see Goldsmith, 2010).

Several serious cases recently before the courts (such as in relation to the scandal of the homicide conviction of the 'Cardiff Three' – from 1988) are frequently a consequence of events some years ago (Lavelle, 2012). In the Cardiff Three case (in a parallel with cases involving IRA suspects in the 1980s), the extraordinary conviction of three suspects on apparently concocted evidence of guilt led to years of incarceration. Public pressure led to their release, and a medley of senior retired officers were found not guilty on a judicially determined 'technicality' despite what seemed to the general public to be a clear indication of serious police wrongdoing.

Similarly, greater cultural and societal tolerance and decriminalization of formerly illegal 'immoral' activities has had positive results: there is no longer a possibility of the resurrection of the 1970s Obscene Publication Squad (also referred to as the 'Dirty Squad', see footnote 24, p. 35). As far as junior officers are concerned, corruption seems no longer systemic but, counter-intuitively, aberrational. Where it occurs, it is normally limited to particular units where commercial gain is readily tempting. Drugs squads are one example. For example, three Merseyside police officers were convicted of serious drug offences at Liverpool Crown Court in 2011. They were part of a plot to distribute more than £75,000 worth of cannabis plants seized in drugs raids (Griffiths, 2010). More importantly, units with specialized access to valuable information are the most susceptible to corruption, such as by officers with direct access to the Holmes computer system. As Punch (2009) suggests, the old style corruption where groups of detectives had familiar relations with criminals and met in pubs to pass on information has decreased because it is too visible and too open to scrutiny. But new opportunities are always being created and exploited. In particular, as Bayley and Perito (2011) argue, large-scale corruption involving police personnel has moved from the domestic to the international setting. They suggest that corruption is a particular problem in international peace-keeping and counter-insurgency operations but particularly in NATO-led police reform missions to Iraq and Afghanistan. Here bribery, expense fiddling and larger patterns of fraud, not to mention the close relationships between state police and the corporate security sector, have created new opportunities for corruption on an endemic scale.

A separate issue, with regard to specialized units, has been the bizarre (see Chapter 5) use and (lack of) control of undercover operators to infiltrate predominantly nonviolent organizations. Such practices contravene a variety of guidelines, including the role played by private companies, and the posting of officers for indefinite periods, with the not-unexpected result that several offices have 'gone native' (see later). A similar undercover operation was disclosed in October 2011 with the revelation that a university lecturer (a former police officer) had worked covertly within a number of anti-racist groups in order to disrupt their activities (Evans and Lewis, 2011b).

The wall of secrecy that successfully concealed the identity of the Special Patrol Group officer who killed Blair Peach in Southall in 1979 is much less evident nowadays. Police culture – or rather 'cultures' – that traditionally supported such deviance is now the product of a much more multi-faceted normative system (Chan, 1996), no longer as pervious to corruption. Thus in the case of Ian Tomlinson at the G20 demonstration (although there was an initial attempt at a cover-up, assisted by the peculiar practices of the police pathologist), a combination of lack of cultural support together with the now-ubiquitous transparency of such events, ensured that the Blair Peach case was not repeated in subsequent proceedings.

Elizabeth Filkin, the former parliamentary commissioner for standards, conducted an inquiry into the ethical issues that arose in police dealings with the media (Filkin, 2012). She recommended in her report that all Scotland Yard officers and staff who meet members of the press make a personal note of that meeting for their line manager. She also suggested a new system to tighten up on leaks and trading of information for personal gain. The culture of secrecy within the organization should also be addressed and a new system implemented to map the ethical risks and any perceived bias towards certain newspapers.

Police absenteeism, injury, and illness

The frequent absence of police officers from duty has customarily raised public concern for several reasons: first, the extent of police 'sickness' compared to other occupations – officers receive their full salary for the first six months and then half pay for the next six months; second, the extent to which policing is a dangerous occupation, meriting special treatment and requirements of staff; and third, the tendency for police officers to suddenly 'retire' when disciplinary measures loom. Other matters have been raised, such as the number of sworn officers on 'restricted duties'. In regard to the first issue, it has been claimed (BBC News, 2010c) that:

> Almost one in 10 police officers in England and Wales is on sick leave or performing limited duties like paperwork and answering phones . . . almost 9,500 officers are on restricted duties due to ill-health, with a further 2,000 on long-term sick leave and off work for at least one month.

In part, the explanation for the high number of officers on long-term medical leave is due to legal restrictions that stipulate only six officers per thousand are allowed to retire from the force on medical grounds in a given year. In a different occupation these officers would have qualified for a medical retirement but owing to legal

---

Box 2.4   The contradictions in disablement and pensions

If you wanted to sort out a lot of long-term sickness . . . if they fell in the disabled box and you couldn't redeploy, you've got massive costs. The quirk on the police pensions, for a civilian, is if you're disabled, and you can't do your job you'd normally qualify for an incapacity pension. The police regulations don't work like that: if you're disabled, and you can't do the ordinary duties of a police officer it then falls on the authority to decide if they can redeploy you. If they can, you don't get a pension even though you're permanently disabled in the meaning of the regs (sic). That's why the police service has lots of people on recuperative duties, permanent and temporary restrictions.

(quoted in Health and Safety Executive, 2007)

---

restrictions in the police they are placed on long-term leave or redeployed elsewhere in the force (Health and Safety Executive, 2007) (see Box 2.4).

As elsewhere in state policing, the data is often flawed: in this case mainly because of varied practices in different police forces. Official data on absenteeism varies dramatically between police areas and is clearly unreliable – from one in seven of the small Warwickshire force to one in twenty-four of the similarly-sized Cambridgeshire police (*Daily Mail*, 2010). In 2009/10, Warwickshire Police reported that it had 13.9 per cent of its officers on restricted or recuperative duties. By contrast, Cambridgeshire and Derbyshire reported none, whilst Cumbria reported 0.4 per cent. Different forces traditionally utilize different processes of measuring illness and injuries. As one chief constable commented (Health and Safety Executive, 2007 p. 42):

> Makes you wonder about how they're managing in other forces, because their sickness is staggeringly low. It can't be can it? So you wonder how they do it. We did find out that we were measuring things wrongly . . . We were overdoing it. We were overemphasizing it. We were doing ourselves no favours at all.

Calculating police injuries suffers from similar problems to other police-related data. Different forces measure police injuries in different ways and award benefits accordingly. For example, for the period 2005/7, the Merseyside Police made injury awards to 14 per cent of all officers who claimed injury compared to the South Yorkshire Police which only acknowledged injury in 0.5 per cent of cases (Health and Safety Executive, 2007). Reports of duty injury appear to follow local subjective guidelines. Data banks containing demographic and absence data were rarely linked to payroll data where the number of days lost was held. This seriously limits the amount of potentially useful cross-analyses that can be made.

International police sickness rates suggest that proportionately more female officers than male are likely to take sick leave, but differences in both international police practices and methodology make it relatively impossible to suggest whether in England and Wales the sickness rate is unusual (Körlin et al., 2009). In the illness context, policing shares the features of other hierarchical organizations:

> you will inevitably get the people who after a weekend, when they're supposed to be back in on the Monday and they're still far too hung-over and poorly to come in. They'll ring in with a stomach upset or a cold or something, and take just that one day off, or they don't want to work the shift and they've been refused leave.

However, officers facing serious disciplinary action have been permitted to retire early and thus avoid potential negative consequences of public and media scrutiny. Over the last two decades, there have been several retirements of senior officers that have appeared to be related to potential disciplinary issues. In the Stephen Lawrence case, Detective Inspector Ben Bullock, second-in-command for the first 14 months of the murder enquiry, retired early. That retirement was described by the chair of the then Police Complaints Authority as an 'abuse of the disciplinary process'. Chief Superintendent David Duckenfield, the senior operational officer at the Hillsborough football ground when ninety-six fans were killed in 1989, retired on grounds of ill health before disciplinary proceedings could be completed. However, given recent procedural changes, the older tradition of police officers allegedly feigning sickness and retiring on pension to avoid disciplinary proceedings appears to be receding. But it is important to distinguish between retirement on ill-health grounds before completion of the 30-year contract, and retirement after completion of that period (see also Box 2.5). In 2004, the senior police officer crucial to a £5 million trial was allowed to retire to avoid disciplinary proceedings. Consequently, five men accused of murder were acquitted (*Stockport Express*, 8 December 2004). The judge claimed that that retirement meant that the Greater Manchester Police had failed to take into account Home Office guidance designed to maintain 'public confidence in policing'. The officer was already suspended because of other allegations, but his suspension was lifted so he could retire after completing 30 years' service. This meant no further disciplinary action could be taken against him. Most of the trial costs were awarded against the police.

As the Health and Safety Executive Report (Health and Safety Executive, 2007) makes clear, the key feature of police absenteeism is related to the ambiguity of the concept of 'stress'. The usual suspects as the cause of stress are wheeled out – including increases in 'paperwork', in 'bureaucracy', in performance-related targets, and in management 'bullying'. Despite rhetoric to the contrary, police work is not especially dangerous as a cause of absenteeism when compared with manual occupations. The ambivalence of stress as a medical category dominated the report's evidence. Typically, research by an occupational psychiatrist to the Metropolitan Police concluded that long-term sickness absence was strongly

---

Box 2.5   Chief officers and gross misconduct

A chief constable who admitted gross misconduct is in line to receive more than £200,000 in compensation after his police authority decided not to renew his contract. It has emerged that North Yorkshire Police Authority would have to make the payment to Grahame Maxwell because he is required to leave his £133,000-a-year post before being able to secure his full pension entitlement after 30 years of service. The payment – which is governed by nationally-agreed chief officer regulations must be made after Mr. Maxwell leaves the force next May unless he obtains another job in the police service.

(Daily Mail, 1 November 2011)

---

associated with workplace disputes: 'Once an officer saw ill health retirement as his preferred option, there was an imperative to maintain the illness presentation until the matter was decided' (Summerfield, 2011). 'Medicalization' of problems led officers to maintain that they were ill in order to obtain appropriate rewards, such as retirement at an appropriate pay level. As Summerfield (2011) suggests: 'The number one predictive factor regarding a return to work and career was whether the officer wanted to, which no psychiatric formulation captures'. The police system perversely creates a barrier to recovery. Work-related injuries were also acknowledged as causing absence, as were psychological trauma – either from a single traumatic event, or a build-up of exposure to such events over time. Taking short-term absence was seen as a way to express dissatisfaction with a situation or decision.

Most forces used some form of incentive, such as extra leave and access to special payment to ensure a health record. In one force, the reward for those with no sickness absence over a 12-month period was a certificate; another gave

---

Box 2.6   Compensation payments 2010–11

Compensation payouts to officers totalling a £12 million has been branded as unacceptable. Many of the settlements – were for slips, trips and minor ailments. They include £120,000 for a bruise, £17,500 for 'noise-induced deafness from computer/keyboard' and £14,000 for a sergeant who claimed a cell buzzer gave him ringing in his ears. The largest single payout of £550,000 went to a civilian employee who sued Hertfordshire Police for chronic pain syndrome caused by a broken elbow sustained in a slip in an icy car park.

(Police Oracle, 27 January 2012)

an extra day of leave. One force applied some form of additional payment as officers with good attendance could become eligible for a bonus. Policy approaches by police forces were varied, from one that took a punitive stance, to others which stressed their duty of care towards staff. The most effective policies were those that accepted that ill health was unavoidable, recognized the importance of a culture where individuals felt valued, and where suitable measures were in place to encourage and support returning to work (Health and Safety Executive, 2007).

We should recognize, however, that work-related injuries are not just experienced by the police as victims. There is an equation to solve. Between 2008 and 2011 police forces across the UK paid out £777,000 in compensation to victims of police dog bites (BBC News, 2011a). In the West Midlands alone, over 680 people had been bitten in the force area in the last three years – the vast majority being 'suspected' criminals. Nine of the incidents resulted in compensation being paid out, after it was later found that the attack victim was in fact an innocent bystander. Curiously, the West Midlands Police seems to have recognized that in those few civilian cases it recognized as worthy of recompense, it only found 1 per cent of its officers who claimed injury on duty worthy of compensation for the period 2005/7 (Home Office, 2008b). More seriously, the then Police Complaints Authority documented in 2004 an 'unacceptable death toll' caused by car chases involving police vehicles (Best and Eves, 2004). Between 2001 and 2003 more than 1 per cent of all traffic deaths in England and Wales involved the police (Best and Eves, 2004). In that period, twenty-seven civilians were killed in police car chases (see Box 2.7).

Box 2.7   Police pursuit

The Independent Police Complaints Commission (IPCC) is independently investigating the management of the police pursuit that preceded the death of 25-year-old Kyle Griffiths from Thornhill, Cardiff, in the early hours of 10 January 2012. At approximately 02:50hrs on January 10, 2012 two police officers in a South Wales Police marked police Ford Focus signalled a blue Fiat Cinquecento to stop in Penarth Road, Cardiff. The driver of the Fiat failed to stop and was pursued through the city centre to Cardiff Bay where the Fiat collided with Mr Griffiths in James Street. Mr Griffiths received serious injuries as a result of the collision and was taken to the University Hospital of Wales where he was later pronounced dead. 'The IPCC investigation will focus on the management of the police pursuit, specifically the actions and decision-making within the control room. Our investigators will also look at this in relation to force training and pursuit policies, which are now subject to the codification of police pursuits on 23 May.'

(*Wales Online*, 2012)

Box 2.8   Early retirement to avoid disciplinary and criminal charges

Hundreds of police officers accused of misconduct and incompetence have escaped punishment by resigning. Almost 500 were allowed to quit with clean records and valuable pension benefits over two years. Critics said the little-known practice is allowing officers facing disciplinary proceedings to leave by the back door, and threatens to damage confidence in the police [. . .] senior officials defended the system, saying it actually saves the public money by allowing officers to leave without spending long periods suspended on full pay. At least 489 officers across Britain facing disciplinary panels were allowed to resign or retire over two years, an investigation discovered. Freedom of Information requests made by the BBC's Panorama programme found that 1,915 officers were found guilty of misconduct during the same period. Of these, 382 were sacked or told to resign for reasons ranging from neglect of duty to improperly accessing information or criminal convictions. Earlier this year Scotland Yard's director of human resources retired with a £180,000 pay-off despite facing 'highly sensitive' allegations by a woman colleague. Solicitor Jocelyn Cockburn, who specializes in cases involving complaints against police, warned of the risks of letting officers leave through the 'back door'. She said: 'If they are allowed to leave the police without any stain on their character then there is the chance they will go and work in another force, and that does happen'.

(*Daily Mail*, 31 October 2011)

Police effectiveness

It is extremely difficult to establish whether the British police are efficient; whether in their own terms or in relation to other public services or in international comparison. No-one knows how many police officers are required to have an impact on policing outcomes such as crime reduction, for instance (Bayley, 1996; Reiner, 2012). Decades of research remains inconclusive. There are many reasons for this impasse. The relationship between policing and crime levels is complex. The research evidence questions any direct relationship between the number of police officers and both the level of crime and police effectiveness in dealing with it. As Reiner suggests:

> Crime is shaped by a variety of factors: shifting definitions of criminality; social, economic, cultural and psychological pressures and seductions motivating potential offenders; the ebb and flow of opportunities and means to offend; and the varying constraints of informal as well as formal social controls. Improvements in crime prevention technology have made an obvious contribution.

(cited in the *Guardian*, 10 March 2011)

Box 2.9   Financial accountability and oversight

In many ways financial accountability within the state police is an oxymoron: whatever the methodology utilized, the data is fundamentally flawed

(a) We do not know how many 'crimes' occur.
(b) Recording by the police is subject to individual (police discretion), occupational (practice of the 'job'), organizational (impression management, resource availability), legal (a £100 burglary may be categorized together with one of a value of £100,000) and judicial variables (guilty versus innocent verdicts).
(c) Reporting by victims varies by offence, by gender assignation, by age, by ethnicity, by socioeconomic class, and by other factors (insurance, access, etc.).
(d) The data cannot be measured by crime reports (subject to (b)) or by victim surveys (subject to (c)).
(e) Performance measures produce contradictory results – response times, forms of patrol and deployment.
(f) Comparisons with private organizations are subject to major flaws – profit motive versus 'public good'.
(g) Comparative measures with other public services are subject to lack of agreement over policing objectives (the National Health Service (NHS) 'cures' patients) (see Chapter 3 on police science).
(h) Comparative measures over time and with other police organizations are flawed by the number of potential variables.
(i) While the Home Office has attempted to centralize and standardize recording practices, the highly devolved nature of policing in the UK means that considerable regional variation occurs in what gets recorded and how.

As some have argued (see for example Manning, 2010; Vollaard, 2006), effectiveness can only be assessed by including qualitative (i.e. subjective) factors, not recognized by accountants and politicians.

Typically, theft of modern cars is now almost entirely restricted to professional thieves.

Policing is only one aspect, frequently a minor one, of an increasingly complex equation of crime and resolution. This realization, despite official rhetoric, led directly to a new emphasis on the fear of crime rather than crime itself, and successively (together with other factors) to a new emphasis on policing the visible petty crime of the 'Other' in public space (Young, 1999). The home secretary, apparently by alchemy rather than by evidence, claimed in 2010 that crime had fallen steadily since 1997, with a further reduction of 18 per cent achieved in the last 4 years, exceeding the target of the 2004 Spending Review. According to the then Labour Home Office minister, Alan Campbell:

> I'm very pleased to see that confidence in the police is increasing and the number of people worried about high levels of anti-social behaviour has fallen to 15% – the lowest on record. The British Crime Survey also shows that the risk of being a victim is at its lowest point ever.[29]

In practice, analysis and recording of crime data is a complex issue and one far removed from questions of police numbers and effectiveness (see Box 2.9). What is established is that apart from at particular times and in particular contexts, and without specialized forms of deployment and expertise levels of police, manpower has (apart from at the extremes) very little impact on the rate of recorded crime and the number and experience of crime victims. So much for problems in reductions in police manpower in the fiscal crisis!

The problems with recorded crime statistics are well known. All the vast volume of research on the issue tells us that reactive police resources and labour force size and composition have a minimal effect on the level of crime (Bayley, 1996; Waddington, 1999). Whatever the partisan caveats, relative increases or decreases in police resources only reinforce the credo that the state police have a minimal effect on the prevention and arrest of offenders – except for the easy pickings of the 'Other' through ASBOs and incivilities. They are subject to arbitrary fluctuation, sieving in the recording process and by local imaginative construction in the attempt to meet police performance targets (now formally replaced by the home secretary to one amorphous target of community safety). Clear-up rates have long been criticized (Gill, 1987; McLaughlin, 2007). Victim and fear of crime surveys have of course their own problems (e.g. Schneider, 1981). Typically, the first attempt to apply the British Crime Survey to Northern Ireland omitted questions around sectarian harassment and victimization which had obvious implications for the depiction of Northern Ireland as a 'low crime' society (Brogden, 2000). But crime data has a different institutional character. Many offences may be recorded but never actually investigated. Transparency has never been a virtue of the British state police. One example will suffice. In 2007, the Metropolitan Police acknowledged that police officers had been told not to bother with follow-ups with nearly half of burglaries. This decision made financial sense – it costs far more to investigate an average burglary than the stolen goods are actually worth (Baldwin and Kinsey, 1982). The decision not to pursue thousands of crimes emerged in guidelines drawn up by the Metropolitan Police (Metropolitan Police, 2007a, 2007b). Similar measures have been adopted by other forces. Officers have been told that only the most serious crimes – such as rape, child abduction and murder – should be investigated automatically. In other cases, investigations will be 'filtered so that resources will only be deployed to futher investigate those crimes that are potentially detectable and/or of a serious nature' (Metropolitan Police, 2007b). That means there must be clear evidence pointing towards a suspect – such as DNA traces, fingerprints or a possible identity – which makes an arrest likely. There are some exceptions, such as where the victim is an elderly person. But the consequence is that many serious cases of robbery, violent crime, car crime, sex offences and so on will be left to gather dust. If there are no obvious clues, the case will be dropped. In 2011 *The Times* news-paper used a Freedom of Information Request to gain access to police statistics in relation to the percentage of reported crimes that were screened for 'no further action' by police forces in England and Wales. The data show that nationally about 32 per cent of offences reported to the police are dropped without further investi-gation. However, the situation in London and the Metropolitan Police is even worse. Of the 824,495 offences reported to the Metropolitan Police in 2010, 463,315 made it to the investigation stage, with 361,180 screened as requiring 'no further action' (PolicyExpert, 2011).

The data in Table 2.1, from the Lancashire Constabulary's website, are presented by the police with little explanation or overall context. There are particular problems here:

1   What is the status of this data – reported to the police, 'cleared-up', convictions?
2   What is the source of the data – the highly unreliable reports to the police, or – slightly less unreliable – local victim surveys?
3   The categories are too broad to be meaningful – a robbery amounting to £10 may be equated with a robbery amounting to £1,000.
4   The category of violence presumably includes a range of quite different types of offences, e.g. late-night alcohol-induced violence versus the quite different domestic abuse.
5   ASBOs constitute half the offences. But they are quite different in legal procedures from offences subject to due process.

Table 2.1 How not to keep the public informed: crime map data from a northern council estate

Offence	Number	Description
Burglary	48	Includes offences where a person enters a house or other building with the intention of stealing
Anti-social behaviour	428	Includes personal, environmental, nuisance, anti-social behaviour, and hoax calls
Vehicle crime	37	Includes theft of or from a vehicle or interference with a vehicle
Robbery	4	Includes offences where a person uses force or the threat of force to steal
Violent crime	88	Includes offences against the person, including common assault, harassment, and grievous bodily harm
Other crime	212	All other crime reported to the police, including criminal damage, shoplifting, and drug offences
Total	817	

Source: www.lancashire.police.uk/ (accessed 2011).

Since the production of the above tabulation, other possibilities have been introduced to local crime maps including limited 'comparative' data by Home Office directive.[30] Sexual crimes are 'dumped' in the violent crimes category when they relate to the specificity of household abuse. Generally, when containing rare accuracies, the statistics increase the gap between the information-rich and the information-poor. Crime statistics have always been used as a rather crude performance indicator, but are likely to become more so under the new local crime and policing commissioners and will therefore be subject to more arbitrary recording and classificatory procedures.

The Metropolitan Police has pioneered a measure of effectiveness based around the question 'Do police do a good job in your local area?' It derives from local victim surveys and uses four measures: perceptions of police effectiveness, fairness of personal treatment, level of police engagement with the community, and local people's concerns with the level of disorder. But this measure, based on shifting subjective data, is a long way from commercial perceptions of efficiency (it is difficult to imagine Tesco or Sainsbury's as commercial enterprises adopting the same criteria!). Amongst many other criticisms is Skolnick's (2005) observation that almost all contact with the police has the potential to be regarded negatively. Similarly, Bradford et al. (2009), for example, report on data from the British Crime Survey to suggest that those individuals who have had some form of contact with the police have also lower levels of confidence in policing overall. As Sir Ronnie Flanagan (former chief constable of the RUC) states in the Interim Report of his Review of Policing, 'every contact an officer will have with a member of the public will leave a trace' (Flanagan, 2007).

Given both the imprecise functions and roles in the British policing system, any attempt to compare agencies in the interest of economic efficiency is doomed to end in failure. The crime data, whether from clear-up rates, recorded crime levels, or from victim surveys, are notoriously suspect. Generally though, the more serious the offence, the more likely an accurate recording is possible. But it is impossible to furnish a comparative critique of crime and successful prosecutions between the common law system of England and Wales and that of similar Western European states. Even within the UK, factors relating to socio-political conflict and high levels of ethno-sectarian tension in Northern Ireland have made it difficult to generalize about crime trends on a regional basis (Brogden, 2000). Different national police forces vary in function, in disparate units and agencies, and in crime definition and recording data. Ideally, within the UK, one should be able to furnish comparisons between different state agencies in terms of 'success rates'. But the nearest comparator to the police service is that of the National Health Service. In the latter context, performance indicators – such as death rates in hospital from varying forms of treatment – are relatively easy to measure. Death, after all, is a pretty definitive item of hard data. Length of queues for treatment is a fairly suspect indicator. But the NHS is beset by a variety of legalized private competitors – from primary healthcare providers to the provision of nursing homes. The prison system offers no comparison in terms of value and effectiveness, despite the privatization of several integrated penal institutions.

In policing, the only competition is with regard to specific tasks, such as guard duty and symbolic targets. In the policing context, only those (at this point in time) at the bottom of the food chain are able to nibble off profitable portions of the public good. Comparative data are regrettably not accessible in objective credibility to determine the effectiveness of policing in Great Britain and Northern Ireland. The problem is best summed up with an estate agency analogy. Estate agents primarily value houses in terms of comparators. The 'for sale' sign value of a house in a British street is primarily determined by the price of a recently sold comparator house in the same street. Only in a few cases of unique properties are estate agents confused. But at least estate agents have a specific, clearly defined objective. The British police system is a unique public service in not having clear objectives nor having comparators with whom to compare efficacy and cost.

Put bluntly, there is no exact science to determine whether the British police are over- or under-resourced.[31] The data is a hugger-mugger. How do you evaluate police performance when the input data, such as clear-up rates, are subject to such extraordinary failings? Nor would it be especially helpful to compare police work with that of other state agencies. Nurses help cure illness and alleviate suffering, but what do the police do and what should be their priorities? Contrasting public organizations in terms of numbers of managerial personnel to rank-and-file often tells us more about the market ideology of those calling for a cull of 'red tape' than it does about the expertise of the critic.

Local police authority effectiveness over financing

Accountability has long been a euphemism in the local police lexicon. An elastic concept, over time, has ranged from direct control by watch committees of the nineteenth century to the recent experience of the RUC where the old Northern Ireland Police Authority saw its primary function as one of 'selling' the police to the communities (Mulcahy, 2006). Despite changes in personnel, LPAs, as committees charged with ensuring the efficacy and effectiveness of the local police, set the police budget and decide how much to raise towards the cost of policing, through the local council tax. However, their financial conduct seems to have little changed since the first academic study (Brogden, 1977). That study depicted the relevant police authority as toothless in practice, honorific in membership, and dazzled and blinded by their incomprehension of police statistics. Occasionally, the then-feudal chief officer would intimidate the chair of the authority by lining the meeting room with his officers as the 'public'. As a financial accountability agency, they were, sometimes by choice, a waste of space. Members were out of their depth. Some things have changed for the better. Bullying by that cohort of chief officers has almost entirely disappeared. The new managerialist chiefs cajole rather than demand, schmooze rather than bully. Financial information is presented in much more accessible fashion. A complex of police public partnerships, such as with 'Lay Visitors' to police stations has intertwined the authority more closely with the outreach of police work. The mantra of 'policing by consent' appears to have been replaced with a similar euphemism of 'policing by active cooperation' under the new mantra of Neighbourhood Policing (McLaughlin, 2005).

The Audit Commission played an increasing role in tandem with HMIC in the search for 'value for money'. But that agency is to be abolished. A recent HMIC investigation (HMIC, 2010a p. 4). was charged with assessing whether the ten police authorities surveyed were 'ensuring value for money and productivity'. The report conceded that little or no assessment is conducted by police authorities of efficiencies or workforce modernization. For example, as formally required, few police authorities are actively engaged in exploring opportunities to work with local strategic partnerships, businesses, and the voluntary sector to drive efficient and effective policing and community safety outcomes. Any such consultation with communities rarely informs their power to shape police priorities. Police authorities lack a comprehensive understanding of the resources available in their area to deliver sustainable policing. They are not active in setting clear long-term priorities in their areas. The Association of Police Authorities often seeks advice over roles relating to different interpretations of the chief constable's operational independence. As with Brogden's 1977 study, the information provided to the authorities by the chief constable is frequently provided in too much detail and complexity to allow effective scrutiny. The more diffuse the area of policing, the less the authorities understand what is actually happening locally. Few police authorities can demonstrate that policing priorities inform local area targets, funding, and resources. However effective police authorities are at delivering annual budgets, HMIC found little evidence of LPAs preparing for the forthcoming period of policing austerity. Currently, the Cleveland Police Authority (which recently passed to Steria UK a £175 million deal to conduct its administrative work and support functions for the control room) is under investigation concerning allegations of nepotism in relation to several smaller contracts (Whitelaw, 2011).

Nevertheless, localism in relationship to accountability remains markedly on the political agenda (McLaughlin, 2005). In 2008 the then Labour government's Green Paper (Blunkett, 2009) caused some controversy by proposing the creation of elected crime and police and policing representatives, who would constitute a majority on police authorities. Accountability should go all the way down the line to the local police officer, with whom most people have a relationship of direct or indirect contact. Some of the LPAs' powers should be devolved to the bottom of the police–civilian pyramid. In any case, 'It is not clear that the public are aware of the powers they (already) have, or the steps that will be taken if the local authority is unresponsive to approaches' (p. 21). The president of ACPO, Sir Hugh Order, responded with:

> If people seriously think some form of elected individual is better placed to oversee policing than the current structure then I am very interested in the detail of how that is going to work . . . Every professional bone in my body

tells me it is a bad idea that could drive a coach and horses through the current model of accountability and add nothing but confusion . . . '

(Orde cited in Blunkett, 2009 p. 25)

The succeeding coalition government approached local elected accountability from a different angle, proposing to introduce new Local Police Commissioners. The right-wing think-tank Policy Exchange furnished the most explicit justification for the proposed commissioners: it claimed, using discredited reported crime data, that the UK suffers from higher crime rates than comparative jurisdictions. The criminal justice system as a whole is largely unresponsive to victims and far too centralized. The police commissioner would be primarily concerned with low level local crime and 'quality' of life matters, arguably largely ignored by current LPAs. The solution is to transfer more decision-making and accountability to the local level along with removing the central state 'monopoly' of minor crime responsibilities. Commercial and voluntary organizations should take over some responsibility. At present the 'weak and invisible Police Authorities' currently cost £65 million a year and some £8 million in expenses. Commissioners will be elected to oversee strategy and set force budgets, including how much local taxpayers contribute towards policing. Somehow, this distinctive British model will make police chiefs truly accountable for the first time.

Criticisms vary. The reforms are a costly distraction in the context of the fiscal crisis. It would 'politicize policing' and potentially increase local corruption. Elected politicians might put pressure on chief constables to investigate or ignore specific criminal cases. Greater political influence would lead to harassment of the minority Other. Two former chief constables, Blair and Condon, claimed that the new police and crime commissioners might be tempted to fire their chief constables for political reasons. Liberal Democrats proposed creating a Crime and Policing Board made up of nominated councillors (in practice, an apparent resurgence of the current LPAs). Nominees for the post might be limited to varied categories of representative, each with their own baggage: figures from the major political parties; uninspiring 'men in suits'; celebrity candidates with a high profile; and professionals with a criminal justice background such as magistrates and even judges might appear. Former chief constables might stand: the police establishment simply reasserts control of the system, ensuring business as usual.

The discourse of reform

The coalition government correctly recognizes that overall police numbers are relatively unimportant in dealing with crime in the context of the fiscal crisis (although its public rhetoric is often different). As HMIC suggests, police numbers do not give the full story. Organizational changes could improve forces' efficiency to allow more officers to be available when there was higher demand. Types of deployment, such as the degree of public visibility among other things, may contribute to assuaging manpower losses. Sir Ronnie Flanagan's *Review of*

Policing: Final Report was regarded in state circles as a watershed in resolving bureaucratic impediments, linking with Cameron's rhetoric on paperwork (Flanagan, 2008). Submerged within this combination of polemic and practice regarding cuts in policing has been a hidden undercurrent – that of privatization – state policing as subject to the laws of the market.

Free market ideology has infiltrated the language of reform, together with a degree of populism – as in the proposal for police commissioners and the release of remarkably unreliable local crime data on the internet under the slogan 'bureaucracy hinders police work'. Pejoratively, cutting paperwork is an important key to releasing 'front-line' resources, one that can mainly be resolved by 'outsourcing' certain policing tasks to private companies; as well as by enhancing the use of digital technology and changes in organization, such as in locally shared force facilities, mergers such as that of the Serious Organized Crime Agency and of the Child Exploitation Service, and local deployment practices. Privatization, according to official legend, can cut police costs by providing specialist services which local forces may be unable to sustain, and can cut labour costs (most obviously, with dubious hiring and firing practices in relation to service and ancillary workers). So-called 'bureaucracy', 'paperwork', and 'red tape' are the usual, easy, monetarist Aunt Sallys. Like other such ideologically based rhetoric, there is some truth in this view. Formally, since the Police Act of 2002, local police forces have been encouraged not just to develop shared facilities but to contract out specialist tasks to private profit-making companies. While such privatization is formally directed towards concern with police efficacy, the process (and its hidden extent) raises major questions both about accountability and legality.

The debate about the growth of directly employed civilians by police forces has concealed the much greater extent to which local forces are now utilizing both older (such as custody maintenance) and new (technological developments) police functions in the hands of a vast array of private companies, whose legal powers are essentially fudged. Together with the Police Reform Act, 2002, the Serious Organized Crime and Police Act, 2005, and the Police and Justice Act, 2006, this has greatly increased the number of non-sworn personnel in custody, investigation and neighbourhood police roles amongst others.

Police forces have long employed civilians – from the old Bridewell keeper onwards. Nevertheless, contracting functions out to profit-making enterprises has given state policing a new combination of capacities and problems (especially over social and legal accountability) over the last decade. A central catalyst for this process was the evidence that less than 20 per cent of uniformed officers' time was spent under the current, transitional, rubric of Neighbourhood Policing. The Police Act 2002 designated four areas in which civilian staff could employ police powers – detention, investigation, escort, and community support. Some of these appointees could be categorized as employees of the LPA. However, many others are staff of private companies. Apart from the justification of releasing sworn officers to direct policing duties and any increase in efficiency (the justification for this process), a hidden rationale lies in the ideology of the free market impact on not-for-profit public services. Police officers, encumbered by rules of accountability and law, are burdened with consequent paperwork that hinders their efficiency.

This ideology underlies much coalition government thinking with regard to policing efficacy, expanding a process initiated by its Labour predecessor. 'Heavyweight' agencies, including the Audit Commission and HMIC, issued a joint report claiming that 12 per cent of central government funding could be saved without reducing police availability. Greater cooperation between police forces, closer matching of crime with the number of officers on duty and better procurement could all cut costs. The recent Audit Commission Report – *Sustaining Value for Money in the Police Service* (Audit Commission, 2010) – offers only euphemistic trimmings in maintaining effectiveness. The rhetoric of reform has been clear.

The subtle expansion of profit-making policing

Privatization of resource provision follows logically. Typically, in a pious inversion of language, the privately funded Serco Institute presents a 'reasoned' corporate rationale 'Contraction . . . optimizes the use of valued personnel through the professionalization of support service roles' (Sotiropoulos, 2008 p. 19). What appears to the policing agency as the 'back office' is regarded by the support service firm as integrated with the frontline. Staff, who would have faced very limited career prospects as supporting members of a police force, are given opportunities to rise to senior positions with a 'service provider'. This move, it is argued, will allow police forces to have a much greater opportunity to retain ' . . . specialist personnel with IT, project management and process reengineering skills' (Sotiropoulos, 2008 p. 17). And, of course, such contracting furnishes private companies with opportunities for increased profit from the public sector without legal accountability – though this is not mentioned by Serco's report. There is also a grey area in which civilians can be employed on direct contracts to act as investigators in interviewing, taking fingerprints, processing detention forms and preparing files for prosecution. Serco notes, reassuringly, that such posts are normally contracted to ex-police officers. A rather curious Home Office report entitled *Reducing Bureaucracy in Policing* (Berry, 2009)[32] paints an idealistic picture of policing before rules 'got in the way':

> people join the police service to do the right thing and make a positive difference, but somehow the system manages to put obstacles and hurdles in their way . . . no policy maker, politician, manager or supervisor goes out of their way to cause unnecessary bureaucracy. But somehow many of the changes they implement – albeit in good faith – end up causing just that.
>
> (p. 1)

In Home Office rhetoric, state policing should be driven by rebuilding trust, making rules more flexible, commonsensical and proportionate and in emphasizing integrity and professional standards. This is a remarkably cavalier approach to legal powers, a notional accountability which seeks to uphold citizen rights. Citizens are 'customers' (directly buying a fixed product) and are 'stakeholders', happily relying in retirement on their investments. Citizens have inherent rights under common law with regard to state intervention, not to a commercially based contract, assuming unequal relations. Critically, without precise determination of the police function, such a system and neoliberal approach is built on a foundation of sand. There is no consensus on what constitutes 'policing', on the functions of police, nor on the social contracts between state, citizens, and communities. (We develop these issues in Chapter 5.)

From contracting out the Metropolitan Police payroll and pensions service in 1998, increasingly local forces have collaborated using a common private contractor. IT and telecommunication work is often the work most prized commercially. Even command–control facilities may be partly manned by private staff, as in Hertfordshire and Merseyside. Other services of local enterprise include those of Air Support and of vehicle Fleet Management. More critical in terms of direct legal impact is the reliance on private companies to run key parts of the detention process, including taking DNA samples and fingerprints. In a few cases, private 'supervisors perform all the functions of a custody sergeant, apart from authorizing detention, carrying out risk assessments and reading a detainee their rights' (Sotiropoulos, 2008 p. 35). Commercial agencies are now also involved in the recruitment process, criminal record checks, and evidence storage, all again sold as allowing uniformed officers to conduct 'front-line policing'. Enterprising former police officers (now bereft of their former police powers and accountability) are foremost in establishing private companies to colonize traditional police work such as police station reception duties, security of police buildings (guarding the guards), management of identity parades and drug-testing, and more generally in the private security industry.[33]

Privatization and the neoliberal economics of state policing

Police tendering (as in other public services) has rarely been an exact science. In Northern Ireland, contract ineptitude under the late RUC demonstrated a structural problem. At that time, contracts were only issued to approved, i.e. security-vetted, private firms, leading to a range of opportunities for 'fiddles' (Brogden, 2000). In England and Wales, lesser but similar problems of police contracts tell us a little about the state of the police. Contracts for the transport and custody of suspected illegal immigrants have regularly been abused by private suppliers, whose staff may conduct actions verging on legality but without the assumed person-handling skills of sworn police officers (see Box 2.10).

A minor example of such incompetence was the ordering of 200 Heckler and Koch automatic assault rifles (costing some £400,000) by the NPIA in 2010. According to a failed contractor, this occured to ensure that the NPIA's budget was used up before the start of the new financial year, even though there was no expressed need for the weapons. The case of Raoul Moat, who had killed a civilian and seriously wounded a police officer, makes a similar point. A Taser had been

---

Box 2.10   Policing-for-profit in transporting illegal immigrants

The system of forcibly removing people from the UK needs a 'complete and radical overhaul', human rights campaigners have said. The Home Secretary . . . should introduce monitors on each and every removal flight and reconsider the use of private contractors . . . The campaign was backed by the widow of Angolan national Jimmy Mubenga, who said her husband would still be alive today if independent monitors had been present when he collapsed on a plane at Heathrow Airport while being removed last October. Adrienne Makenda Kambana said: 'If someone had been monitoring how Jimmy was being treated on that flight, I'm sure he'd still be alive today. The other passengers said he was crying out for help. The system must change to stop this happening again. No-one should have to go through what me and my family have suffered, and no-one should be treated like my husband was that night in October.' Amnesty called for the Government to consider the systems used in other European countries such as Germany where law enforcement personnel are used for enforced returns of individuals, including those who have overstayed their visas and foreign national prisoners . . . with so many reports of improper treatment.

(London Evening Standard, 6 October 2011)

---

used immediately before Moat's death. The Taser in question – an X12 model – had been handed over in person to the Northumbria police by the owner of a monopoly private company, Pro-Tect Systems.[34] However, this model had not been authorized for use by the Home Office Scientific Development Branch (Home Affairs Committee, 2011). As well as criticizing a clear breach of the rules governing the provision, use and transportation of Tasers, Select Committee MPs questioned the wisdom of a monopoly supplier business model in police procurement. Such monopoly provision is a major problem, as in the Greater Manchester Police's utilization of a single company in the supply of interpreters, to the chagrin of potentially competing providers. Inter alia, the police admitted that the Race Relations Act had been broken in the tendering process. The size and extent of this warped tendering is further illustrated by a recent Metropolitan Police Authority advertisement for renewal of a variety of civilian services. Up to £20 million has been allocated for a fully managed support service to cover the continued operation of the Metropolitan Police Service's custody and management information system (MIS) (Laja, 2011). Custody and case preparation functions are intended to be covered by the new civilian supplier. The NPIA proposes a remedy: all such local purchasing processes be centralized, though inevitably within the orbit of a private procurement agency. ProcServe has announced that they are providing a purchase-to-pay and an e-marketplace service for all forty-three police forces across England and Wales. The NPIA negotiated a deal with

Siemens Enterprise Communications so forces could buy equipment at a reduced cost. More important is the extent to which private companies are involved, not so much at the periphery of policing but at the centre. Charter Systems claims proudly that it now runs a single database solution by which five South West police forces 'will have access to a central repository for all covert operations that are carried out across the five forces, with the option for intelligence sharing across the whole South West region'. In a marketing statement it claims:

> Since 1994, Charter Systems Ltd have worked alongside our police partners to develop and maintain a software application capable of meeting the regulatory demands of managing Source and Covert Authorities policing and surveillance activities, which is now used in four out of five police regions in England.[35]

Some forms of coordination with policing-for-profit have been financially, if not legally, desirable. The NPIA's value for money efforts have helped forces across the UK make combined savings of more than £6 million by using the agency's Identity Access Management (AIAM) national framework. It enables authorized police officers and staff to access national police databases securely using one unique password or smartcard and pin. AIAM also creates a common security platform for information-sharing between forces, giving the private contractor access to full use of the Police National Database. Additionally, other functions are proposed – for example, using AIAM for other national applications such as IDENT1 (the national fingerprint database) and development work with CRASH (a computerized accident recording system).

On the local front, Kensington residents employ private security firms to patrol their streets in an attempt to reduce violent crime (see also Box 2.11). It is not uncommon to see private security guards patrolling the affluent grounds of gated communities. The number of private security guards armed with some police powers seems set to rise in London, with at least fifty affluent districts patrolled. Under the Community Safety Accreditation Scheme (2002), these officers can issue fines, confiscate alcohol or tobacco, direct traffic and demand someone's name and address. Whereas traditional private security had no legal authority to enforce the law over any British citizen, the government has quietly granted security companies working for councils, hospitals and private establishments some of the same powers as fully qualified police. (Their numbers now seem set to rise, from 127 accredited guards in 2010 to 400 by May 2012.)[36] The wealthier the district, the more likely it is to employ private security patrols, ensuring that policing as a whole becomes differentiated in terms of socioeconomic status. New small companies emerge on the margins, such as Sparta Security (twenty occasional staff), Garde UK, and Atraks, to pick up the leavings of the corporate firms to operate in more diverse constituencies, with a charge agreed with local council households (Davis, 2010).

At the other end of the scale Securitas, a leading global security company, offers commercial monitoring and emergency response patrols in the UK and is

---

Box 2.11 Multinationals enter the private policing sector

The Burger Bobbies: hard-up police force patrols streets with McDonald's marshals to beat crime

McDonald's is helping to pay for a team of police officers and civilians to patrol the streets of a city centre at night. The 'street marshals' are being funded entirely by local businesses, including the fast food chain, to try to control alcohol-fuelled violence. While towns across the country use street marshals or 'angels' to patrol on busy Friday and Saturday nights, the scheme in Leeds is the first totally funded by private businesses. West Yorkshire Police insists all the marshals are 'licensed and professional' door staff whose job involves controlling troublemakers anyway. Since July, up to 29 street marshals, wearing high-visibility jackets, have been going on patrol at key weekends alongside police officers, community support and special constables.

(*Daily Mail*, 19 November 2010)

---

contracted by the police to help secure particular events, such as festivals and football matches. If, however, you operate under contract, as Sparta does, a license from the Security Industry Authority (SIA) is required. Private security firms guard police stations and provide protection for politicians, judges and other possible terrorist targets from Northern Ireland to North Wales.

Private firms now largely furnish and staff custody suites. MPs demanded an urgent inquiry into such practices after a series of deaths and serious injuries in police custody suites staffed by private security companies. Their demand followed an investigation by the IPCC into how a man suffered brain damage and permanent paralysis after falling into a coma while in a Brighton police cell in 2008. Responsibility for custody was by employees of the Reliance Security Group, which has a 39-year contract with the Sussex Police to run its custody centres and similar contracts with four other police forces. The incident followed deaths in custody in Brighton and in Crawley. The IPCC recommended disciplinary action against three Sussex police officers but it has no authority to make similar recommendations to Reliance. Reliance was founded and is chaired by Brian Kingham, one of Britain's richest men and also a prominent Conservative Party donor. The MPs said it constituted an 'accountability vacuum' (Lakhani, 2011a).

In 12 months, the West Midlands Police paid £1.51 million to ISS Facility Services, a Surrey-based firm which provides everything from security to catering. In the last 3 years the amount it has spent on private security contractors has increased by 25 per cent.[37] Following its acqusition of the Cotswold Group (specialists in surveillance, fraud analysis, intelligence and investigations services), G4S – Britain's largest private security company – may now dominate serious investigations with its available (mainly) retired 12,000 former police 'freelancers' (Boxell, 2009). John Shaw, Managing Director of G4S, claimed that 'We have a team of 30 of our guys in one force on a major investigation right now, practically doing all of the roles except that of the senior investigating officer' (cited in Boxell, 2009). G4S has also been hired to assist counter-terrorist officers at Birmingham International Airport by providing video surveillance and monitoring capabilities (Oldham, 2011). Private firms, such as Evensure Management, are used to guard crime scenes in Sussex. Evensure furnishes staff to stand watch outside premises or land where a serious incident has taken place (Hall, 2002). G4S hopes to build thirty custody centres in the UK over the next 3 years and is in talks with police forces to provide what it says would be the UK's first privately built and run police cells. Under G4S's plans the firm would build, own and run the cells, which could then be rented by police forces and other agencies. Under the scheme, suites would be staffed by G4S employees, but overseen by police custody sergeants.[38] Scotland Yard has licensed Ultimate Security Services to provide guarding duties at several major transport hubs in London with the powers to request a name and address for a string of offences including criminal damage, begging, and antisocial behaviour, to confiscate alcohol being consumed within a designated public place or by a person under the age of 18 years, and also to confiscate cigarettes from under-16s (*Belfast Telegraph*, 2011).

Criticisms of these schemes are not lacking. The Police Federation makes several salient points about the employment of private security officers to conduct police functions. It undermines the crucial distinction between the police as the statutory law enforcers and the private security industry. It regards many private security officers as poorly trained, unqualified and inexperienced. Private companies are responsible only to their shareholders. Typically, how would complaints against them be handled? (BBC News, 2009). The previous Metropolitan Police commissioner, Sir Ian Blair, stated that 'What private security does best is the guarding of factories, or retail, or goods in transit. We do not want private security to become quasi-police'.[39] Many local problems have been documented, such as a private security manager impersonating a police officer and gathering details from witnesses of a major incident (he was later fined for impersonating a police officer).[40] The private security industry has responded with unverifiable claims about its success in street patrols with regard to crime.

Overview: value for money?

This chapter has furnished a necessarily selective account of the financial wastage of the British police. There is no way of comparing it to other police forces, internationally, or to other public agencies in the UK. In focusing on internal practices and measures or organizational efficiency, the findings are not good. Ineffectiveness and value for money is of course not simply the preserve of the police service: the then home secretary in 2005 wasted some £10 million on an abortive attempt to induce amalgamations of smaller forces. Reform is happening, as much due to competent senior officers (sensitive to international developments in policing), like the former head of the NPIA, as it is to the structural realities of contemporary neoliberal economics (see Chapter 3). The incremental, largely opaque infiltration of private security into state policing poses more questions than answers. The critique in this chapter has been largely limited to an account of the economic and fiscal reality of the UK police services, not of individual agents. Analysing the cuts in state policing requires a deeper account of the impact of the police role. We turn to this in the following chapter.

3 Smoke and mirrors

The cuts in policing and the technological fix

Home Secretary Theresa May and Policing Minister Nick Herbert have assured the public that 'frontline services' will be protected in spite of budget cuts of 20 per cent. But, in response to a Freedom of Information request, their department responded saying it could not define the term, adding: 'There is no formally agreed definition . . . although these are terms in relatively common use across the police service'.

(The Times, 15 March 2011)

The purpose of this essay is to show how finance ministries and cabinets in parliamentary documentaries can reduce both crime and police costs, simultaneously. By using a new strategy called 'evidence-based policing', governments can transparently work with police and the public to invest in police tasks that are cost-effective. These investments can be made by putting an end to expensive but ineffective police tasks.

(Sherman, n.d. p. 1)

Introduction

It is early days in the policing cuts. But some truths are apparent. There will be no common standard of cuts across the country. Few sworn police posts will be lost. Even fewer police officers will lose their jobs. The bulk of redundancies will be arbitrarily culled from civilian support staff. Staff cuts will relate not to essential competence by civilians but according to pragmatism and local/organizational politics. Privatization and outsourcing will increase. Much less than the expected sum will be saved. The public will probably not notice any difference: the police institution has shuffled its cards well. Science and technology can contribute to savings in manpower but their potential benefits are limited. The re-emergence of the Other, as in the August 2011 riots (we are assured by a government minister), will not occur again. However, the claim by the new breed of evidence-based police scientists that practice-directed research can, in part, assuage cuts in personnel, has little merit. The policing crisis will not be resolved without clearer determination of police goals, not decontextualized and pseudo-scientific remedies.

Major reductions in police resources have been decreed as one component of government reaction to the Western financial crisis. Nearly two-thirds of expenditure in the UK on criminal justice relates directly to police service expenditure (Mills et al., 2010). In real terms, police expenditure increased by nearly 59 per cent in the decade from 1998/9 to 2008/9 (ibid.) as compared with 33 per cent in the previous decade. The 24 per cent or so cuts to be implemented in policing between 2011 and 2014, undermine, indeed, shatter the facade of 'business as usual'. This economically-induced 'downsizing' (the euphemism of neoliberal discourse) has no obvious precedent (except, perhaps, during wartime emergencies) in modern societies. In jurisdictions where state policing agencies have been markedly reduced in size, this process has been the result of political imperatives such as a change in regime: in former Eastern bloc countries, in South Africa,[1] and of course, in Northern Ireland.[2] In the latter, a political raison d'être informed the final objective of the process. In Great Britain, the cuts are almost directly a function of economic exigencies (though in other state institutions such as the National Health Service, ideological opportunism to privatize is also evident). Consequently, there is no model to follow; no game-plan to 'seize the day' to modernize the police service. Drastic changes are measured almost solely by financial criteria and the vox pop to 'save the frontline', as determined by the relative influence of different lobbies. Critically, to repeat, cutbacks in policing should have provided the space within which to rethink the process of governance and security for a notional community of democratic equals. Crime and the larger concept of social harm (Hillyard and Tombs, 2007), and the role of the state police together with that of other agencies, could have been considered, evaluated, and implemented. The skeleton of a notional modernization needed to have meat fleshed out on its bones.

The modernization programme should have been coordinated nationally, rather than in an ad hoc mix of local and central decision-making. Context, the relationship and potential effects on interagency relationships, should have been considered. Policing changes have ramifications for the judiciary, penal agency, social services and many other institutions. But, in practice, the case for modernization, the skewed policing of the Other, has been largely ignored in the search for 'easy' cuts within an abysmal understanding of truly democratic policing.

Large reductions in police resources were an inevitable part of UK government reaction to the financial crisis – some £100 million in 2011 and £545 million by 2014/15. The home secretary declared that she wanted officers' pay to be frozen for two years along with that of other public sector workers, saving £350 million (Winsor Report, 2011 Part 1) (see Box 3.2). But police were expected to take cuts in other payments, including overtime, which as we noted in Chapter 2 had spiralled to almost £400 million a year, and housing and travel allowances. As Theresa May, the home secretary, acknowledged: 'No Home Secretary wants to cut police officers' pay packages' (cited in Travis, 2011a). But with a record budget deficit, these were extraordinary circumstances.

There is no precedent for these cuts. Arguably, only a Conservative government could make such savings, as the historic 'owner' of the constituency of law-and-order. Opposition to the financial imperatives by the various policing lobbies was feeble, disjointed, and apparently self-interested. There was no evident attempt to dress up such savagery as part of a planned twenty-first-century policing system. When push came to shove, in the face of the revival of the ideology of the market economy, opponents were supine, limited to such clarion calls as 'Christmas for criminals' by Paul McKeever of the Police Federation.[3] Even criticism from the inner circles of chief police officers did not avoid the dissipation of the complex functions of agencies such as the Child Exploitation and Online Protection Centre (CEOP) being merged into the new National Crime Agency (NCA). CEOP was limited in its powers. It could not direct local forces to conduct appropriate operations. But like the Forensic Science Service (FSS), it had created an integrated corps of specialists from different disciplines to deal with the reported increase in internet child abuse. It is difficult to see how such integration can be maintained as a micro partner in the new NCA.

Assessing the depth of police cuts is not a simple exercise. There is little objective transparency. No central register existed given the token localism of provincial decision-making. Different lobbies proclaimed different figures. Some forces like South Yorkshire had reserves to draw on. A few forces had already made major cuts independently of the new crisis. Others were already committed to costly building projects. Some LPAs distinguish in their decision-making between police officers, PCSOs (none in Scotland), and 'civilian support'. Others simply referred to 'manpower' reductions. For some forces, the cuts were frontloaded and their figures only cover the first two years of the four-year process. There is a variation of some 7 per cent between forces that commit most expenditure to personnel salaries. A few LPAs had already suffered relatively severe local cuts. The small contribution by local councils in most cases was frozen. But a few proposed to increase their contribution. A small minority of police forces, such as the Metropolitan and Surrey, receive enhanced grants because of their unique extra duties, such as diplomatic protection. Some forces include special constables in their listing of staffing, others do not, similarly with the use of volunteers in police work.

There is, however, serious criticism of the forced redundancy of those officers who are coming to the end of their 30-year service. The Labour shadow justice secretary claimed from Home Office data that the proposed extent of savings is false. Forced retirement in the first year of an estimated 2,000 officers could cost up to £200 million. A forcible retirement of a constable would incur the taxpayer a bill of £115,600 (£149,000 for a superintendent) in the first year and save only £7,333 a year later (with other parts of the local public sector consequently subsiding policing from the council tax).[4] Given that a proportion of these officers would have retired anyhow, her claim had merit but also contains that flaw.

Apart from the proposed loss of some 800 police posts and 1,000 civilians, a typical large force like that of Merseyside planned to make savings from dog squads, CCTV, information handling staff, the Force Operations Unit, which plans for the response to emergencies and pre-planned public events and operations, and training staff. Virtually all forces were considered for cost savings to be applied to the 'extended police family', which includes volunteers, cadets, Home Watch, PCSOs and special constables. Antisocial Behaviour Units, horse patrols and

---

Box 3.1 Curious expenditure

The Metropolitan Police spent more than £35,000 on 110,000 calls to the Speaking Clock and £200,000 on calls to Directory Enquiries over the past two years. There were 'evidential and operational reasons' for the calls a spokesman for the Met said.

(*BBC News*, 18 January 2012)

---

control room staff, witness care, scientific support, roads policing and call-handling departments are also in the firing line.[5]

And of course, civilian staff cuts begs the question, who would conduct that civilian work in future – police officers on fixed salaries? The response lies in a statement from the public sector trade union, UNISON. According to the regional officer for UNISON's Strathclyde Police branch:

> We have discovered that 36 per cent of the jobs in Strathclyde Police Area Control Rooms – which are essentially specialised call centres – are being done by police officers rather than the expert staff who are trained for the jobs. The Chief Constable claims that more than 400 extra frontline police have been added since 2007 to meet the government's target. In fact, 126 officers are not deployed on frontline duties, despite being counted in the total claimed by Strathclyde Police.

(*The Scotsman*, Wednesday 14 July 2010)

Table 3.1 provides an indication of the likely extent of the cuts among police forces which will not be uniform in their impact. Those forces at the top of the table that receive higher levels of funding from local council tax will be least affected by the central government cuts. Surrey Police Authority, for example, receives 51.5 per cent of funding from central government and the rest from council tax. Conversely, those forces at the bottom of the table that receive proportionately more of their funding from central government sources are likely to be hardest hit. Such forces are invariably in poorer parts of the country. Merseyside, for instance, receives over 80 per cent of its funding from central government grants. Local councils can vary their own contributions to the police from council tax. Even after a freeze in council tax as the government has required, the cuts will remain unequal (Gash, 2011). Northern cities with higher levels of social problems will place more demands on an already overstretched police. Furthermore, higher levels of unemployment in such areas as a result of the economic crisis more generally mean that local council tax coffers are not replenished, further depleting police resources. According to Gash (2011) more affluent areas such as Surrey, supported by a strong council tax base, have seen real-term cuts of just 12 per cent while others endured the full real-term budget reductions of 20 per cent.

Table 3.1 Central–local police funding 2010–2011

	Government	*Council tax*
Surrey	51.5%	42.9%
Warwickshire	56.4%	30.9%
Dorset	58.7%	38.0%
North Yorkshire	59.6%	40.4%
Lincolnshire	60.6%	33.6%
Gloucestershire	60.8%	36.3%
Nottinghamshire	60.9%	36.6%
Dyfed-Powys	61.3%	34.3%
Northamptonshire	61.9%	32.1%
West Mercia	61.9%	34.7%
North Wales	62.1%	35.1%
Wiltshire	62.8%	31.7%
Norfolk	63.6%	33.8%
Suffolk	64.5%	32.0%
Thames Valley	65.2%	30.7%
Hertfordshire	65.3%	31.1%
Essex	65.6%	26.9%
Sussex	65.7%	27.8%
Cambridgeshire	65.9%	32.5%
Staffordshire	66.2%	30.7%
Devon & Cornwall	66.9%	29.8%
Hampshire	66.9%	28.2%
Avon & Somerset	67.5%	30.0%
Cumbria	67.5%	27.0%
Kent	68.5%	25.5%
Derbyshire	68.8%	28.4%
Leicestershire	69.3%	27.3%
Gwent	70.1%	26.9%
Cheshire	70.7%	26.3%
Metropolitan Police	72.1%	17.8%
Bedfordshire	72.2%	25.4%
South Wales	72.6%	24.0%
Lancashire	74.3%	21.7%
Humberside	74.3%	24.7%
Cleveland	75.2%	21.7%
Durham	75.2%	21.5%
West Yorkshire	78.0%	16.7%
South Yorkshire	79.5%	17.8%
Greater Manchester	79.5%	16.6%
Merseyside	80.3%	16.0%
Northumbria	82.0%	10.5%
West Midlands	83.3%	11.4%
City of London	84.4%	0.0%

Note: Total central government provision is comprised of revenue support grant, national non-domestic rates, Home Office police grant, and specific grants.

Source: Police Estimates Statistics 2010/11, CIPFA. Available: http://www.cipfastats.net/news/newsstory.asp?content=13904

Box 3.2   Winsor's primary proposals for cuts

Two years' freeze on police and civilian salary progression
Abolition of Competence Related Threshold Payments (CRTP)
Suspension of chief officer and superintendent bonuses
Abolition of Special Priority Payments (SPP)
Reductions in overtime/mutual aid for officers and staff

A perspective on the financial reduction

The very nature of the police organization, especially the fixed employment of sworn officers, ensures that there may be some benefits in terms of progressive initiatives, such as encouraging police forces to coordinate their resources and activities. But that example hardly reflects the core financial problems. Neoliberal political ideology underlies such changes and has two obvious manifestations. Privatization, as with other state agencies, is a major undercurrent (see Chapter 2). The model can most obviously be seen within the NHS, where proposals for hiving off functions such as catering, long-term care, and many other processes are most clearly signalled. With the police, the key indicator noted previously was the UK government's announcement that it was to close the FSS and contract out many of its responsibilities to the private sector (Lawless, 2011) against the almost united opposition of the lobby of chief constables (described by one as 'like closing a major university'). Into this mess has been thrown a different political card: that of political populism (localism) and the proposals for the election of police commissioners. But the central problem relates to reductions in the labour force.

Police officers

First of all, the number of police officers who are actually losing their jobs over the period will be relatively small – far less than the predictions of the Police Federation. It is not just legally difficult to make police officers redundant. It is also very costly. Second, the current cohort of officers (having served 30 years) available for redundancy over the cuts period, is a relatively small proportion of overall staffing levels. Third, the Police Federation is an extremely powerful lobby. Its outcry about the cuts is not quite a case of crying 'wolf' too often: it has undisputed expertise and serious political muscle. It is the shock of its previous law-and-order political allies in the Conservative Party failing to make its members a special case. Federation rhetoric disguises substance. Further, police officers are supported by the ideological myth of the effects of the uniformed police patrol officer in dealing with the Other. Police patrols have minimal evident impact on violent and property crime. While the simplistic equation between numbers of sworn officers and impact on crime is little more than a pipedream, it does have popular support (like capital punishment and the castration of sex offenders!). Pragmatic chief officers faced with a normally compliant police authority (now with an apparently simple statistic to get their teeth into), and by shrill media support for uniformed presence on the streets, have found it near-impossible to enforce redundancies. The easiest option, as adopted by the vast majority of chief constables, has been to freeze recruitment for 2 years (as recommended in the Winsor Report) including, of course, PCSOs. This hidden cut in police establishments is easier for powerful lobbies to swallow than the political fallout from police redundancies.

The myth of the frontline: easing the way for privatization

Downgrading of civilian posts in the police service is extraordinary in several ways. It is bound up with an 'interesting' depiction of the frontline (frequently code for policing the Other in public space). The general principle of Conservative governments, with regard to the provision of public services, has been to increase civilian inputs into specialist agencies like the police to conduct administrative tasks.[6] This notionally would 'free' up officers to perform beat and instant response duties. In policing, civilianization has been equated with 'back-office' administration. Paul McKeever, of the Police Federation for England and Wales, has suggested:

> It is extraordinary that the Home Office and Government have actually followed a policy for the last few months of reforming the police service through cuts by saying they will protect the 'front line' when they, nor anyone else, can say what that is . . . Recently I've even heard the terms 'back office' and 'middle office', but no one in policing knows what they mean. As far as I am aware it is terminology used in the banking world. But, like the phrase 'front line', they are phrases that have been coined by the Government.
>
> (cited in Hughes, 2011)

The Home Office, however, seems unable to agree on a definition of what constitutes 'frontline', 'middle office' and 'back office' services, suggesting merely that 'these terms are in relatively common use across the police service' (Hughes, 2011). Winsor in his report (Winsor Report, 2011) provided even less clarity, suggesting that the 'frontline is partially visible and partially invisible' (cited in Hughes, 2011). Generally, however, the 'frontline' seems to imply a combination of Neighbourhood Policing, criminal investigation and response policing.

A curious official document[7] recently attempted to translate the vox pop of the frontline into a more definitive discourse. Attempting, like an old steam-train spotter, to decide on the priorities between engine driver, fireman, and guard is

Table 3.2 The official demarcation of the frontline

Role	Type of work carried out	Percentage of total workforce (officers, PCSOs, civilian staff) in these roles	Percentage of officers and PCSOs in these roles
Visible	999 call response, attending traffic accidents, patrolling neighbourhoods	41	61
Specialist	Investigating crime, bringing criminals to justice, crime scene investigations	19	21
Middle office	Managing or supporting those in visible or specialist roles, running specific processes e.g. answering emergency calls from the public, holding prisoners in custody, processing intelligence	24	14
Back office	Support services e.g. finance, information, technology, human resources	15	5

Source: HMIC, 2011.

obviously fraught with problems. Briefly, after utilizing varied methodologies, the Report initially determined four different types of police role: visible, specialist, middle office, and back office (Table 3.2).

HMIC then attempted to define the 'front line' by consulting with police sector representatives, analysing data provided by forces and conducting a small public survey that used two essentially subjective criteria: everyday contact with the public and direct delivery of police services. These criteria, as practice shows, do not hold up to objective assessment. Consulting police officers leaves out the many other interest groups such as victims and offenders. Contact with the public varied between the positive and the negative, and delivery of services begs the question of both quality and purpose of service. However, from this initial premise, HMIC concluded that around 68 per cent of the police workforce is in the frontline (including 7 per cent in middle office roles). HMIC correctly recognizes some of the limitations of this demarcation. Measuring quantity is not the same as ensuring quality or indeed purpose in policing (though only assumed in the report). Though qualified in HMIC's report, contact with the public and visibility appear to be the key indicators of the division between the various sectors of policing staff. Drawing conclusions from one subjective-based set of data, the HMIC report then deduced equally problematic conclusions about the division between 'Public Facing Police' and 'Supporting Processes'. It concluded with the following vacuous definition 'the police front-line comprises those who are in everyday contact with the public and will directly intervene to keep people safe and enforce the law' (p. 18). The delineation of the 'frontline' is hardly helped by HMIC's vague emphasis on themes of discretion, of visibility, and of sensitive decision-making that apparently is peculiar to the frontline. It remains inscrutable what these specific factors have to do with dealing with the whole variety of different types of crime, from domestic disturbance to bank fraud. Tellingly, the report also notes that that those police forces that have privatized some of their support functions have fewer people in the back and middle office, and appear to have a larger frontline. The consequences for comparisons of police manpower and efficiency in relation to crime are evident. You cannot compare different forces on this dimension. It is difficult to see any value in this demarcation, apart from a politically driven expedient to privatize the support functions and ensure that in a time of cuts some staff are more surplus to requirements than others. Who needs a fireman and conductor, when you have an engine driver? The primary police function is defined by implication as 'contact with the public'.

Civilian staff composition in different police forces ranges from 36 per cent to 50 per cent of the total personnel. Together with the 16,000 PCSOs, spread across different forces, they (by implication from that discourse) constitute a surplus and sometimes dispensable population, which can sometimes be either privatized or subject to redundancy. They are legitimized by the official metaphor as being on the wrong side of the frontline. However, because individual police forces are complex, integrated, interdependent organisms, any division between the frontline and the assumed 'rest' is arbitrary at best and misleading at worst. Generally, the notion of a 'frontline' is a different kind of myth, feeding to a kind of populism, but having little value in developing a modern police force in the context of the present financial crisis.

As Winsor points out in his Report, unlike police officers, civilian police staff can be offered voluntary severance and early release packages and be made redundant, if necessary, in large numbers. 'It is therefore inevitable that they will bear the greatest burden of workforce reductions, which may be unfair' (2011 p. 12). The HMIC report referred to above codifies and legitimizes political rhetoric over the 'bureaucracy' and 'paperwork' to which 'frontline' police officers are subject. The relative disdain shown by some politicians for civilian so-called 'support staff' makes them an easy target. Given the variety of such roles, from IT specialists to PCSOs, civilian employees do not have the same defined trade association influence as do Police Federation members. Nor can they be identified in public mythology as crucial to the 'fight against crime'. Political opportunism has labelled them as 'second'- and 'third'-line police staff. A few will receive popular support for retention independently of the value of their contribution (such as PCSOs). Others, especially the *bête noir* of Conservative backbenchers, diversity training officers, have little chance of justification for their retention. The *Guardian* (12 January 2011) furnishes one anecdotal account of the bizarre nature of the cuts in the Greater Manchester Police (see Box 3.3).

Box 3.3   A GMP example of functional distinction as a means of cost-cutting

A few weeks before Christmas staff working for Greater Manchester Police (GMP) received a letter telling them whether they were in green-land, blue-land or red-land – a perplexing management consultancy-created code indicating the likelihood and imminence of redundancy. If your job was located in green-land, you could sleep easy for a while. For people like Anna, an IT specialist (who prefers not to give her real name), the letter made clear that her job was being scrapped. Her department was in red-land, an area of the force facing 37% cuts, and her own role was classified as category three, meaning it will be discontinued within months. 'The term "red-land" means you're for the chop, basically', she says, devastated after 20 years with the force. 'I've given half my life to GMP, helping keep the community a safe place. Now I'm being told I'm no longer needed'. Anna's job, for example, involves installing software and hardware for police staff. If a team of officers is launching a major investigation, she might be called in to install the violent and sex offenders register on their machines. Colleagues whose jobs are also being discontinued work on maintaining the telephone system and radio network, she says. After May their work will be shared out among other staff. 'IT employees are going to be over-stretched. Staff are going to have to take on more work, so police officers will have to wait longer if they need IT support, if they need their computer fixed. This will have an impact on frontline policing – on how long it takes to respond to an incident', Anna says.

(Gentleman, 2011)

Closure of the FSS

After several years of attrition with regard to funding certain contracts, in December 2010 the government announced that the FSS in England and Wales was to be closed. (Its practices were far removed from that of evidence-based policing promoted by others – see below.) The arguments regarding that closure are complicated, but it furnishes a primary example of the way the coalition government has sought to commercialize existing policing expertise. While a lengthy history is not of itself justification for continuity, the FSS had been in existence since the 1930s. Initially, it was relied on reactively by most police forces to furnish scientific evidence in court to support other evidence. More recently, its approach has been proactive, such as searching for suspects through its pioneering DNA Bank. Closure was officially based on several factors: it has been increasingly involved in loss-making activities, as private companies 'cherry-picked' the more lucrative aspects of forensic science activities; as civilian employees of a

---

Box 3.4   Promoting privatization of forensic science

At the present time, the near-monopoly existence of the FSS inhibits desirable competition. *Inter alia*, technology in the field is progressing so fast that eventually a Custody Sergeant will be able to conduct DNA analysis. At a time of Police Authority financial restraints and Police Service budget cuts, the market for forensic science appears to be rapidly shrinking and some police forces are considering in-sourcing much of the traditional forensic science provision.

(Steve Allen, managing director, LGC Forensics)[8]

---

government agency, its work can rapidly be privatized without major redundancy costs; and it has internal rivalries with the Metropolitan Police Force Forensic Service (to whom 120 of the national service staff were eventually transferred), whose chief executive regarded the FSS as replaceable by more individual agencies such as those in the private sector. LGC Forensics, which profits from varied state and commercial needs across Europe, perceived an opportunity to increase the profits to their shareholders and investors (see Box 3.4).

In its evidence to the Parliamentary Science and Technology Committee (House of Commons Science and Technology Committee, 2011) the FSS made a number of claims in its defence: that the service contributed markedly to academic scholarship in the area; that the coalition government ideologically valued only visible outputs; that there would be a loss of scientific expertise to the criminal justice system in the country; and, that many more miscarriages of justice would likely ensue if forensic science services were privatized.

The FSS employed experts from a variety of disciplines allowing a 'total' rather than 'partial' view of a complex case, and as such many FSS staff would be unlikely to be find alternative employment with private companies. Such a reduction would be bound in any case to adversely affect research and development, and the speed of specialized, sophisticated response to police enquiries. Commercial companies would not bid for the less profitable forensic work and, in any case, they could not guarantee the degree of impartiality in criminal cases to which the FSS is committed (a claim denied by the private companies). If a company is to make a profit from forensic science, there will be a temptation to achieve cost savings by carrying out an incomplete examination or employing inexperienced staff who can be paid a lower wage. The FSS had, at the time of closure, about 60 per cent of the market share of work from provincial forces. This work could not be absorbed within the 12 months within which the FSS was scheduled for closure, without major long-term investment. Its abolition would mean that England and Wales is the only police jurisdiction in Western Europe without a state forensic service. In-sourcing by provincial police forces is inefficient because of the economies of scale.

There were many complaints from provincial police forces about the closure of local FSS laboratories that prevented immediate response in relation to the investigation of cases. The impending closure of the FSS provoked a major outcry among international forensic scientists. Joseph Bono, president of the American Academy of Forensic Sciences, had urged that the coalition government stop the closure, claiming that handing over forensic science responsibilities to an untested privatized system will have 'serious repercussions' for Britain's capacity to solve compex criminal cases in the future (Lakhani, 2011b).

But pragmatically, the rationale was simple. A government committed to neo-liberal economics promotes private competition in the belief that such positioning is an incentive to efficiency. Second, given its disparagement of the benefits of higher education in the UK, support for research by the FSS was heavily discounted. And, of course in the context of major cuts in policing, the FSS was easy to dispose of, irrespective of policing consequences, in the quest for quick savings.

Incremental effects of cuts

There has been much hyperbole about the efficiency of local criminal justice partnerships. As noted in the previous chapter, the relationship between crime causation and the number of personnel in the criminal justice system as a whole is tenuous at best. But existing populations of offenders, even assuming the effectiveness of the present system, are likely to result in major problems. An integrated system at local level (admittedly a utopian vision!) has long been a goal of both major political parties. It has also been a necessity. Integration operates at several levels. Since April 2011, all domestic murders are to be subject to mandatory case reviews by all the agencies involved, including police, health and probation services, and relevant voluntary agencies (Johnson and Morgan, 2011). There is no apparent assessment of the availability of the appropriate staff from each agency to be involved in that process in future.

Typically, the number of suspects arrested by the police affects the ability of the prosecution and judicial system to cope. Decisions in the latter context affect the processes of prison and probation agencies, and social services (also suffering cuts). And of course, policing affects the voluntary agencies, as in drug rehabilitation projects, similarly top-sliced. In reality, the research evidence often shows more dislocation between the local agencies than coordination. For example, the police often play a dominant role in such relationships, partly in terms of ranking officer appointed and partly because of their more eclectic command of resources. However, changes in resources and staff personnel in one agency affect all other agencies, in a circular process.

Financial cuts are occurring across the board in the criminal justice system and related structures. Figures are inexact, due to a variety of circumstances. In the judicial system, between 100 and 149 local magistrates' courts were due to close across England and Wales to save approximately £45 million per annum (BBC News, 2010d). Whatever the savings in efficiency, local problems will occur with cases transferred from one district to another with consequences for suspects, witnesses, and in legal fees. Existing building contracts will be curtailed resulting in contractual costs, as in Birmingham's loss of a planned £81 million new criminal justice centre. Conveyor-belt justice may also increase. Delays in processing suspects will affect the potentially criminogenic population, increasing the demands on policing. Legal aid is being cut drastically (though that affects more civil cases than criminal). It will have unknown effects on other criminal justice agencies.

Similar problems are occurring in the National Probation Service, with a loss of 20 per cent of income (BBC News, 2010b). Caseloads for individual officers had already increased by 50 per cent over the decade from 1997. Consequently, many convicted offenders will not complete their community supervision, offenders being 'stacked', waiting to undergo local supervision.[9] In one example (from 2006), courts in south London sentenced 488 offenders to domestic violence programmes in 2006 even though there were only 300 places in the whole of London. Like state policing, probation is labour intensive: some 80 per cent of costs are on staff. Cuts can only be achieved by making existing staff redundant and limiting the number of new entrants.

The CPS was required to undergo a 25 per cent decrease in funding over the 2011/15 period (Hanman, 2010). Plans were afoot to encourage the swifter processing of guilty pleas and merger of regional offices. Again the effects will have both internal and wider criminal justice implications. The Warwick University Rights Centre, like the Law Society, argues that this will have a particular effect on vulnerable victims, such as in rape cases. Again trials will inevitably be delayed, with incremental consequences elsewhere in the criminal justice system. An increasing number of prosecution decisions will be made by the police (see Chapter 5) rather than by the CPS, a further backwards move given the original mandate of the CPS. Intended to save time, money, and 'bureaucracy', it will inevitably add to police tasks, quite apart from rolling back the binary rights system of separation of policing and prosecution functions. Victims will not escape the cuts. Reductions in the (largely) voluntary victim support system will require more attention by police family liaison officers, amongst others. Decreases in prison service resources have been equally severe. Half of its £2.6 billion building and maintenance plan has been shelved, while it is facing a spending squeeze of 28 per cent between 2010 and 2014. Two-thirds of the country's prisons are overcrowded and a number of major prisons are 50 per cent above 'certified normal accomodation' (Wright and Morris, 2011).

In many ways, this wrecking ball is on a controlled swing. The justice secretary, a penal reformer, wished to curb the previous government's commitment to the custodial sanction with a consequent record number of inmates. But his own political party rejected what would have been, in the long term, a cost-saving measure. Prisons will increasingly recycle offenders, with evident consequences for policing. Fewer police officers may result in fewer arrests and an eventual decrease in inmates. But this is long-term guesswork, given the indirect relationship between policing and crime figures and successful prosecutions. The penal system, without new facilities and without legislative innovations to decrease the use of the custodial sanction, is likely to become even more involved in a simple process of warehousing for crime prevention through incarceration without rehabilitation. The justice secretary's innovative commitment to community sentences, such as the new restorative justice schemes (although they are not without their problems – for example see Hoyle and Noguera, 2008) may not help, given the relative lack of difference in success rates between custodial and community sanctions (Pease, 2010). The unknown factor lies in the criminological debate about whether or not increased social and economic inequality does or does not affect the substantive rate of crime (e.g. Taylor, 1999). All we do know is that certain forms of violent offence (and arguably, the most difficult areas of state policing), such as domestic, child, and elder abuse, are largely impervious to socioeconomic factors, the numbers recorded being simply a function of the proactive practices of the police and social service departments. Elsewhere, the increasing expansion of the arbitrary ASBO process (given increased police powers in such matters – see Chapter 5) may be as likely to lower the threshold at which suspects enter the criminal justice process as to deter them.

The police forces in England and Wales depend on a variety of other agency contributions. Generally, the cuts in policing with their bias towards redundancies for civilian staff is entailing sworn officers assuming, to a limited extent, previous civilian posts for which they may not have the required expertise (as above). But it will also involve a series of complications with other criminal justice agencies. Coordination between the different agencies (except in particular local cases) has always been a long way from a success story. Cuts in specialist areas of cooperation may not coincide with complementary cuts in other agencies. The focus of the cuts, agency by agency, may vary: there is no requirement on the agencies to coordinate cutbacks. One police force might withdraw from a local community partnership while other agencies create redundancies elsewhere, creating new problems of cooperation at the local level. While formally the Home Office has no legal authority to ensure coordinated cooperation in the locality, Home Office circulars have accrued directive powers. But central direction of such matters has been marked only by its absence. Decision-making over complementary cuts in the locality has been left to ad hoc district improvisation, within a kaleidoscope of local interests. The Home Office has 'passed the buck', as indeed have other departments of state with regard to the relevant public service that they provide. Confusion will prevail in the community partnerships that the coalition government has made a priority for localized crime and anti-social behaviour reduction efforts.

The 'appliance of science' as a response to a decrease in police resources

In the 1850s, local English watch committees frequently debated the relative effectiveness of a police constable versus the new gas streetlights as alternatives in crime prevention in the local 'hotspots'. There is little new in the alliance between policing, science and technology – or in the use of technology to substitute for police staff. For example, August Vollmer's *The Scientific Policeman* was published in the 1930s (Vollmer, 1930) while Vollmer was himself appointed to a professorship of police administration at the University of Chicago a few years earlier. But the utility of a such misnamed police 'science' is itself problematic, given the vagaries of much policework, the absence of reliable data and of appropriate comparators to produce reliable and verifiable results. In this section, the terms 'crime science', 'police science' and 'evidence-based policing' are treated as coterminous. The 'science of police' (Reiner, 2010b), that quaint post-Rousseau attempt to rationally order society according to positivist principles, has returned with a vengeance. The most recent manifestation (e.g. see Sherman, 1998) makes the case for the latter. Sherman refers specifically to the way such an alliance can save police costs in general, and by implication, the size of the police labour force. The new 'sciences' represent a strategy by which police cuts in personnel can be compensated for by more efficient use of technology and the application of technical know-how. Clearly, one response in justifying and responding to the cuts in staff employed by the police is linked to assumption that there are more technical and scientifically based ways of 'doing policing' than approaches that depend upon the use of labour alone.

Just over 20 years ago Clarke and Mayhew (1988) pointed out that the simple substitution of nontoxic North Sea gas for traditional coal gas in households appeared to have caused a drop in the suicide rate owing to lower levels of carbon monoxide. More recently, technology has saved much police time. For example, in 2010, 107,000 vehicles were stolen in the UK compared with some 600,000 20 years earlier (Travis, 2011b). Various devices have been developed by manufacturers to prevent vehicles being started and subsequently stolen by means of relatively crude devices such as a coat-hanger or a screwdriver. Thus it is not because of the increase in police staff that car theft no longer constitutes a major problem. Similarly, improved technology applied to mobile phones has curbed what a few years ago was an epidemic of petty thefts of such devices. Technology can deter much minor opportunistic crime, curbing specific demands on policing. It is frequently argued that scientific developments such as in DNA testing can vastly speed up the detection of offenders via the use of a national database. New communications system such as e-mail and the real time sharing and analyis of documents offered in the Cloud[10] can dramatically enhance police investigation communication. As with car immobilization devices, crime science has utility elsewhere. Simple devices have been cited to prove the point. Graham Schleyer, of Liverpool University, constructed a blast-resistant litter bin, which would contain explosions and avoid the harm that has followed from flying fragments when bombs have exploded in traditional cast-iron structures (though it is difficult to recognize the relative costs of such devices replacing every litter bin in that way).[11]

A new discourse has emerged of crime science, with its variations in police science and evidence-based policing: 'Studies that focused police resources on crime hotspots provide the strongest collective evidence of police effectiveness that is now available' (Weisburd and Eck, 2004 p. 58). As the first director of the Jill Dando Institute stated at the time of its foundation, 'crime science is about applying established scientific approaches and techniques to crime control' (cited in Smith and Tilley, 2005 p. 9). Labour force cuts, by implication, can be massaged by the 'appliance of science', neglecting, however, natural science's commitment

---

Box 3.5   Police drone crashes into River Mersey

A drone used by police on Merseyside crashed into the River Mersey during a routine training exercise

The Unmanned Aerial Vehicle (UAV), which was fitted with CCTV, apparently lost battery power while being flown by officers in Aigburth in February 2010. Attempts to make an emergency landing failed and it crashed into the water. Merseyside Police said it would not replace the £13,000 drone due to problems with its performance and the cost of training staff to use it. It said full aerial cover and support was now provided to police by the North West Air Operations Group. A spokesman said: 'Despite the conditions a search of the area was undertaken but unfortunately the unit was not found. The force has since received compensation from its insurers to cover the cost of the vehicle.' He added: 'Initially the force identified the potential benefits of a UAV within operational policing. However, during its use officers recognised certain technical and operational issues including staff training costs and the inability to use the UAV in all weather conditions. These issues in conjunction with the current financial climate resulted in the decision being made by chief officers not to replace the unit.' The remote control helicopter came into use in November 2009. It was also fitted with thermal imaging equipment and was used by police for criminal surveillance. When it was launched police said it could be used for anything from hostage situations to monitoring large public events. Shortly before the crash, police were forced to take it out of service temporarily as they discovered they were using it without an appropriate licence. They needed permission from the Civil Aviation Authority (CAA) to fly within 50m of people and within 150m of buildings. A licence was later granted by the CAA, but soon afterwards the device plummeted into the river and could not be found.

BBC News, 31st October, 2011. http://www.bbc.co.uk/
news/uk-england-merseyside-15520279

---

to empirical proof. But, as the new applied police scientists recognize, technology and scientific investigation as a substitute for the use of police personnel have their downside (see Box 3.5). New technologies can create opportunities for crime that never existed previously (as with the development of the internet, for example). As Peter Grabosky (1998) suggests:

> What has changed and what will continue to change in our lifetime, as sure as night follows day, is technology. This has, and will, generate new opportunities for crime. In the words of Willie Sutton, 'That's where the money is'. Fortunately, for us honest folks, technology will also create new opportunities for crime control.
>
> (p. 2)

Box 3.6   The case of Tasers

In favour:

- The US producers of the weapon claim that there have been no injuries in 99 per cent of cases.
- Tests on pigs' hearts (more sensitive than human hearts) show no ill effects.
- They allow police officers to 'fill the gap' between batons and guns in violent confrontation – a 'non-lethal' incapacitation device.
- They are only used by officers trained for 18 hours.

Against:

- Proliferation – all English and Welsh forces now possess them.
- Like all new policing technology, they tempt officers to use them in relatively non-threatening situations – lowering the threshold for use.
- Officers using them have no idea whether the target is suffering from epileptic fits or forms of mental incapacity. In such cases, use may have long-term effects.
- Although available for crowd control situations, they are quite unsuitable because of inaccuracy.
- The new Metropolitan Police commissioner encourages Taser use by recommending that they be carried by instant response vehicles.

> Paramedics were called but, as the 41-year-old father of three writhed in agony, so were Greater Manchester Police. As a disorientated Swarray struggled with those restraining him, an officer racing to the scene was recorded on police radio saying: 'If he's getting aggressive I am sure 50,000 volts will stand him up'. Swarray (an epileptic) has no memory of what it felt like to be shot with an electric stun gun but his medical notes recorded that a Taser was used against him five times. Swarray was so heavily sedated with ketamine by an attending doctor in order to transport him to hospital that he spent eight days in a coma. He was subsequently diagnosed with kidney failure [and remains traumatized].
>
> (*Guardian*, 9 November 2011)

Suspect profiling is typical of the new evidence-based policing. There are two types of criminal profiling – inductive (inferring unknown characteristics such as demographic, physical, emotional and behavioural characteristics of past offenders); and deductive profiling (interweaving forensic evidence and criminological research to reconstruct crime scene material to infer personal characteristics of the offender). Both include inferential subjective 'case construction' material, which raises serious doubts about the validity of such methods. (The case of the unfortunate Colin Stagg, 'befriended' by an undercover female detective in a murder enquiry, requires little retelling.) At best, the profiling process may marginally contribute to successful apprehension. The latter's importance is often inflamed by media sensationalism. There are now a number of studies from the UK and elsewhere claiming the effectiveness of criminal profiling (e.g. see Canter, 2000; Kocsis, 2006). However, since many studies are conducted by self-interested practitioners this taints their reliability. Copson and Holloway (1997) have conducted one of the few meta-analyses of profiling studies in the UK. They found that in the 184 cases they examined profiling led to a direct result in only 2.7 per cent of investigations, and was 'helpful' in a further 16 per cent. Like Hotspot Policing, profiling smacks of a witchfinder-general's pursuits rather than Kuhnian social science.

However, in several ways the contribution by Sherman and his colleagues demonstrates correctly that the police staffing problem can, in part, be compensated for and made more effective by the appliance of science. Sherman (see Sherman, 1998) makes several points with which critical academics would agree. Evidence-based policing scholars demonstrate the failure of previous scientific applications to policing. The authors find that many policing practices applied broadly throughout the United States have either not been the subject of systematic evaluation for effectiveness, or have been examined in the context of research designs that do not allow practitioners or policy makers to draw very strong conclusions. Critical comparative research has not been conducted. Sherman, in particular, correctly, makes the point that that scientific applications often fail to be directed to the primary foci of policing. Professionals and citizenry are offering diffuse views of what we expect the police to do.

But the technologies raise public expectation of their success. There is little point in the police continuing with activities such as Neighbourhood Policing, which escapes any viable measure of effectiveness and which has little evident value (Brogden and Nijhar, 2005). The adjunct to the new Neighbourhood Policing (see Chapter 5) of Problem Solving Policing, like Hotspot Policing, is old wine in new bottles. Its annual celebration, via the curious Tilley Award, demonstrates how to achieve local minor successes at considerable cost. Local business communities voraciously support a system of CCTV first popularized in the UK via its contribution to the capture of the youthful killers of James Bulger in Bootle. But the most recent evidence on CCTV is that it has negligible effect on property crimes. At best, CCTV may marginally displace crime; it also requires a veritable army of surveillance staff to monitor the system. Certainly, the riots of August 2011 appeared to highlight the value of CCTV (as it had, according to senior officers [personal communication] in the earlier poll tax riots). But the cost of such surveillance and its subsequent revelations was extraordinary. Working from a database of between 25,000 and 50,000 suspects, officers were engaged in trawling through some 200,000 hours of recordings. The costs in police time (an officer could be expected to scan some 4–5 hours of recordings a day), leaving aside any subsequent, judicial, penal, and probation costs, were astronomical. By any normative standard, the financial commitment was quite unjustifiable outside a state, moral and political panic over disorder. The contribution of DNA databases to the capture of burglars has had a negligible effect because there is an estimated probability of a 'cold hit' detection using DNA retrival in less than 1.3 per cent of cases (National DNA Database, 2009).

New discoveries lead to expectations of greater success and, like the now disregarded Home Watch schemes (and their variants), may simply result in more crime reporting rather than better crime prevention and investigation (Packwood, 2002). Lifestyle and geographical analyses continue to produce far too many potential multi-causal factors to determine whether anything other than commonsense accuracy would be cheaper in specifying criminogenic populations. Suspect populations with the same profiles most evidently do not follow predicted patterns of deviance. Ostensibly, the new comparative, longitudinal, and geographical methodologies offer more serious prospects. Geographical Information Systems (GIS), potentially involving the latest satellite technology, can inform police about the regular incidence of crime at certain locations. Home Watch schemes fell into disrepute partly because of the largely inconsequential data reported from such domains. However, as the contributors to Chainey and Thompson (2008) make clear, the efficacy of GIS crime mapping depends to a large extent on the quality of data generated. In the case studies evaluated there were inaccuracies due to differences in methodological approach adopted across police force areas; the size of the area used for mapping often varied; and the quality of the information coming out was only as good as the quality of the information going in – which was based on the vagaries of police-recorded data. Fundamentally, though, there are issues with how the data are interpreted. As Betsy Stanko (cited in Blunkett, 2009) reminds us, 'You can look at a clump of dots on a map, but you need to know what they mean'.

A central concept in the most recent evidence-based approach is that of the 'hotspot'. Police labour – in patterns of deployment and in retaining officers in reserve – can be better utilized. Comparative analyses of crime data show where many crimes are regularly committed. Crime 'hotspots' are defined as 'small places in which the occurrence of crime is so frequent that it is highly predictable, at least over a one-year period' (Sherman, 1995 p. 36). Such 'hotspots' include street corners, malls, apartment blocks, subway stations, and public parks that generate a large number of complaints to police. While both repeat victimization and 'hotspots' have undoubtedly been around as long as crime itself, 'hotspots' have been formally recognized in literature, albeit in various guises. In 1751, Henry Fielding recommended the focusing of efforts upon crime-prone locations to deter offenders. Frankly, there is little new about such recognition.[12]

Current research shows that about 3 per cent of all places generate more than half of all citizen complaints about crime and disorder to the police. In this sense there is a congruence with the 'Hotspot Policing' approach but the police need to distinguish between short-lived concentrations of crime versus those hotspots that have long histories (see Weisburd and Eck, 2004). Indeed, Weisburd and Eck (2004) suggest that if hotspots of crime shift rapidly from place to place, it makes little sense to focus crime control resources at such locations. By contrast, the police would be most effective by identifying and targeting resources at those hotspots with long histories of crime.

The most recent study by Weisburd and his colleagues (Weisburd et al., 2010) is the *Police Foundation Displacement and Diffusion Study*. This intends to rectify some of the initial failures of the appliance of science to crime and policework. Their study of drug users and prostitution in Seattle makes two key points. Better methodological studies are more sensitive to stable hotspots, and especially that better use of resources does not apparently, according to the previous conventional wisdom, simply displace such crime to other areas. There is a net reduction in such crimes. However, their example of such effectiveness is unfortunate and shows the problems of policy transfer from one jurisdiction to another. Ultimately crime 'hotspots' are a subjective rather than objective concept. Apart from major questions about the reliability of police data, the determination of the importance of the crime being committed there reflects policing assumptions, devoid of wider criminological concerns with the partisan selectivity of police forces. Typically, members of the Other, drug users and prostitutes, that feature in Weisburd et al.'s (2010) most recent work, might be regarded by some as engaging in victimless crime. The proverbial Martian might wonder, given the gamut of crime, why select such a marginal group as a hotspot problem?[13]

There are few locales involving such offences in the UK that could not be determined by routine police commonsense; perhaps late-night disturbances after the closure of bars, and a few minor locations of pickpockets and transient events such as conflict in the crowd at football matches. Remarkably, evidence-based policing informs us that incidents of drinking and driving tend to occur at certain times and locations! Residential burglaries occur most often when residents are absent. Despite Sherman's caveat, evidence-based policing and police science, somewhat tautologously, take society as currently policed as adequate justification for various interventions. Unlike natural scientists, they concentrate on offenders with minimal impact on the larger crime problems, typically components of the Other. Devoid of a wider appreciation of criminological theory, of history and of context, the new applied police science seems to contribute little with regard to the more serious crime problems. No hotspots, to which evidence-based policing could readily have been applied, appear to have been subject to analysis such as in the major banking centres that caused the current recession. Wall Street is not a hotspot. Crimes of the household, the most serious forms of violence, are as yet impervious to significant scientific advance, despite recent progress in policing interventions. The partisan commitment of state police to the policing of the Other as demarcated by stratification, socioeconomic class, ethnicity, gender, and age is followed without questions about the sociological, political, and economic issues regarding the object of police focus. Fundamentally, the quality of data in evidence-based policing, such as recorded crime rates, would be disparaged by any researcher in the natural sciences.

Box 3.7   How to improve police data – an older lesson revived

Two detectives have been found guilty of misconduct after giving a 17-year-old youth strong cider in a 'crude inducement' to make false confessions. Sean Wall was picked up at 9 a.m., driven to crime scenes around Cardiff and plied with two bottles of cider before police interrogated him about a string of burglaries. He confessed to several crimes he could not possibly have carried out because he was in custody when the thefts happened. Detective Constable Neville Bradbury and Detective Constable Geraint Jones, from South Wales Police, both kept their jobs, despite a harsh report by the Independent Police Complaints Commission. The two faced a gross misconduct hearing last week, which heard that the detective had given alcohol to Mr. Wall, a 'vulnerable male' who had a drink problem. He asked 17 times to see his solicitor, Nadeem Majid, before his request was granted. Mr. Majid said 'getting my client to admit things he hadn't done in the hope that it will improve crime figures takes policing back 25 years'. Despite the evidence, the CPS has declined to prosecute the officers.

(BBC News, 16 January 2012)

The sensitivity of qualitative research as opposed to quantitative has generally been ignored. Researchers carry with them, like students in the wider criminological field, a body of primary assumptions about the problems worthy of study. Evidence-based policing simply ignores the structured biases in state policing and criminal law and in generic social control.

Evidence-based policing has been applied to domestic violence and household abuse (Sherman, 1992). This suggests that there is a clear relationship between socioeconomic class and decisions to arrest. But research conducted by one of us (Brogden and Nijhar, 2004) suggests that the sex of the complainant is a more important configuration. In such calls for help, local station instruction to officers tends to assume that whoever, male or female, calls for help, the presumption is that the male should be arrested. Similarly, using stop-and-search powers to prevent gun violence may work in the United States (Sherman, 2001). But it may also (as Sherman seems to recognize but dismisses) generate more antagonism to the police than benefits, and it is (as widely recognized the copious literature) often based on partisan police stereotypes. A different school of criminology might ask a different question: 'Why is American legislation so lax about gun control and the availability of personal firearms?'

Evidence-based policing points to the failings of the judicial process in contributing to future youth delinquency. Stan Cohen made the same point in the UK 30 years ago with regard to the danger of lowering the threshold for youths entering the criminal justice system – without the benefit of such science (Cohen,

1985). The current deployment of PCSOs may simply add to that process, as problem behaviour becomes translated into legal misdemeanours. It is not clear how scientific techniques can offer labour-saving as an expensive alternative to Gramscian 'good commonsense'.

These examples are hardly a definitive response to evidence-based policing claims for practices that might compensate for decreases in the labour force. But they do reveal that such approaches raise more questions than answers about the application of such a policy-driven and technocratic approach to subjectively messy questions of crime, disorder and policing. As a basis for replacing sworn police officers and their civilian colleagues, the appliance of science to labour shortages seems to be making only a minimal contribution (and one that cannot be disentangled from the promotion of privatization). Evidence-based policing reflects the quality of the data on which it draws, and on its failure to tackle primary assumptions about what the police should 'do'. It relies on a methodology inadequate to construct controlled evaluation. Its studies, following assumed police priorities, maintain a policy, rather than normative focus on the policing of the marginal 'Other'. The debate over whether science and technology can adequately compensate for the loss of police (and especially, civilian) staff has hardly started.

The above critique is limited in its coverage of the many diffuse studies conducted under the evidence-based policing rubric. Geographical profiling, high crime areas (actually large hotspots with less precise locations, such as large council housing areas) and repeat victimization are commonly (and rightly) confused in their relationship with hotspots policing (see Box 3.7). Among many other methodological problems, they share common problems. Typically, we should ask 'How does the Other experience policing?' The clarification of such issues and the related concepts seems to be more than just a matter of academic semantics. Unless policing has clear working definitions and concepts, and understands the relationship between them, the strategies and tactics that emerge to tackle crime may reflect that lack of understanding.

Long live Ned Lud!

The original Luddites were frequently portrayed in institutional histories as 'machine-wreckers' intent on frustrating inevitable technological progress. However, as revisionist histories tell us (as epitomized by the Chartist movement), they had a major social, economic, and political agenda, concerned with the ways that such 'progress' would benefit a few at the expense of the many and do little to redress existing socioeconomic inequalities (Thompson, 1963). Evidence-based policing frequently makes many of the same mistakes. It takes as given existing policy-driven formulation of policing objectives, often following vox pop. (The invention of the contraceptive pill appeared to benefit women. But, of course, it placed the onus on women, not on men.) The most obvious recent use of police technology for directly partisan purposes was in Birmingham in 2010. Under the formal guise of a crime prevention initiative (with minimal community consultation), 218 cameras (including a facility to read car number plates) were installed in primarily Muslim areas of the city (despite higher recorded crime rates in other city areas) (see Lewis, 2010). In the event, it appeared they had been paid for by a £3-million special government anti-terror fund. No other residential area in the UK had such a concentration of cameras. In effect, they targeted all local Muslims as potential terrorist suspects under the pretence of crime prevention. After major community protests, the system was terminated. Where science in policing-for-profit has been efficacious, it has mainly been through the methodology of the natural sciences in high-profile cases (as in the contribution of the private company LGC Forensics to a partial resolution of the Lawrence case).

Many (but not all) of the exponents of evidence-based policing and police science make the assumption that police policy and practice is impartial, driven by a given public good. There is little suggestion that evidence-making policing ever challenges that assumption. As the politics of policing have demonstrated historically, some groups always bear the brunt of police action. In postcolonial theory, the Other is a consolidation of those groups. It is difficult in the UK to discover what such partisan 'science' can add to existing police knowledge and deployment.

Overview

Research on policing is only as good as the quality of its data. Evaluating the net effect of a decrease in police resources is beset by the major problem of a lack of reliable data. Research is beset by major quandaries regarding the quality of information at its disposal. It is also, in England and Wales, stranded on the rock of different police force practices. It is debatable from wider research whether relative changes in police resources affect levels of substantive crime and their successful prosecution, we have no idea of what the concept of 'relative' means in this context. Certainly the changes that have been made to date in Britain in resolving the financial policing crisis have little bearing on a successful resolution. Within the parameters of current police assumptions – practices, procedures, and purpose – we remain clueless about the consequences. The absurdity of the many ways of defining frontline policing is merely one amongst many questions that have been raised. No commercial organization that wished to survive in business would act in the ways depicted in this chapter. Beyond these parameters, questions about purpose and futures of state policing have not been addressed.

The new policing 'sciences' have little to offer. Living in a taken-for-granted world, from quality of data to police functions, they offer only incidental resolutions, common to other parts of social life. Principally the major feature of this ramshackle process of change has not challenged the major problematic to be developed in subsequent chapters: why is British policing still committed to the primary object of the policing of the 'Other', to the neglect of serious matters of violence and of other forms of major social harm? The priority response to the riots of August 2011 demonstrates not just a largely incompetent organization but, more importantly, little appreciation of the key problems to which a more democratic policing should be directed.

4   Commodifying state policing

The export of the 'UK Police plc' brand

UK policing is held in high esteem throughout the world. The UK's long history of civilian policing, of working with members of the public from different communities, and of upholding the rule of law, has proved invaluable in the development of democratic, civilian policing practices in transitional/crisis nations around the globe.

(Home Office, *Overseas Deployment
Manual for Police Officers*, 2004, p. 2)

'UK Police' is one of the most recognized and highly valued international brands. The police service has a long and successful history of assisting other countries to develop their policing, and restore law and order following conflict. With the increased danger to the UK from a range of threats such as terrorist groups or failing states, engaging with international organizations/governments works towards reducing harm to the UK. The contributions made by police officers and police staff from UK police forces are widely recognized and valued by international partners as serving officers provide credibility of current working practices and accountability.

(UK Foreign and Commonwealth Office)[1]

Introduction

At a time of fiscal crisis the international market economy and neoliberal economics demand that all services be commodified. Public services are given a price tag. They are sold on the market, to customers home and abroad. Britain sells policing – and also imports.[2] Lessons about policing the Other accumulate in a policy transfer process (Brogden and Nijhar, 2005; Jones and Newburn, 2006). Like other goods, the only criterion for the sale of a product is what the customer will accept. The goods become branded and mythical qualities are attributed to them. The salespeople dwell on their historically sanctified virtues. Historically, the goods might have been given for free, or imposed on the locals by an imperial power, in effect preparing the ground for future commercial ventures. Policing as export business has a long history. The East India Company did not charge for its early policing of the sub-continent – security was necessary for its profits from other commercial ventures.

Britain has long been in the police export business, with its hallowed expertise at policing the Other. In an age of austerity, the sale of such an apparently valuable product is even more crucial. In that process, state policing adopts a privatized function. Social ordering goods have a value beyond the public space of the locality. Expertise, personnel, and police technology take their share of the export market. But the international market is a competitive environment and many states are currently clamouring to sell their brand of policing on the global stage.

Considered historically there has been widespread exportation of British policing ideas, knowledge and practices internationally – particularly to the colonial context (Anderson and Killingray, 1992; Brogden, 1987a, b; Sinclair, 2006). Colonial polic-ing thus represents an early form of police globalization that was to refract a set of ideas developed in the metropolitan core, the practice of policing developed in Ireland, but also hybridized forms of policing that were to develop across the Empire and inform intra-colonial practice (Brogden, 1987a, b; Emsley, 2012; Sinclair, 2006). Of course, it wasn't only to the Empire that British policing knowledge was exported. The British were involved in a restructuring of the Ottoman gendarmerie in the late nineteenth century (Swanson, 1972). Geo-strategic concerns in the con-text of an emergent Cold War (post-1945) saw a high level of British involvement (with Irish police personnel) with the Allied Control Commission, as well as the British Policing Mission to Greece (Ellison and O'Reilly, 2008a; Sinclair, 2012). The purpose of this chapter, therefore, is to situate this history in the present context of policing the local Other, by focusing on contemporary developments in the inter-national export of British policing. The past decade in particular has seen British policing recast as a 'brand' for export (see also Sinclair, 2012). There remain, how-ever, remarkable historical continuities between historical practice and present-day developments. In light of what we have discussed in earlier chapters our argument is that the increased exportation of British policing knowledge and expertise – whether officially or via any number of policy entrepreneurs – needs to be set in the overall domestic context of the increased marketization and commodification of policing and security (Loader, 1999). What is occurring at the global level is, in many ways, an extension of what has already occurred locally. Furthermore, the export of the brand relies on a number of Peelian myths about community policing and an assumed relationship between the police and the public, for example, that are simply unwarranted in terms of the majority practice of overseas missions.

The chapter develops as follows: we first provide some idea of scale by outlining the proliferation of British police agencies and personnel involved in overseas missions and the exchange of policing knowledge and practices. Drawing from an analysis of the marketing and branding literature, we then link these developments to a discussion of what Assistant Chief Constable Colin Firth has termed the 'UK Police PLC brand'[3] and efforts by the Foreign and Commonwealth Office (FCO) (among others) to project the brand globally as an aspect of soft power. We decon-struct the 'brand' and consider what its key components are and what the ostensi-ble purpose of its promotion is. We suggest, however, that the branding process and the brand itself contain a number of flaws and contradictions. While the ideo-logical and rhetorical underpinnings of the brand are rooted in a Peelian/Reithian reading of British police history, its actual practical application owes more to an alternative history – one derived from the Irish colonial tradition. In many overseas missions it is the RUC/PSNI that provide the core personnel (Sinclair, 2012) owing to their experience of counter-terrorism, high level public order, and in policing the Other.[4] One of the key proposals of the ICP (1999) was that the size of the RUC be reduced from 13,000 to 7,500 officers, so there is no shortage of potential recruits for such missions. The chapter concludes by suggesting that we are seeing the emergence of what Jean-Paul Brodeur (Brodeur, 2005) termed 'terror orientated policing' as the dominant export paradigm. Arguably, it is the War on Terror that in recent years has provided an unprecedented focal point for the exchange of policing knowledge and expertise on the international stage (Ellison and O'Reilly, 2008a). However, there is also a domestic resonance in the traditional policing of the Other – the original core function of the export business: one that neatly meshes with the current policing of the youthful Muslim 'Other' on British streets.

British policing for export

There is now a global cottage industry devoted to police and security sector reform and international police assistance in weak or failing states, humanitarian missions, post-conflict reconstruction, and other democratization efforts. David Bayley (cited in Kempa, 2010 p.273) estimates that, globally, around $200 billion is spent annually on policing, and of this around a third is devoted to police reform in post-conflict and transitional states. Unfortunately however, in spite of the energy, resources, and time devoted to these endeavours, successes in instilling democratic policing internationally have been few and far between, and have not been particularly sustainable. Much of the extant literature has been heavily practitioner focused and self-referential. The potential pitfalls, hazards, and sheer difficulties involved in transplanting models to widely different political, historical, and cultural contexts have only recently been addressed in the research literature (Brogden and Nijhar, 2005; Goldsmith and Sheptycki, 2007; Pino and Wiatrowski, 2006).

Nevertheless, the UK continues to be a major player in overseas assistance efforts (Home Office, 2004) and as well as seconding officers to various UN, EU and Organisation for Security and Co-operation in Europe (OSCE) missions, UK police have also been active in providing training in democracy, human rights and community policing to Central and East European EU accession states via the Twinning Programme and also via the work of the UK's Department for International Development (DFID) in local capacity building. The UK Home Office has provided technical assistance to the Turkish Ministry of Interior in relation to a police complaints machinery closely modelled on the IPCC. The UK has also played a major role in the European Union Police Mission (EUPOL) police missions to Afghanistan, Kosovo, Georgia and Palestine, while it has been particularly active in Iraq since 2003. In Iraq the UK has developed a national policing strategy led by the Home Office, while officers have been involved in the provision of police training via the Civilian Police Assistance Training Team (CPATT), the ACPO, and also the Joint International Police Training Centre (JIPTC) in Jordan (Flanagan, 2006). In addition, the member states of the EU have established provisions for joint investigation teams under the EU Convention on Mutual Assistance in Criminal Matters (articles, 13, 15 and 16) that involve British police in cross-national investigations should the need arise (Home Office, 2004 p.22).

There is no single provider of international police in the UK and officers are drawn from across the fifty-two regional forces, although the NPIA, ACPO, and SOCA have attempted to provide some degree of centralized co-ordination (Sinclair, 2012). ACPO for instance has established a Police Overseas Assistance Group (UKP-OAG) that seeks to co-ordinate requests from different countries and maintain a database of UK police personnel available for secondments or missions. As well as providing the 'police' for the Pitcairn Islands, the British Ministry of Defence Police (MDP), established in 1971 from the remnants of various Royal Air Force and Admiralty constabularies, also provides pre-deployment training for UK police officers seconded to missions, and has sent its own officers to Sierra Leone, Bosnia, Kosovo, Afghanistan and Sudan (Button, 2002).

As we discuss later in the chapter, the conflicts in Afghanistan, Iraq and Kosovo, as well as the broader context of global insecurity and domestic/international terrorism, have also spawned a huge increase in the corporate security sector (private security companies, private military companies – see O'Reilly, 2011). These have attracted influxes of retired (though some have taken a leave of absence from their main job) officers from the MDP and the RUC/PSNI (because of their firearms training), as well as retired army personnel. In these highly volatile security conditions their skill-set is seen as a prized commodity, with potential tax-free earnings of around £100,000 per annum not including bonuses – several times that of a regular UK police officer (personal communication, ex-RUC officer in Afghanistan). Importantly, however, there is something of a state–corporate symbiosis at play here and the line between state and private/corporate policing agencies has become increasingly muddied in the context of global insecurities and the 'War on Terror' (O'Reilly, 2011; O'Reilly and Ellison, 2006; Whyte, 2003). Increased privatization, marketization, commodification and hybridization have all problematized the very nature of policing and its delivery across myriad domains. One cannot, for example, analyse the counter-terrorism 'performance' of the police either in the US or the UK separately from the huge corporate infrastructure (security consultancies, security contractors, risk advisors, and so forth) that has grown up around national security, counter-terrorism, and policing public space. Even ice-cream and hamburger vendors are getting in on the act and are being trained by Westminster Council and the London Metropolitan Police to spot 'terrorists' during the London Olympic Games in 2012 (Meikle, 2012).

Geo-branding, soft power and the promotion of British Police plc

Until the late twentieth century, branding was synonymous with advertising and was associated mainly with physical objects such as consumer goods. However, branding is now linked to efforts to create a particular identity and personality for a product, service, organization or state (Ellison and O'Reilly, 2008b p.336). Branding is about the creation of meanings that come to define the symbolic embodiment of the product (or service) in question – the National Health Service in the UK with its logo comprising stark block text is widely recognized as one of the country's most powerful and recognizable brands and one that elicits a powerful emotional empathy among consumers (Nuffield Trust, 2011). In a highly influential article in the magazine *Foreign Policy*, Peter van Ham (2001) notes that we can talk about a state's 'personality' in much the same way as we talk about commercial brands ('unreliable', 'ally', 'friendly', and 'Other') and as he acknowledges 'geo-branding' (how a state markets and projects itself globally) is increasingly used to supplant traditional diplomacy as a mechanism of soft power. States (and countries) are no longer areas that one might point to on a map or atlas but are associated with a range of meanings and imagery that invoke an emotional reaction amongst a global audience of consumers. Thus several states have embarked on wide-ranging attempts at enhancing their 'geo brand' – Estonia, for example, has carried out a 'Brand Estonia' project, availing itself of the services of Interbrand in an attempt to shrug off the perception of the country as a target destination for stag parties and all night drinking sprees (Gardner and Standaert, n.d.). In the 1990s, and not particularly successfully, the then New Labour government in the UK hired the global branding and corporate identity firm Woolf Olins in an attempt to market Britain as 'Cool Britannia' (Ellison and O'Reilly, 2008b).

The policing developments we have described above are pretty commonplace in the era of transnational and increasingly globalized policing. Many states deploy their police on overseas missions, while the emergence of what Otwin Marenin (2007) has termed the transnational policing policy community has witnessed a huge proliferation in the movement of police personnel (either officially, or more informally) as part of joint training programmes, seminars and secondments, as well as bilateral and multilateral assistance missions. Much is humdrum and routine, for officers immersed in the British and Northern Irish traditions. However, what is not routine, and is something that goes above and beyond the regular toing and froing of police personnel internationally, is the increasing marketing and projection of British policing as a global 'brand'. Reference to the British Police plc brand was made by Assistant Chief Constable Colin Firth (above), but earlier (in 2008) ACPO established the International Police Assistance Board (IPAB) whose flyer announces that 'UK Police is one of the most recognized and highly valued international brands' (cited in Emsley, 2012 p.1). Comparatively speaking, the only national police agencies that come close in their attempts to market themselves on the world stage in a similar fashion are Canada's Royal Canadian Mounted Police (RCMP) and perhaps the FBI.

Selling the myth of policing the Other

The degree to which officials perceive a brand value for the British police also extends to the activities of individual forces, where local privatization of social

---

Box 4.1   The New Scotland Yard brand

One symbol and one symbol alone represents the rich heritage and sophistication of British policing. Established in 1829, New Scotland Yard is legendary around the globe for strength, courage and steely determination . . . a name recognised throughout the world; yet perceived as quintessentially British. It conjures up thoughts of mystery, excitement, strength, justice, and determination . . . The new brand gave the Metropolitan Police Service an excellent opportunity to introduce communities to the police in a more positive way. . . . New Scotland Yard appeals to all age ranges and has the potential to flourish in different markets.

---

ordering has developed relative expertise. For example, the London Metropolitan Police have appointed the image consultants John Anthony Signs to 'produce their corporate signage manual [and] acting as their brand guardians'.[5] In its Articles of Association provided under the Companies Act (1985) ACPO claims that a key aspect of its work is to 'develop our business activities to ensure that the ACPO brand name is recognized globally as a mark of excellence in policing' (ACPO, 1997). In the mid-1990s police services in England and Wales were accorded powers to generate revenue from sponsorship and commercial licensing. The Metropolitan Police have licensed the New Scotland Yard brand – which is actually the name of their London headquarters but often used metonymically to refer to the entire organization – and the 'brand story' is told on its website (see Box 4.1).

The Metropolitan Police's website claims that the brand is now available for license in several (unspecified) territories and makes an appeal for commercial sponsorship. Thus far the Metropolitan Police have licensed the brand to a toy and games manufacturer to market a 'New Scotland Yard Forensics Kit' and a 'New Scotland Yard Forensics Jigsaw Puzzle'. Both, it claims, will provide young children with a fascinating insight into the world of crime scene investigation and forensics.

What is clear from these various branding and marketing endeavours is that the British policing 'brand' is increasingly linked to those Peelian qualities and characteristics of policing the Other in public space that are said to give British policing its unique and benign character, and as the Home Office suggests, 'the UK police are held in the highest regard in most other countries' (2004 p.41). Clearly, as several commentators have acknowledged (and as we discussed in Chapter 1), the British police 'brand' is tapping into the myriad ways in which British – though read 'English' – policing acts as a symbol that condenses the national character and is associated with attributes such as tolerance, decency, fair play and unflappability (Emsley, 2009; Loader and Mulcahy, 2003). The emphasis on a decentralized, localized and unarmed community policing tradition is trumpeted in accordance with Peel's foundational principles. However, as we have seen, the emergence of the New Police in 1829 is premised on a doctrine of public consent that is largely mythical (see Chapter 5) but which nevertheless remains an important discourse of legitimation (Brogden, 1982; Gatrell, 1990).

Our argument, then, is that recent attempts to promote the UK Police plc 'brand' globally need to be set in the context of broader processes of geo-branding and the establishment of an identity for policing that is linked to abstract notions of how the UK projects itself to the world. This is linked both to self-ascribed national characteristics of the Occident as expressed in notions of tolerance, decency, and moral virtue, but also an imagining of a quintessentially British civilian constabulary (Emsley, 2009) that is rooted in widespread public consent and that wields a high level of symbolic power (Loader, 1997). As Ian Loader (1997) argues, the police – or more accurately the symbolism associated with the British Bobby – is one of the 'principal means by which English society tells stories about itself' (p. 2). It is this symbolic capital that forms the core of the brand and the basis for its suggested international appeal. As Emsley (2012 p. 2) acknowledges:

> there appears to be a sincere belief that there is something distinctive about British policing and something worth exporting to others. And while it is possible to be sceptical about multinational corporations, the deployment of British police officers to educate and to train the police offices of other states in a style of policing suggests a genuine belief in the brand's values, look and idea.

We are, however, a little less sanguine about what is being exported. In many respects it is in the international policing arena where the Peelian myth lives on. The brand involves promoting and marketing a consensual notion of 'British' policing when in reality the ideology (and practice) of the policing model that is being exported is rooted (more) in the Irish experience (especially so given the high numbers of RUC/PSNI that are involved in many missions), not to mention the growing emphasis on counter-terrorism and public order. Thus while the export model may emphasize its 'British' identity, in reality it is an 'identity' that derives just as much from Britain's colonial experience in policing the Other.

In the past two years British police officers have trained police in Bahrain, Libya, Abu Dhabi, Qatar and Saudi Arabia through a programme organized by the NPIA (Taylor, 2011). The NPIA has also seconded three full time British police advisors to the Bahraini police. While the NPIA insists that the training it provides internationally is human rights compliant, the violent crackdown by the police and military in a number of these countries in response to civil society protests and the so-called Arab Spring has raised serious questions about exactly what kind of training is being provided by British officers or indeed what aspects of the brand are being promoted (Taylor, 2011). Elsewhere in the Middle East, Sir Ronnie Flanagan, who was previously chief constable of the RUC, and Her Majesty's Chief Inspector of Constabulary, has landed what is in effect a corporate sinecure as strategic advisor to the Ministry of Interior of the United Arab Emirates. Sir Ronnie has brought his own team of officers with him, many of whom have previously served in the RUC or PSNI (personal communication with ex-RUC officer).

We are not suggesting that British officers eschew any attempt at transplanting community policing overseas (however that can be defined or taken to mean), nor that an emphasis on 'democratic' policing and policing by consent does not constitute a component of the brand. Rather, all we are suggesting is that this is *one* aspect of the brand. Arguably in the context of global insecurities and the 'War on Terror', and in an era of neoliberal globalization where policing has become a commodity for sale on the open market, the content of the brand has shifted to one that has less to do with its Peelian antecedents (however tenuous in the first place) to one that increasingly looks across the Irish Sea for its inspiration (see Box 4.2). This has been facilitated by a number of interrelated processes: changes in global (in)security that prize those skill-sets that emphasize counter-terrorism and high-level public order experience; the intense promotional activities of the PSNI in recent years and the movement of senior Northern Irish policing personnel or 'policy entrepreneurs' (cf. Jones and Newburn, 2006) to occupy key policing positions in Britain; the marketization of policing and security globally and the high number of ex-RUC/PSNI personnel who work as private security operatives for the British state in international missions; and the role played by international policing missions in constructing regional security corridors to contain the 'Other'. As Sinclair (2012 p. 4) suggests, 'more generally it is felt that this [international policing] helps prevent the globalization of crime through the identification and containment of criminal activity at source before groups or individuals have become established in the UK'.

What we are describing, therefore, is not simply a case of policy transfer but rather reflects a more complex process of what marketing analysts term 'market segmentation' where a global audience of consumers are seen to have different needs and requirements and where the brand is specifically tailored to meet divergent tastes and interests. A parallel can be found in the marketing and branding of the ubiquitous Coca-Cola, which while ostensibly representing a single product (a fizzy drink) nevertheless tastes slightly different in each of the countries where it is sold as a consequence of consumer preference. Turkish consumers have a preference for a slightly sweeter taste compared to their British counterparts, for instance. As we outline below, the UK Police plc brand does not represent a single product but is similarly tailored both to the requirements of global 'consumers' and is also skewed by the strategic interests and foreign policy requirements of the UK government. Indeed, this linkage of overseas police assistance to national interest/security has been highlighted by Chief Constable Colin Port, lead officer for ACPO International Affairs, when he suggests:

> The UK government remains committed to international policing assistance as highlighted in the 2010 National Security Strategy. ACPO International Affairs supports these national security and overseas development objectives that promote global stability and keep the UK secure from serious organized crime, terrorism, drugs and extremism.
>
> (Port, 2011)

The implications of this are clear. It is difficult to see how the provision of training to some of the regimes mentioned above – Libya, Saudi Arabia for instance – sits with the principles that are said to normatively underlie British policing. Even if we were to assume (at a stretch) that policing systems in these states could be democratized this is notoriously difficult to realize in practice. For Peter Manning (2010) in order to be properly 'democratic', governmental institutions, including the police, must be rooted in an enabling legal framework that is normatively committed to the upholding, preservation and protection of 'rights'. Ultimately, as he suggests, however, it is 'a democratic state and culture that produce democratic policing', without which a contentious 'rights based' conception of state policing can have no validity (2010 p. 7).

Our argument in this section is that contemporary developments in Britain in relation to the marketing of policing as a brand for export have accelerated as a consequence of developments in Northern Ireland, and in particular with the activities of the PSNI, who moved with breakneck speed to harness the opportunities for international promotionalism in the context of the ongoing Northern Irish peace process and the reforms of the ICP.[6] 'The fiscal crisis has given this export process a practical utility in a time of local financial cuts. This of course has been facilitated by the movement of key British policing personnel between Northern Ireland and Britain: Sir Hugh Orde, Sir Ronnie Flanagan, Stephen White, and Paul Kernaghan to name but a few. All these officers have experience of policing in Northern Ireland, with three of them – Flanagan, Kernaghan and White – assuming senior roles in British policing missions in Iraq and elsewhere. (Two – White and Flanagan – have also moved seamlessly between the state and international corporate security sectors (discussed below).) Developments in Northern Ireland have thus influenced those in a broader UK context. During the August 2011 riots the PSNI were contacted by the Police National Information Co-Ordination Centre (PNICC) and asked to deploy a fleet of the armoured Land Rovers used for riot control in Northern Ireland as well as PSNI officers to assist the Metropolitan Police in London. In the event no officers were deployed and it is unclear how many Land Rovers were eventually provided (BBC News, 9 August 2011).

In terms of international promotionalism there is no police organization anywhere in the UK (including perhaps even the Metropolitan Police) that has been so proactive in promoting its activities to a global audience, organizing fact finding trips, seminars, training sessions, conferences, and selling the 'lessons' of Northern Ireland police reform to any number of overseas government and police officials who fly into Belfast with monotonous regularity. Furthermore, as we noted above RUC/PSNI personnel are actively headhunted for British executive policing missions given their firearms and public order experience and also their knowledge of counter-terrorism (see Box 4.3).

There are, of course, historical continuities here. As several commentators have pointed out, the (policing) knowledge exchange between the metropolis and the Empire, and Ireland in particular, was never one-directional. Rather it circulated in a much more dynamic and processual fashion, with lessons learned in the colonies impacting on the development of policing in the metropolis (Brogden,

---

Box 4.2   From the Northern Irish Policing Model to UK Police plc

In terms of our experiences gained in Northern Ireland, we are very popular in terms of providing aid to other parts of the world and with support from our Police Board ... we have worked over the last three years in Bosnia, Kosovo, Ethiopia, Gaza, Palestine, Jamaica, Guinea, Estonia, New Zealand, Iraq and Hungary, to name just a few. We have some incredible best practice, which we are happy to export, and we benefit in the longer term from doing that.

(Sir Hugh Orde, chief constable of the PSNI, speaking before the Select Committee on Northern Ireland Affairs, 9 November 2005)

1987a, b; Sinclair, 2006). Key here was the role played by Irish policing personnel, or officials who had knowledge of Ireland in some way who flitted effortlessly between the metropolitan context and the Empire and vice versa (R. Williams, 2003), in the policing of the Other 'home and away'.

In the aftermath of the paramilitary ceasefires of 1994 the RUC found its core raison d'être challenged and in the context of a debate about the force's future it began to look for new areas in which to channel its expertise. One such area was in the field of international policing, and by the late 1990s the RUC was playing an active role in overseas policing missions to Bosnia, Kosovo, Ethiopia, Mongolia and the Commonwealth of Dominica (Ellison and O'Reilly, 2008a p. 338). However, following the publication of the *Report of the Independent Commission on Policing* (ICP) in 1999 – which made a number of recommendations for reform of the RUC including a change in name to PSNI – the force's international activities went into overdrive. Thousands of overseas visitors, from government officials to police chiefs, have visited Northern Ireland to witness the policing transition first hand, while in one year alone the force spent over £1 million on air fares in order to promote its activities around the globe. What has been termed an NIPM (see Ellison and O'Reilly, 2008a; 2008b) has emerged in Northern Ireland that has been strategically harnessed and promoted by the PSNI as a model for overseas emulation. The NIPM is not monolithic but bifurcated and targeted at two principal categories of overseas consumer. First, there are the lessons from Northern Ireland's relatively successful domestic policing transition that allow the PSNI to promote its expertise in democratic policing reform to any number of post-conflict and transitional states globally. Second, in the aftermath of the mass-carnage terrorist attacks in New York, London, and Madrid, the PSNI is availing itself of the institutional memory of the RUC and the counter-terrorist experience it garnered during 'The Troubles'. In the context of global insecurities and threats from Islamic terrorism this skill-set has been heavily in demand and the RUC/PSNI has both participated in British overseas missions (Kosovo, Afghanistan,

---

Box 4.3   The NIPM as a model for transitional and post-conflict states

The PSNI has made huge strides in policing reform and has acquired a reputation throughout the world for setting the agenda in terms of good policing practice. That is evidenced by the number of international visitors and police officers from services around the world who come to Northern Ireland to find out firsthand what has happened in policing here. In the last few weeks we have had visitors from Pakistan, Kyrgyzstan, Israel, Latvia and Slovenia. Indeed we have also hosted a high powered delegation of politicians and police officers from Kazakhstan, and I can assure you that they were not here to attend the current screening of Borat.

(Vice Chair of the Northern Ireland Policing Board Barry Gilligan, in his address to PSNI recruits, 3 November 2006)

Iraq) and also provided counter-terrorist advice and training to any number of national governments and police agencies, including the US and the FBI.

As noted above, the police reform programme in Northern Ireland has resulted in a high volume of traffic into Northern Ireland with visitors observing the transition process at first hand. However, it has also resulted in a phenomenally high outward traffic of Northern Irish policing personnel promoting the transition at any number of international conferences and symposia, as well as officers deployed and seconded to various overseas missions. The degree to which retired RUC and current serving PSNI officers are capitalizing on the reform programme can be seen in the large number of officers who are taking courses in human rights, conflict resolution and transitional justice at Northern Ireland's two universities (Ellison and O'Reilly, 2008b). This is a strategic career move: without any hint of irony many retired RUC officers have established themselves as consultants in democratic police reform and human rights, while currently serving PSNI officers nearing retirement are thinking about 'what next' in terms of their career development such as a lucrative secondment or consultancy.

The PSNI have provided training advice in relation to democratic and transitional policing to police organizations in Latvia, Sweden, South Africa, Brazil, France, Hong Kong, Canada, Portugal, Sri Lanka, Afghanistan, Iraq, the USA, Belgium, Georgia and Russia. In 2007 the Northern Ireland Policing Board (NIPB) sponsored a 3-day conference entitled 'Policing the Future' at Belfast's prestigious Waterfront Hall, attended by a 'who's-who' of police dignitaries from Britain (Sir Ian Blair and Sir John Grieve) the United States (William Bratton, John Timoney) and across the globe. Northern Ireland is now seen to provide a clear example of democratic policing transition and a model to be lauded on the global stage.

Much has changed in relation to policing in Northern Ireland. The PSNI is a much more accountable, transparent and representative organization than the RUC ever was. Nevertheless, we need to be sceptical not just about the lessons that can be drawn and transferred from Northern Ireland's peace process to other similar contexts, but also the lessons of the policing transition itself, and question the degree to which these are exportable to overseas markets. There is an assumption in the peace and conflict studies literature to assume a symmetry in ethnic conflicts that is rarely borne out in practice. Northern Ireland was never a failed state: it had good hospitals, schools, communications links and a functioning infrastructure (Bayley, 2008), which makes it a far cry from the situation in Iraq, Afghanistan or Kosovo. There has been of course, the level of peace support funding provided by the British government and other international donors which has run to billions of pounds. Precise figures are difficult to obtain but the EU has contributed £800 million to the peace programme thus far, with a further £180 million to be allocated by the end of 2013. The International Fund for Ireland has contributed over £500 million to enhance local capacity building (for an extended discussion see Ellison and Pino, 2012). Certainly, while many individuals within Northern Ireland have worked tirelessly for peace, the level of funding devoted to the broader peace process is simply beyond the capability of many developing and conflicted states to provide. It is a similar story for the much lauded policing transition. The corporate financial services firm Deloitte has estimated that the ICP reforms have cost the British government £100 million annually since 1999, over and above the annual £1 billion spend on policing and criminal justice in Northern Ireland (Deloitte, 2007). Many officers have taken advantage of a generous voluntary and compulsory severance scheme (older officers were encouraged to leave to make room for new recruits) that has already topped £500 million. As we discuss below, many retired PSNI/RUC officers have now found lucrative consultancies, have been seconded to British overseas policing missions as advisors or alternatively are working for private security contractors in Afghanistan and Iraq.

The NIPM as a model for countering global terrorism

The second aspect of the NIPM is targeted at those conflicted states (Kosovo, Iraq and Afghanistan) that have experienced (or are experiencing) high levels of inter-communal strife and where the RUC/PSNI's public order experience is called for. However, the context of global insecurity, as well as threats from domestic and international terrorism, has also re-energized the RUC/PSNI's[7] counter-terrorist skill-set, with officers in demand for British executive policing missions as well as providing training and advice to national governments and policing agencies. Indeed, it is this aspect of the NIPM that is in demand domestically to fulfil officer quotas for British overseas assistance missions as well as provide advice, guidance and training in counter-terrorism (discussed below). One of the paradoxes of the reform process in Northern Ireland has been that while the ICP reforms curtailed the RUC/PSNI's counter-terrorist activities locally (by merging Special Branch into a Crime Operations Department) they created the operational space for senior figures in the RUC/PSNI to market their skill-set globally. Senior officers, including Sir Ronnie Flanagan, have participated in a Harvard University Research Project entitled 'A Long-Term Strategy Project for Preserving Security and Democratic Freedoms in the "War on Terror"' (see Ellison and O'Reilly, 2008b p.345). Curiously, the PSNI organized a training programme bizarrely entitled 'Policing and Terrorism in Democratic Societies' that was attended by senior police officers from Jordan, Algeria, Lebanon, the Philippines, Pakistan and Sudan (see Ellison and O'Reilly, 2008b p. 345). It is not obviously apparent what the point of this training programme was since the participating countries are not exactly noted for their adherence to democratic values.

A number of senior officers with experience of Northern Ireland, but in particular Sir Ronnie Flanagan and Stephen White, have also moved from the state sector into the corporate security sector. As we noted above, Flanagan and his team of advisors are currently providing strategic guidance on security matters in a private capacity to the United Arab Emirates. Stephen White, who held senior command posts in Northern Ireland and Britain as well as heading the EUJUST LEX mission for Iraq, is currently vice president for Europe of the Soufan Group. The Soufan Group is headed by Ali Soufan, a former FBI supervisory special agent with a background in international terrorism. According to its website the Soufan group provides security services such as Strategic Intelligence Reports, Crisis Management, Cultural Intelligence, Investigative Support, Interrogation Training, Situational Forecast and Critical Event Survival. Most of the Soufan Group's staff appear to have a background in special operations and counter-terrorism.[8]

More recently the PSNI has upped its international ambitions with a vengeance. The long-term plan appears to be to recoup some of the cost of the force's new £140 million training facility by offering at-a-price training packages (mostly it seems around counter-terrorism and public order) to national (i.e. from Britain) and international police agencies. The facilities available at the new 250-acre site will apparently include an aircraft fuselage, a ship's hull, a train carriage, a practice decontamination unit in the event of a chemical, biological or nuclear attack, and a 'mock' streetscape for urban guerrilla warfare and riot control (*The News Letter*, 29 December 2011). The FBI has already expressed an interest in availing itself of these training facilities, and as Assistant Chief Constable Judith Gillespie stated:

> There are all sorts of opportunities opening up for us to have residential training for national and international colleagues, not just in policing but in fire and rescue and prisons as well. This will be a truly unique state-of-the-art, best-in-class facility ... The FBI are already expressing an interest, our colleagues in An Garda Síochána and the rest of the UK as well.
>
> (Cited in *The News Letter*, 29 December 2011)

The myth of the brand

This section has explored two key and perhaps mutually incompatible dimensions of the NIPM and suggests that each has been promoted by the PSNI depending on target audience. Lessons from the ICP reform process are promoted in the context of democratic policing transitions, while lessons from the conflict in Northern Ireland are promoted in the context of global insecurities and the War on Terror. It is this aspect of the model that is in the ascendency and has become of a core component of the 'British' policing brand given the increasing role played by RUC/PSNI personnel in UK executive policing missions (Ashraf, 2007; Sinclair, 2012). Again, there are historical parallels. It was always the Royal Irish Constabulary (RIC) (not the New Police) that the British authorities regarded as their finest export model (Brogden, 1987a, b). Ashraf (2007), who served with a UK police mission to Iraq, questions the utility of sending 'ordinary' UK police to conflict zones such as Iraq and Afghanistan and argues that in such contexts the skill-set of RUC/PSNI officers (whether official or as a private security operative) was seen as a prized and highly valued commodity:

> A debate raged and continues about the appropriateness of UK police forces imparting their doctrine to countries in the grip of acute civil violence and possessing fragile governance capacity. Many felt that a Third Force such as the Gendarmerie or Carabinieri was more relevant to Iraq's needs. The argument has some merit, as those UK volunteers who had served with PSNI or the RUC tended to be amongst the most effective in understanding the Iraqi situation and in contributing to their counter-terrorism capability. These officers had experience of counter-terrorism in a sectarian environment. They understood the threats and pressure that Iraqi officers faced. They also understood the crucial importance of acquiring and using intelligence effectively in a terrorism context, and they knew how to coordinate action with the Army. Whether these officers were recruited directly by the FCO or via a private security contractor, the senior British police officer in Iraq would invariably deploy them in posts that exploited their valuable talents.
>
> (Ashraf, 2007 p. 108)

Furthermore, as Sinclair (2012) notes, one of the effects of the current fiscal crisis has been to severely limit the number of officers available for overseas deployments. However, the slack has been taken up by the corporate security sector, staffed again by mainly ex-RUC/PSNI personnel.[9] A recent Amnesty International report into the scale of the defence and security consultancy industry in Northern Ireland notes that:

> many private security and military companies regard former Royal Ulster Constabulary (RUC), PSNI and Royal Irish Regiment (RIR) personnel as possessing desirable skills in counter-terrorism and urban conflict operations. This has led to many of these personnel working overseas in conflict zones as trainers, security guards and advisors . . . One such private company is Task International . . . [its website] states that 'TASK has trained over 500 military and police special forces units and individual team members from friendly

countries all over the world and its instructors are ex special forces, Metropolitan police and Northern Ireland specialists'.

(Amnesty International, 2007 p. 22)

We have no doubt that in many ways the RUC/PSNI have order-maintenance skills that are more suited to problematic security environments such as Iraq and Afghanistan, where the establishment of community policing or indeed democratic policing is likely to be little more than a pipedream. Nevertheless, there are several problems with the promotion of this aspect of the brand in particular. And while it is clear that that both the RUC/PSNI model and personnel are lauded by British officials internationally (see Sinclair, 2012) we should remember that the RUC has cast a long shadow in the domestic (Northern Irish) context.[10] Indeed, the force's role in exacerbating the conflict in Northern Ireland is well documented, and as Brendan O'Leary reminds us:

> We must not, of course, ever forget that over 300 police officers were killed in the current conflict, but we must also not forget that the outbreak of armed conflict in 1969 was partly caused by an unreformed, half-legitimate police service, responsible for seven of the first eight deaths.
>
> (O'Leary, 2000 p. 14)

The international policing of the Other

We have argued in Chapter 1 that the core practice of the police in Britain relies less on its mythical Reithian/Peelian foundations and should be seen instead in terms of policing the domestic Other. This chapter suggests that the UK Police plc brand – while rooted in a Peelian mythology – can be similarly construed in terms of policing an international Other. It forms part of an expanded process of policing-for-profit that is itself a consequence of the impact of globalizing neoliberalism and where overseas training is seen as an important revenue stream, or where missions themselves are seen to have a strategic benefit (as in containing the international Other, for instance). In this sense the promotion of the brand is intimately tied with the political economy of aid and development assistance that, more often than not, reflects narrow geo-strategic concerns (Pino and Wiatrowski, 2006).

More generally though, the UK policing brand is conceptually inadequate in the context of twenty-first-century policing. It insists on imagining the brand in terms of a reified vision of nineteenth-century policing that is deeply contested historically (see Chapter 5). It also insists on imagining the brand as a statist function performed by identifiable state functionaries. Even in the national/domestic setting this bears little relation to reality, given what Sir Ian Blair referred to as the 'extended policing family' – that includes everything from PCSOs, traffic wardens, local council officials, neighbourhood wardens and commercial security (Crawford and Lister, 2004). We noted in Chapter 3 that the policing landscape has become increasingly fractured over the past two decades, a situation that has accelerated as a consequence of neoliberal globalization. It is impossible, there-fore, to make any assessment of domestic policing without considering the role played by civil society, and private as well as state police actors.

However, this state-centred model of public policing provision and its location *within* the UK police brand is of even less relevance in the international context. Neoliberal globalization has thrown open the door to any number of auspices and providers of security (Johnston and Shearing, 2003) who market, promote and sell their services in a global marketplace as part of a mixed economy of policing (Crawford, 2006b p. 111). Even in those contexts where an overseas mission is primarily the responsibility of a national or supranational organization there are myriad civil, police, military and commercial security actors, making any claim to the ownership of the mission by any one organization (for example, the state police) or indeed national government, futile in practice. The British brand for export process is comprised of any number of functionaries: some in the state sector, some in the corporate security sector, some straddling both; as well as associated advisors and gurus who are hired by national governments and entrepreneurs who often work in a private capacity[11] (see Box 4.4). In Iraq and Afghanistan we might as well say that the British police brand is represented just as much – if not more – by Aegis Defence Services, Armorgroup or Control Risks, given the key role that these firms play there on behalf of the British government.[12]

Furthermore, there are few international missions that rely solely on UK police officers, and in various EU missions what you are more likely to find is brand competition along national lines, with, for example, French, Italian and Spanish officials tending to favour police reform models organizationally structured along the lines of a gendarmerie compared to the British preference for emphasizing a sharp distinction between military and police units (Hills, 2009 p. 65).[13] Again, it is difficult to say with any certainty that the British brand will be the dominant one.

Box 4.4   A typology of international policing personnel[14]

The Fixer The fixer has a long history in British policing missions. Fixers flit from conflict zone to conflict zone and are usually involved in major policing or security sector reform programmes or are despatched in a troubleshooting capacity. Historical examples of policing fixers range from Sir Charles Wickham and Sir Charles Tegart to the more contemporary role played by Sir Ronnie Flanagan, who was sent to problem-solve policing in Iraq on behalf of the British government. Fixers can also utilize their experience elsewhere; e.g. Sir Ronnie Flanagan's activities with the International Cricket Council's anti-corruption and security unit.

The Advisor Some overlap with the guru (below) but are arguably more technocratic. Advisors can be currently serving police or more usually recently retired senior officers with experience in a particular area. Advisors are seconded to overseas missions to advise on security sector reform endeavours. Most advisors sell their services for a fee.

The Guru Like fixers and advisors, gurus flit from place to place depending on where their expertise is needed. Gurus are characterized by a sense of mission and are perceived to hold a preternatural insight into international policing problems. They believe that they and they alone hold the solution based on many years experience of doing the same thing. Gurus have carved out expertise in counter-terrorism, democratic policing, and also zero-tolerance policing. Gurus will work for a fee, but in some instances if they are feeling magnanimous will freely share their knowledge.

The Secondee Often a currently serving officer who is released from his or her own force for a short to medium term to participate in an international mission. Increasingly, however, secondees are released on a 'fee basis' to a national government – as with the crop of officers working in Libya and other parts of the Middle East. There may be some overlap here with advisors.

The Journeyman Some overlap here with private security operatives and secondees. They do not have the same sense of mission as gurus and advisors. They are quite happy to take a lucrative salary and don't mind the risks. They are not normatively committed to the job, or to the international policing operation itself. Any money that is earned is usually put down as a deposit on a new house or used to purchase a new car.

The Entrepreneur Generally a less successful guru. Usually older retired police officers who have found a niche (say in community policing). Attach themselves to host police force in a remote area which they come to feel 'own'. Tend to be rather territorial of this force and resent any intrusion by other entrepreneurs. Most are paid a consultancy fee by an international development agency.

The Private Operative Some overlap here with the journeyman. Usually recently retired police (mainly from PSNI/RUC) or British Army or younger officers on a career break. They are recruited by one of the international security consultancies and are attracted by high salaries in dangerous places. Roles vary depending on age. Older operatives advise on threats and risks and usually have counter-terrorism experience. Younger operatives are at the coal-face and perform guarding and protection duties (often of their own country's state forces). Increasingly such operatives are hired by national governments, given the interpenetration of policing forms.

Overview

This chapter has deconstructed what is termed by senior British police and government officials as the UK Police plc brand. We have pointed to a number of problems with this conceptualization: its linkages to a mythical notion of 'British' (though in reality English) policing that did not exist in the nineteenth century and bears little relationship to what is practised in terms of international policing missions anyway. Furthermore, in the mixed economy of twenty-first-century policing (Crawford, 2006b) there is no British brand, or at least no brand that can be uniquely associated with state personnel. As we have seen in conflict zones such as Kosovo, Afghanistan and Iraq, the brand is just as likely to be represented by the corporate security sector.

It is often easier to sell a commodity to an often appreciative international audience rather than to whingeing and contrary locals. Given its history, tradition of export of social ordering to the previous colonies, legitimized mythology, and British Northern Irish policing personnel, state policing has become an international brand in which defects in practice and in principle are concealed by the salespeople. Building upon the 'gift' to the Orient in colonial days, sales talk meets a relatively welcoming consumer market, especially in those states that wish to conceal their autocracy behind a facade of 'public good' when confronting their own internal Other. In an age of austerity, such an export serves several functions. It helps fill the state's coffers, replenishing in part resources cut as a consequence of the Western capital crisis. It also links with the neoliberal commitment to privatization by blurring the state–private divide. Privatization can occur by stealth in that process. Third, it provides new sources of employment for police officers (and others) who need to enhance their pensions after 30 years of service. There are major personal rewards in such an export business. Much of this export remains opaque, given the questionable sales (like military equipment) to states without a notionally democratic record. British and Northern Ireland policing resources are massaged in the transitional context to provide relief for other governments that see the Other as a local problem, most effectively dealt with by a Western brand of expertise. What is missing from the argument, of course, is the extent to which the Occident strikes back – in the import of postcolonial and transitional society expertise in policing their own local Other.

5 Policing the Other through law

The 'Office of Constable' is the bedrock of British policing – the office of constable, whereby a police officer has an original and not a delegated jurisdiction, and is himself directly answerable to the law for his actions, is far from an historical adornment; it is a fundamental part of what makes British policing an essential and extremely powerful protection of the citizen in his relationship with the state and its agencies, and ensures that our country could never become a police state. A system under which senior police officers and management make decisions as to the efficient and effective deployment of police officers, and evaluate those officers in the ways in which they work and the jobs they do so as to ensure they always meet the needs of the public they serve, is entirely consistent with the integrity of the office of constable.

(Winsor Report, 2011 Part 1)

It is difficult for a civil community to identify with anything labelled a Basic Command Unit, especially as these become bigger and bigger. The local police committees of such forces hardly constitute local involvement, while community liaison teams. . . do not find that such involvement is keen on, or funds much of local relevance in some of the policies and targets identified by the Home Office or the Inspectorate. Perhaps the time has come to recognize that the Home Office police forces largely constitute a national police institution and to endeavour to work out how small community links can develop the kind of tight community links that everyone claims to want.

(Emsley, 2009 pp. 295–6)

Introduction: law and democratic policing

In this chapter, we explore the neglected role of criminal and common law in constructing and sustaining a state police institution designed to emphasize the policing of the Other. There is a curious notion that democratic state policing is a 'good thing'. Accountability to the 'community' via the mechanisms of law and popular assent is assumed to be a desirable, if utopian, target. The prescient alternatives are not evidently pleasant. Policing-for-profit in which the rich get richer and the poor get prison, can be discounted. Similarly, the caricature of Stalinist state policing is not just a caricature. Informal agencies of maintaining social order vary from the whimsical and the romantic to the infinitely regressive inclusion of various agencies of social order (within or without the extended police family). Shearing and Stenning's dystopian Disneyland model rightly gives rise to conspiratorial soft panopticon concerns (Shearing and Stenning, 1987). Accountability through professionalism, as in the Police and Criminal Evidence Act of 1984, entails determining behaviour on the street according to the subjective experience of senior staff (Jones, 1985; Maguire, 2002). The Potemkin house of democratic accountability, in relation to the modern state, shields more than it reveals.

In modern society, accountability is a peculiar concept. At face value, the problems are obvious. At worst, democratic control of that key state social ordering device by a majority of the notional citizenry can lead to the legal oppression of the minority by the majority. At the other end of the scale, as in the UK, accountability can simply be lost in the vacuous fog of tautological mechanisms of public consent through law, professionalism, and the ballot box. The confusion will only be compounded by implanting police commissioners. As we have argued in earlier chapters, scholars face three key problems in attempting to develop an appropriate way to understand the concept of democratic policing.

First of all, it depends upon a clear definition of state police duties. There is almost a total absence of such agreed duties within Anglo-American policing. As Manning (2010 p. viii) says in his recent erudite study:

> What are the police good for? How can we know and evaluate democratic policing? What do we know about such policing in Anglo-American democracies? If democracy rests on equality, justice, and basic rights and responsibilities, what role do the police play in shaping them?

Second, Manning reiterates the question central to this text: if such societies are characterized by deep structural (and increasing) economic inequalities, exasperated by the fiscal crisis, how can the police act other than to sustain those fissures? The regulation of the Other is the state police rationale, as determined through practice and legal process. Given that any superficial overview of the practices of criminal justice, as evidenced by data from judicial process, shows that the vast majority of offences as processed by policing agencies are conducted by members of the lower economic social classes, irrespective of the level of social harm.

Third, discretion is a critical if a peculiar aspect of the common law inheritance. For example, the judiciary commonly 'makes' law by interpreting statutes with considerable discretion. One typical argument against the discretionary powers of the constable on the street is that it can lead to subjective practice in relation to stop-and-search powers. This potential abuse of street powers has influenced police forces to conceive of such bias as remediable by diversity training in an attempt to mediate the more pernicious aspects of police occupational culture (Chan, 1996). If this is the case, such training has been ineffective, given the continuity of that bias (Cashmore, 2002). One conclusion is that constabulary discretion is the wrong target for reform, that the problems are structural (institutional) rather than aberrational. Legal structures are the key problem, not the easy target of officers' street behaviour. In this chapter, we explore the neglected role of criminal and common law in constructing and sustaining a state police institution designed to emphasize the policing of the Other.

A pastiche on the Office of Constable

The Office of Constable (see Box 5.1) necessarily sustains inequality. It is an oxymoron in several ways: principally because of the amorphous original; common law powers of arrest and prosecution. The Office is a remarkably flexible tool, all smoke and mirrors in practice. It allows the holder to conduct a range of undefined duties with vague limits. Legal accountability is problematic. It allows for the officer to uphold a legal notion of equality on one hand while promoting inequality on the other. He/she draws legitimacy for practice under (primarily) common law powers as a citizen amongst citizens. The Constable, as discussed below, is unique to England and Wales, in failing (opposed to practice in other common law countries and in Roman Law Western Europe) to balance the interest of state and citizen in the criminal justice process system, with an independent office of prosecution.

The emphasis on the importance of the constable in front-line policing practice during the current fiscal crisis makes the point more strongly. The evidence of such discretion appears from 1829 through to the present day. Emsley (2009) quotes from the notebook of Metropolitan PC Hennessy, between 1857 and 1880, listing his arrests. They consisted mainly of being drunk and disorderly, vagrancy, drunk in charge of a vehicle, omnibus offences, and petty larceny. During that period, Hennessy records only three burglaries. Following the 'domestic missionary' pattern identified by Storch (1975), policing was concerned with a more general social

---

Box 5.1   Where is this office?

The above quotation is not made up. It was actually said by a Member of Parliament upon hearing the term the Office of Constable . . . The Office of Constable has evolved over the centuries and the 'British Bobby' is recognised across the world, but what is it that makes it so special, so endearing, so different? . . . But what is at its heart, and why does it remain a recognised and trusted brand leader around the world? Why does it conjure up feelings of safety and security, and why do the public want to see more 'bobbies'? Why do those of us who hold this proud Office of Constable go forward into dangers when others go back? The answer is simple; it's about integrity, impartiality, and most importantly, political independence. It is the tie breaker, the ultimate check and balance in our democracy to protect against a tyrannical abuse of power.

(Police Federation for England and Wales)[1]

ordering of the lumpen-proletariat, including policing their morals and cultural practices (see also Petrow, 1994; Dixon, 1997). That practice represented what is now called the frontline (or the policing of the Other). A similar pattern of such policing practice is evident in Edwardian Liverpool (Brogden, 1991). A constable's work routine consisted of 'moving-on' loiterers outside a public house, curtailing street-betting, dealing with the occasional prostitute, and checking ('milking') locks. Subsequent penalties reflected the same pattern. A remarkably consistent social ordering of the lower classes is evident in the present day (with the addition of a display of ASBOs). Normal frontline duty allows the constable to concentrate his/her duties on policing the most socially unequal. As Steve Box says in his text on crime and the recession of the 1980s, 'Through their deployment, arrest and prosecution practices, the police supply the judiciary with an increasing number of persons to process, and among those proportionately more are young, unemployed and/or black' (1987 p. 148). But there is a curious recent, postcolonial twist in the use of the constable's original powers.

Law and the continuity of summary justice for the Other

We now recognize, from the work of many critical historians, that the myths (still held and promulgated on institutional websites) about the period of the birth of the New Police were exactly that: romanticized folk legacies (Brogden, 1982; Emsley, 2012; Reiner, 2012; Weinberger, 1995). The Metropolitan Police was not 'newly' formed in 1829. It drew on many previous experiments – from Colquhoun's River Thames Police to the Dublin City Police. Like them, its primary function was to control, at the general level, the 'mob' and individually the uncivil poor and its itinerant components (see Box 5.2). Peel may have regarded it as having a primary 'crime function' in the Metropolitan Police Act of 1829. But social ordering of the Other, the poor and the street economy, stands out as primary in the records of the time (Emsley, 1991; Gatrell, 1990; Palmer, 1988; Roberts, 1988). In such a process, it maintained (initially in tandem) the street patrol and guard duties of the old Watch. In other ways, the New Police were not particularly 'new': their beat style had been in use long before 1829 and older practices of the Watch continued long afterwards (Storch, 1975). The 'blue locust', both as oppressed (by his disciplinary code) and oppressor of the street Other, was not a novelty in 1829 (Gatrell, 1990; Storch, 1975). At that date they simply became considerably larger as an institution and more structured in terms of ranks, duties, and form of control. They were not locals policing locals (Roberts, 1988). Many were drawn from Scotland, Wales, and Ireland, or frequently from cognate rural areas. Others were dislocated ex-seamen and ex-soldiers, long cut adrift from their parish of origin. They were drunk as often as not (judging by the discharge data – Brogden, 1991). The myths that legitimize the present neighbourhood style of policing have long been exposed as fairy tales. They played little part in crime prevention (in the normative meaning of the term) and in crime resolution. They simply dominated their beats by coercion although more often by threat. Their targets were not criminals but the lower classes of the street – the Other. Officers might respond (and give deference) to their betters in return for the occasional unofficial rewards. They subverted the secondary economy of public space by regulating the livelihoods of the poor – from betting shops to gambling houses to brothels and second-hand shops (often fences) to gin parlours. They were available en masse to deal with occasional eruptions from the rookeries (London slums). Knowledge of law was limited: training was essentially drill. But that absence of legal powers did not stop them conducting summary justice, either within the permissive legal framework or outside it. Their authority reflected the uniformed status, as backed by coercion or rather the threat of it. In court cases they were often the only witness, and over the years they came (by accident rather than by design) to act as prosecutors, thus doubling their formal authority. Organizationally, they were neither new in principle or practice.

Unrepresentative provincial watch committees were appointed by council elites (Brogden, 1982; C. A. Williams, 2003). With the political and economic decline of the authority of urbanism, by the end of the nineteenth century watch committees were little different in values and economic interests from their representatives at Westminster. Despite the initial (overrated) opposition to the 'French model', watch committees were not as much concerned with the locality of policing but rather with reinforcing their own economic and social power bases. Socioeconomic values of class and normative practices of the watch committees were to be little different in future from those of their supposed opponents in Westminster. Such bodies were democratic only in the sense that male ratepayers over the age of thirty were enfranchised, thus continuing the disenfranchisement of the vast majority of local population who had no input into police policies and procedures.

When Westminster attempted a degree of urban local control, it first (in 1857) furnished a quarter of urban police costs, which it increased to half in 1874. The counties were funded (initially by the promise of financial support) in return for a degree of central inspection. That inspection, when extended to the provinces, was the price paid by localities for receiving central funding, and was a token affair. As the Bramshill Library records demonstrate, the new Home Office Inspectorate simply matched the number of sworn officers of the approved local police establishments (itself an arbitrary euphemism[2]), and inspected both polished buttons and manicured records. Williams (C. A. Williams, 2003) rightly highlights the early centralization by the new Inspectorate but fails to document its procedural reality. As late as 1981, inspectors' reports on local forces remained confidential. In that year, the then MP for Bootle, the late Alan Roberts, at one of the authors' instigation (Brogden), asked the then home secretary to reveal the contents of the reports. Willie Whitelaw answered with a blunt 'NO'! Times have changed a little over recent years with regard to the disclosure of the detail of such anodyne inspections. This lack of democratic accountability was even more evident when unelected county magistrates appointed former military officers as police chiefs, as the key to their unilateral control of both city streets and rural lanes inhabited by the street populations of the Other. Unchanged legislation continued for the Other and its imposers until the 1970s. For the rest of the century and up to the end of the World War I, unelected local watch committees appear rarely to have overruled the head (later chief) constable. The Nott Bower case of 1896 in Liverpool, when the local watch committee fruitlessly tried to impose its wishes on the head constable, was the exception rather than the rule (Brogden, 1982).[3] The autonomy of a non-democratic local elite was challenged by a new emerging collective of the new chief officers of the police (see Stallion and Wall, 2011). Similar but exceptional, limited cases, appeared occasionally (Jefferson and Grimshaw, 1984), from Birmingham (1880) to Nottingham (1958). They were different in character from the Nott Bower case in that the chief officer appeared to be intervening in the practices of watch committees, rather than the other way round. Localism, this was not. But police street practices remained the same (Brogden, 1991).

Certainly, at several times, Westminster did attempt to impose central control of local forces, although some historians have noted correctly that the Victorian ruling class was hardly a unified elite over policing practice, divided both horizontally and vertically in relation to the urban elites (Philips and Storch, 1999). But there was a Delphic implication. In governance, unelected county magistrates frequently appointed former military officers as rulers of both city streets and rural lanes inhabited by the Other. By the latter part of the nineteenth century, unelected local watch committees appear rarely to have overruled the head constable in processing the socially disorderly. Local 'democracy' encompassed only a minority until female enfranchisement after World War I. Urban governance was to be little different in future from central governance (apart from a brief interlude between the early 1970s and mid-1980s when local Labour municipalities dared to challenge certain feudal policing practices).[4]

For a century and a half, police officers were formally disassociated from local communities and intentionally isolated. Officers patrolled the streets at night, sundered from colleagues and locals. External recruitment practices ensured lack of fealty to the locals. Rights to marry and choice of accommodation were monitored by CID until World War II. In turn, they recorded, observed, and spied on lower-class communities. Typically, indulging in conversation with a local person, fraternizing to break the tedium of a night-time beat, could be met with severe retribution by senior officers (Brogden, 1991). Given the level of police pay until the Desborough Report of 1919, itself precipitated by legitimate attempts to develop police rank-and-file bargaining rights, the police as Reiner once acknowledged (Reiner, 1978) were in a contradictory class position. Despite conditions of work and wages only slightly above those of an agricultural worker, they were expected to conduct largely meaningless night-time tasks policing the Other, forbidden social intimacy with the locals, and enjoyed no legal rights as wage labourers.

The construction of new metropolitan provincial forces after 1964 opened a Pandora's box of intrusive social ordering under the mythology of the citizen-in-uniform. Constables' discretionary powers are again critical in understanding the continuity of the policing of the Other. The Victorian police had haphazardly accrued new infinite duties, legitimized by common law, and that office provided an historical justification for current intrusive community and Neighbourhood Policing (Brogden and Nijhar, 2005). Legislation, both the older summary policing by character rather than by category of offence, and police discretion, continued in parallel with elements of the new adversarial practices. Such legislation did not introduce democratic policing to the locality, but merely perpetuated the relative legal inequalities, eventually to be reinforced by the new police and crime commissioners. The essential bilateralism of informal justice practices in the abodes of the Other was increasingly replaced by unilateral state police determination. In sum, this process was facilitated by the enabling Office of Constable: a lack of specification of police duties, and organizationally-based discretion. Constables could go where constables had rarely been before, under the rubric of 'community' and latterly Neighbourhood and Reassurance Policing. The rudimentary 'clip around the ear' was replaced by permissive extension of police powers.

The concept of *localism* also aided the process of incorporation of traditional informal structures. Localism is a curious notion containing an assumption of local harmony, an odd thesis given that local society simply reflects the inequalities and differential power structures of the central state. Social order is appealing in its relative simplicity, its articulation of a previous *golden age*, and its relative expedition of justice. But it has little value in furnishing justice in arrest and victim experiences for the Other.

'Citizens' versus the 'Other' in contemporary criminal law

A fundamental problem owing to the Enlightenment development of the concept of the citizen is that the constable, supposedly an equal amongst equals, structurally underpins a system that in practice is heavily weighted against the accused (McBarnet, 1981). The assumption of legally equal citizens structures and reinforces social inequality within the criminal justice process. Legal equality has little relationship to social justice and to social equality. Critical jurisprudence has long recognized the structural inequalities innate within criminal law, none more evidential (and forgotten) than in the conflated heuristic work of the socialist jurists Pashukanis (2007 [1924]) and Balbus (1977). Drawing on the latter, the key reason that the criminal justice process operates under a formal veneer of equality is the assumption of the peculiar notion of equal citizens before the law in Western democracies. State functionaries police all citizens under an independent body of impartial legislation. Especially in the adversarial system, citizens engage in mutual combat before an impartial officer (jury or judge). Citizen juries in serious cases are intended to prevent a more powerful entity, the state, taking advantage of its overwhelming power against the accused. Rather differently, under the varied inquisitorial processes of continental Europe, suspected citizens are investigated by an independent judge and his/her policing staff to establish the 'facts' of the case (see below on Prosecution).

But critical theory suggests that such approaches depend upon a 'false equivalent', an artificial construct, 'the citizen'. The latter within Western democracies is assumed to be the equal of all other citizens in that jurisdiction. Communities, societies, are conceived of as being constructs of equal citizens before the law. Neighbourhood Policing relies on the same false representation about the equality of citizens of locality, connecting with a form of social capital; the empowering social networks and the norms of reciprocity and trustworthiness that arise from them. As the Tottenham riots demonstrated, in the context of mass youth unemployment, there are few organic local structures and forms of social capital through which police might meaningfully communicate and, euphemistically, 'lead', given the tradition and legacy of policing the Other. In many respects, Neighbourhood Policing seeks to engage with 'imaginary communities of citizens'.

Equality in law as a citizen is a quite different entity from equality in relation to social/economic persons and social formations, which vary considerably in relation to ethnicity, age, gender, economic resources and so on. But the criminal justice process in particular (with rare exceptions, some positive, some negative) treats social unequals as legal equivalents. Limited other areas of law markedly differ. Steve Box phrases it well: 'Law is like Christmas chocolates: hard on the outside and soft in the middle' (Box, 1987 p. 17). Criminal law (summary) for the poor, administrative and civil law for the more affluent. Taxation law, for example, recognizes the economic inequality of social actors. Criminal law may also occasionally deviate from the principle of legal equivalence (as in the judicial tariff system). The unit (or day) fine system, common in Scandinavia and certain Commonwealth jurisdictions,[5] punishes offenders not as legal equals but as economic unequals. In those exceptions, the rich pay more than the poor for the same offence. Conversely, the legal equivalence principle may be breached in the opposite direction. Under what seems to have been a deliberate expedient process of pre-trial punishment, justified by policing procedural rationales, suspects arrested during the riots of August 2011 were ten times more likely to be held in custody than suspects accused of similar offences in different contexts. They were also more likely to have previous convictions widely circulated by the police, consequently making them more liable to serious penalties. Commodity form theory suggests that a democratic policing system based on a notion of equal citizenship results in a structural bias in police enforcement structural bias (Balbus, 1977). In that sense, democratic policing is an oxymoron.

Studying British policing without reference to the enabling powers of law is like the proverbial design of an elephant through a committee. Marginal people – the Other – are unequal in the criminal justice process and most likely to be on the receiving end of summary contact with the state, and in their status as victim. The principle of equal rights is not apparent in relation to the socially excluded, a problem that will be exacerbated by the recent cuts in Legal Aid.

Street law

Historical pragmatism in the development of the state police and the accompanying body of law (almost an *accidental* history – Brogden et al., 1988) is coupled with the structural inequalities of criminal law. At the serious end of a social harm continuum, billionaire tax avoiders, environmental polluters (typically regarded as civil rather than criminal offenders), and much political chicanery, are rarely arenas of state policing intervention. Some are more equal than others. Policing follows the contours of the inequalities inherent in an unequal legal system. Indeed, if the criminal law is skewed against the poor, impartial policing under that legal rubric will always be partisan. Statutory definitions of the police function in Anglo-American societies were tautologically absent within the traditional Metropolitan Police model, irrespective of the phrasing of Peel's Nine Principles. There was a complete lack of any regulation for state policing under the 1829 Act and its immediate successors.

Despite the Benthamite formulation of the trial as an adversarial contest between equals, the Victorian criminal justice legislation inexorably contained the assumptions of the previous system. Criminal justice and policing specifically were directed at the lowest strata. There are many well-known aphorisms to summarize that picture, but the following astutely sums up the spirit and the practice of state policing: 'The law, in its majestic equality, forbids the rich as well as the poor to sleep under bridges, to beg in the streets, and to steal bread.' (Anatole France, *The Red Lily*, 1894).

As we note above, the eighteenth-century criminal justice process had formally been discarded with the advent of the New Police. But Becarria's influence in Continental Europe in constructing a modern codified system of criminal law, drawing upon clear basic principles, had not been an easy act for Samuel Romilly and Robert Peel to follow. As John Lea (2004) acknowledges, the dispersed tradition of English common law did not lend itself easily to codification under Bentham's tutelage. Criminal law remained (and remains) cluttered by traditional common law practices. British and colonial law, during the Industrial Revolution, drew heavily on the procedures of an earlier period (Palmer, 1988; R. Williams, 2003). This differentiation in law was evident as far back as 1823 with the notorious Masters and Servants Act, which determined that if an employer broke the law he could only be sued in the civil courts, while if a workman broke a contract he could be disciplined by the full forces of the law spearheaded by the police.[6]

Box 5.2   The summary process of early street policing

. . . the new police were able to set about establishing a new level of order and decorum on the streets, partly because of their numbers but also because they had a relatively simple task, though often unpopular with the working classes who passed much of their leisure time in the street. The advent of the new police in a district invariably resulted in an increase in arrest for petty offences and misdemeanours: street traders were ordered to move along, as were groups of loitering youth, prostitutes and vagrants; street games and gambling were stopped; drunks were dragged to the police cells to sleep of their inebriation; fighting drunks were dragged with much force. Traffic was better controlled; carters, cab and omnibus drivers were forbidden from loitering . . .

(Emsley, 1996 p. 60)

Legal flexibility

In local practice, like the original constable, state police operate with a mix of legal and extra-legal powers. The Vagrancy Act, like the Habitual Offenders Act, occasional legislation such as the Contagious Diseases Act, and similar legislation such as that against homosexuality in 1880, have long been permissive common law instruments. The Vagrancy Act, in its various manifestations since the sixteenth century (Chambliss, 1964), has been and gone, but the permissive common-law and statutory powers continue, appearing later with the increasingly divisive practice of stop-and-search powers as one precipitant of the riots of August 2011. Stop-and-search powers have an unwritten history. Largely useless at preventing crime, they are a political response to moral panics. They target suspect populations almost randomly, according to majority hysteria and a frenzied media. The usual 'strike' rate is one-in-twelve of those stopped. But the normal arrest in such circumstances is usually one of the police-constructed offences of 'obstruction'. Typical of such practices is one in the North Wales policing area in 2008. A media-inflated panic about the possession of knives by young people resulted in a major overnight operation by the North Wales Police. Three hundred and twelve young people were stopped and searched. No knives were found, and oddly – to the cynic – no arrests were made for obstruction (Scott, 2008). No other offences were responded to during that period. Police overtime payments were appreciated.

Such legal practices were reinforced by the police cultural reliance on what Robert Reiner jokingly termed the 'Ways and Means Act' (Reiner, 2010b). As above, use of permissive powers was most recently exemplified in the August 2011 riots with the extraordinary use of pre-trial custody, on police request, and the subsequent use of the stop-and-search powers contained within Section 60 of the 1994 Criminal Justice and Public Order Act. Some two-thirds of non-tried suspects were held in custody compared with the usual one-in-twenty. Clearly such deprivation of liberty may be legal within permissive summary legislation and depends on local justice agreement. But there are some questions about the political intervention of the prime minster, in deliberately promoting that and similar practices of eventual sentencing.[7] Failure to appreciate the legal context of police practice is a major lacuna in both traditional and revisionist histories.

How to expand police powers without really trying: the example of incivilities

The Office of Constable, with its lack of specification of duties, is an extraordinary facilitator of the expansion of police powers of intervention. When coupled with statutory expansion of law, such as in the in the instant justice of fixed penalties, it has grossly enhanced the demands on policing resources. Typical of this process is the recurring problem of responding to a combination of high recorded crime rates and a similar rise in levels of fear of crime among the public. Answers have to be found to this conundrum. Broken Windows theory[8] was formally intended as a strategy to promote community integrity, to support existing social capital, and to encourage better relations between police and public. In practice, it was reduced to a zero tolerance approach, one that perceived minor local deviance as a stepping stone to serious criminality (Young, 1999). Major criminals start as small, petty, offenders. Physical dilapidation encourages social deviance such as drug use. Curtailing that career should occur at its inception, in the same way that decrepit buildings should be improved to avoid social malaise. Previously tolerated minor misdemeanours may inexorably lead to more serious criminality. Thus in New York in the early 1980s, the commissioner embarked on a long-term project in which police resources were directed away from the traditional focus (though this is debatable) – on serious crimes to minor offences such as in the practice of 'squeegee' merchants, arbitrarily cleaning car windows at traffic lights and demanding payment (see Young, 1999 for lucid critique of Broken Windows).

To Broken Windows exponents, adoption of the strategy was successful. Eventually, more serious forms of crime in New York (the most quoted example) declined. However, experiments elsewhere variously did or did not validate this conclusion (Dixon, 1999). Typically, other cities such as Boston experienced similar falls in serious crimes without recourse to that strategy. The experiment in New York coincided with a major decline in the birth rate of the presumed primary criminogenic population of the Other and a major reduction in the use of crack cocaine (Bowling, 1999).

However, social scientists (and especially evidence-based policing practitioners) rarely produce negative results from their investigations. Methodological haziness is assisted by the fact that the thesis requires long-term investigation of criminal careers to produce notionally clear results. It takes a long time for minor offenders to graduate into more serious crime. Paradoxically, however, in the Broken Windows case, many were fast-tracked into the criminal justice system by the new ambitious commissioner, Bill Bratton, and by local political pressure for publicly digestible 'successes' in the war against street crime. In the UK, the zero tolerance variation was adopted in tandem with several processes. Fear of crime as opposed to crime itself became *the* major problem through the increasing use of victim surveys (e.g. Lea and Young, 1993). The majority of respondents (subject to methodological weaknesses in such studies which notably exclude the supposed socially illiterate) demonstrated that they commonly appeared to believe that crime was a more serious local problem that alternative indices suggested. There was a major disjunction between state police perception of crime levels and civilian perception. Further, respondents appeared to be more worried about local misdemeanours than about more serious forms of crime. Consequently, state policing increasingly came to focus on fear of crime (a fear partly exaggerated due to the presence of the Other in public space) rather than crime per se. This transition was aided by the new commitment to community policing and eventually, its more narrowly focused British brand, Neighbourhood Policing strategies (as above) committed to the 'local' nexus. Out of the latter emerged, in the early years of the century, Reassurance Policing, a strategy intended by the use of various signifiers both to persuade locals that crime was not such so much a problem as a social construction and, second, to direct more police resources to relatively trivial offences – the euphemism for misdemeanours – the seeds of criminal careers (Goldson, 2002). The latter became legally translated into summary (mainly) ASBOs, in the Crime and Disorder Act 1998, and more colloquially, into 'incivilities'. Later legislation strengthened their application across the UK, although in 2010 the home secretary, Theresa May, announced that ASBOs would eventually be abolished in England and Wales in favour of community sentences.

In many respects, ASBOs were a doomed legal entrepreneurial venture. Their subjectivity, based on a perception of a behaviour or conduct, was always a rather shaky footing from which to authorize official sanctions. They were populist, supported by the 'silent majority' of the Occident, and therefore fickle, subject to local moral panics and intermittent 'unease' (Goldson, 2005). They also became something of a badge of honour among young people (Meltzer, 2011). Officially, ASBOs were designed to deal with

> conduct which caused or was likely to cause harm, harassment, alarm or distress, to one or more persons not of the same household as him or herself and where an ASBO is seen as necessary to protect relevant persons from further anti-social acts by the Defendant.
>
> (Crime and Disorder Act, 1998 s.1)

However, as the *Guardian* sardonically lamented about their eventual demise, ASBOs have been responsible for some of the daftest stories in the mass media for a decade (Meltzer, 2011). In addition to the behaviours listed below (see Box 5.3), ASBOs have been issued for singing, wearing low-slung trousers, naked opera singing, jumping into a canal, laughing, staring, slow-clapping, goose-stepping, singing in the bath, bee keeping, keeping chickens in a backyard, and climbing the side of a tower block as a stunt (Meltzer, 2011). These matters may appeal to a local councillor seeking re-election. But they impinge only marginally in the current financial crisis, with respect to serious social harm and its resolution.

The new policing of incivilities meshed with an older concept of situational crime prevention. Home Office crime prevention required serious attention to the practices of the 'natives' in the 'locality' by policing agencies. Methodological

---

Box 5.3   Expanding summary justice in relation to the Other: current ASBOs

noise pollution – playing music persistently too loud or persistently making other loud or intrusive noise
drunkenness
abandoned cars, burned-out cars, joyriding
stealing/mugging/shoplifting
begging
vandalism, graffiti, criminal damage to property
loitering

ethnography (of the lower-class indigents of the council estate rather than in the City of London) and Problem-Solving Policing are the keys to resolving the crime/ fear problems of late modernity. 'Disorder' has crept into the discourse of crime control as a key policing issue problem. Formally, ASBOs are civil remedies in which evidence is not required to adhere to the criminal court standard of proof 'beyond reasonable doubt' but rather the alternative civil court standard of proof 'on the balance of probabilities'. This lower standard of proof, a summary process of decision-making, and a vague and often highly subjective definition of anti-social behaviour, ensured that on breach of the Order the police would continue as the dominant local agency, further empowered to discipline and control the tradi-tional Other. Typically such Orders might involve bans on entering certain areas, conducting particular control practices, and involving night-time curfews of pre-sumed offenders. The latter were added to in 2011, by proposals for the police to enforce unilateral curfews on entire areas. Being obviously lower class and present in a politically/economically sensitive area could be an offence in itself. While the Orders themselves are not formally part of the criminal justice process, oddly, as noted earlier, breaching an Order constitutes a step on this ladder. Attention to 'incivilities' was accompanied, of course, by the creation of an additional layer of street policing. PCSOs were developed as a supplement to state policing both to reassure and to police such (primarily) public space behaviour. The Crime and Disorder Act itself was a product of a conflict between a traditional crime preven-tion policy (essentially a fenced-off police legal compound) and one of community safety (one in which other local agencies might assume limited policing powers). The Act, under the new Labour government, came down in favour of the latter. The emphasis on community safety was formalized in Community Safety and Crime Reduction Partnerships, extending legal powers to, inter alia, probation and health agencies among any number of statutory authorities. It was a reaction to a political debate over moral panics in which crime control reflected a hothouse political climate (Hughes, 2002). Local 'problems' sprang up quickly. Action was demanded and, very soon, government initiatives launched (Squires, 2008a).

The development of ASBOs was originally not intended to apply to young peo-ple aged less than 16 years, but 'within a very short time in England and Wales, the notions "ASBOs" and "problem youth" seemed to have become virtually syn-onymous. Anti-social behaviour had become, almost inadvertently . . . a youth problem' (Squires, 2008b). That process was aided by a combination of two factors peculiar to common law policing and the Office of Constable. An ill-defined polic-ing mandate allowed police forces to explore quasi-legal forms of criminality – drinking alcohol in public places, problems of street behaviour by young people, and so on. Second, the flexibility of police discretion enabled local police to expand legislative powers without requiring a new mandate. The import of problem-solving policing gave this commitment a further intrusive boost. Fear of crime could be overcome both by reassurance practices and by devoting more resources to highly visible local incivilities, the practices of the Other.

Of course, such legal flexibility was not the only easing mechanism in the exten-sion of police powers. In Britain, ASBOs and related approaches (fixed fines and incivilities) were backed by new legislation, by both New Labour and coalition governments. Home Office reports had produced some (frankly, fairly desperate) taxonomies of incivilities to assist such permissive policing powers and the measurement of the new performance-based policing. Traditional police discretionary cautioning and stop-and-search powers, often directed summarily at the same target, in retrospect were obliquely largely subsumed (though not denounced) as a long-term, failed, net-widening strategy. Reports, and research by entrepreneurs, police (often officers seeking an academic way round the organizational log-jam of promotion) and administratively-oriented academics, gave this policing tradition a new boost.

At this point, certain doubts crept into the perception of more critical commentators. As we have noted, shifting police priorities to misdemeanours away from serious crime required, in practice, greater police resourcing of ill-defined tasks. A bank robbery is a bank robbery is a bank robbery. An incivility is – what? Subjectivity, discretionary judgement, holds many dangers in developing legal clarity in policing practice, and in public reporting. The new taxonomies were subsequently extended.

As with other forms of policing entrepreneurship in constructing criminality, ASBOs were broken often and may have become a 'badge of prestige' (Squires, 2008a) with current breach rates of some 50 per cent. Finally, the development of ASBOs extended the police mission further. It reinforced the problem-solving approach (and by implication, expanding the vacuous powers of the Office of

---

Box 5.4   Mission creep (or how to expand the demand for state police services)

- find a vague area of the criminal law – say, anti-social behaviour (incivilities)
- ensure that the police agency has no limit on duties – such as in the Office of Constable
- recruit an aspiring police officer who wishes to obtain an academic credential as primary researcher
- ensure funding and cooperation of policing agency
- survey all local police forces for their records of such offending
- develop typology to organize incivilities – say five major categories with some fifteen sub-categories
- analyse responses and place them in categories
- chastise those forces who appear to be recording fewer incivilities than others and encourage them to record more
- if successful, more ASBOs will be issued, more people 'protected' from incivilities – and more young people from deprived backgrounds will enter the criminal justice system – net-widening has been achieved
- and more police attention directed away from serious crime.

Constable) by giving police a statutory (as opposed to common law) legal mandate in a non-criminally defined context. More generically, ASBOs reinforced the highly stratified notion of crime as a problem of the locality, of the Other, rather than having structural origins. They reinforce through statute the traditional practice of policing in an unequal society. The local lower-class young become increasingly the object of policework. Most recently, ASBOs have fallen foul of both critique and of coalition government responses. New measures are intended to replace them. The Crime Prevention injunction will target anti-social behaviour before it becomes a bigger 'problem'. Curiously, there is to be the introduction of a 'community trigger' where police will be compelled to follow up incidents reported by five or more members of the public. Outside the boundaries of due process, the police are to be given powers that include the confiscation of personal items such as iPods or other electrical items. Officers will also be given more discretion on how to deal with incidents, including forcing offenders to make immediate amends, such as repairing a damaged fence, rather than taking more formal action. A recent online opinion poll found that voters think anti-social behaviour should be the key priority for the new police and crime commissioners. Doubtless a similarly phrased question on the introduction of the chemical castration of sex offenders would have elicited a similar result – as long as respondents were not also asked informed questions on effective and valued use of resources.

Mission creep is a curious phenomenon enabled by the Office of Constable and statutory supplementation (see Box 5.4). Von Hirsch and Simester (2006) have focused on an important area for research – one that extends beyond penal theory and ethics to wider philosophical, jurisprudential and criminological study. Quite simply, what actions or speech can be regarded as uncivil or offensive, to the extent that they necessitate criminalization or regulation? In Utopia, such matters would be a case for negotiation. In dystopian neoliberal societies, where police action is skewed within the law, this is a contribution to a manifesto for serious unrest.

In addition to unilateral policing, extending its mandate to so-called quality of life issues, summary justice is increasing elsewhere with the prairie fire of fixed penalty notices for a variety of vaguely-defined offences. Justice, and especially the targeting of particular strata and social groups, is being transferred from the realm of due process with the assumption of innocence, to discretionary police practice which involves the prior presumption of guilt. In the aftermath of the relatively minor riots of August 2011 – at least by the comparative standards of the 1980s and early 1990s – features of the old Riot Act (repealed in 1973) are to be restored. At police instigation, a new public order power is proposed allowing the police to impose arbitrary curfews (as above). The legislation will furnish a new public order power allowing them to clear the streets and tell the public to leave during a riot or 'disorder'. A police superintendent will be able to declare a specific district a 'no go' area for a limited time, making it an offence to refuse a police instruction to leave the area. Locals are to be penalized simply by virtue of their presence outdoors.

Incivilities

ASBOs are merely one example of the extension of police powers in recent years over the traditional Others. The range of potential forms of civil intrusion is broad. Extraordinary statistics have been produced: Sir Denis O'Connor, the current chief inspector of constabulary, warned in 2010 that police have lost control of the streets as figures showed that an estimated 14 million incidents of anti-social behaviour take place each year (HMIC, 2010b).

Such an official imprimatur is clearly a pioneering breakthrough in evidence-based policing. The number of ASBOs actually issued grossly underestimates the number of police interventions in incivilities. Thus in 2004, the police intervened in some 100,000 cases of incivilities while only issuing 2,633 ASBOs and 418 dispersal orders. Legislation extended the bizarre list of incivilities on behalf of Middle England: noise pollution – playing music persistently too loud or persistently making other loud or intrusive noise; drunkenness; abandoned cars; burned-out cars; joyriding; stealing/mugging/shoplifting; begging; vandalism; graffiti; criminal damage to property; loitering; dropping litter or fly tipping; dog fouling; drug dealing or drug taking; intimidation and bullying; and spitting.

Second, the lower the threshold of the criminal justice system (though formally not recorded as part of a criminal record) the more young people were regarded as a problem worthy of contingent attention and targeting by the criminal justice authorities – net-widening. More policing resources were required. This may have been possible at a time of police expansion but not during a process of contraction and cutbacks. The mission of policing incivilities laid the groundwork for debates about the importance of the frontline, the old beat. In a vicious (uncivil) process, the more police acted against incivilities, the more the public (despite the new Reassurance Policing) became aware of such matters as a policing problem and of the way they should be reported the police. As noted in Chapter 3, such a process resulted in the redefinition of 'non-crime' problems, often varied quality-of-life issues, as criminal justice (and hence policing) problems.

The power of prosecution

Before the development of a minimalist independent prosecution system – the CPS – the authoritative study by Lustgarten (1986) had described the police institution of England and Wales as one of the most powerful in the Western world: 'viewed from the east, the scope of their authority, and the lack of control over its exercise is awesome . . . the species Anglica contains virtually unique features, whose effect is to extend the range of unchecked police powers still further' (1986 pp. 4–5). In particular, it avoids the dominant structural principle of most continental authorities: the centralization of powers under which state authorities can issue binding directives to local officials and can give specific instructions on the handling of a particular case. The CPS is much less powerful than prosecution agencies elsewhere, and according to recent coalition government proposals, its powers may be diluted even further. In 2011 the home secretary, Theresa May, announced that the government was finalizing plans to return the decision on whether to prosecute over 80 per cent of 'minor' cases – though quite what these are is not specified – back to the police. This will apparently save an estimated 2.5 million hours of police time and 'get the Home Office off the backs of the police' (May cited in Travis, 2011a).

Equally important in departing from practice in other domains, from Scotland to the United States, the police almost accidentally and spasmodically absorbed prosecution duties between the 1830s and the 1930s. The citizen's original power of prosecution became in practice, if not in law, a state policing function. In England and Wales, this represented a major divergence from other common law countries and from those drawing on the Napoleonic Code.

Ironically, while much mythological attention has been directed to the value of Peel's Nine Principles of Policing, little has been noted about the failure to implement his key other proposal. Peel, amongst others, had tried to import the Scottish system of an independent prosecutor as a check on police powers into England and Wales. Opposition from fixed interests, such as the legal profession and propertied interests, squashed that first proposal (Brogden, 1982). As the New Police gradually assumed prosecution functions, this has been little remarked previously (although Emsley, 2009, claims it benefited the local working class, although not the Other in saving victims from the onerous responsibilities for prosecution). It further determined English and Welsh policing as peculiar, in conflating the roles of arrest and of prosecution.

The initial part of the criminal justice process involves several clearly separate functions: arresting, prosecuting (involving, under the inquisitorial system, establishing the 'facts'), the judicial, and the sentencing. While district magistrates in British colonies were expediently required to conduct all four functions, to combine even two of them, within Western jurisprudence systems, is anachronistic. Other common law domains, such as Canada and the United States, avoided the peculiarity of this English and Welsh system much earlier. In Wales, although a national director of public prosecutions had been appointed in 1879, this major unique British problem with the powers of the constable was not formally modified until the development of the Crown Prosecution Service.

The Royal Commission of 1981 made two key points. The police should not investigate offences *and* decide whether to prosecute. The officer who investigated a case could not be relied on to make a fair decision on whether to prosecute. Second, different police forces around the country used different standards to decide whether to prosecute. The anomalous nature of that combined role (in effect, giving the arresting police a personal interest in a successful prosecution) only received the attention it deserved with the subsequently overturned convictions of the so-called Guildford Four, amongst several public cases. It appeared that the Surrey Police had, for understandable if unacceptable reasons given public pressure, constructed improper cases against the defendants ('fitting them into the frame'). Together the 1984 Police and Criminal Evidence Act and the 1985

Box 5.5   'Prosecuting the messenger'

Scotland Yard failed to consult the Director of Public Prosecutions or the Attorney General; before invoking unique provisions of the Official Secrets Act to try to force The Guardian to reveal journalistic sources. . . . [in] . . . the phone-hacking scandal . . . police are not technically required to get the DPP's permission at an early stage of enquiries. This extraordinary and devious ruse to mount a prosecution against a Guardian journalist who had initially revealed the illegal phone-hacking would not have been permissible under the normal legislation regarding journalist sources. The Guardian sources had revealed a scandal that eventually resulted in the related resignation of the two senior officers of the Metropolitan Police, arrest of many alleged culprits, multi-million pay-outs to victims and the closure of a major national newspaper. Eventually dropped after a public outcry and the eventual intervention of the DPP, it occurred after the Metropolitan Police had earlier dismissed the case as of little importance.

(*Guardian*, 20 September 2011)

Prosecution of Offenders Act resulted in the establishment of a central CPS in 1986, with some local staff. But that was no solution to the national problem of installing a 'neutral' figure in the prosecution process.

The perceived lack of independence of the CPS has resulted from a variety of factors, but is mainly attributed to a lack of resources to investigate police files and reliance on the police 'gatekeepers' for information. This has led to criticisms that the CPS is merely facilitating the fulfilment of the police service's agenda, which is what the CPS was established to prevent. Since the inception of the CPS, it has been beset by funding problems and criticisms that it is centralized, bureaucratic and ineffective, and too close to the police. The most serious allegation against the CPS is that it has failed to fulfil its function as an independent body from the police, and has acquired a predisposition to prosecute. Lea (2004, 2006) notes several deficiencies in the CPS compared to independent prosecution processes elsewhere. It does not possess Scottish or Continental independent powers to direct or supervise a police investigation. The accusatorial and inquisitorial roles of the CPS are incompatible, giving the CPS an anomalous position of working *for* the police, at the same time as having to work *on* them. The CPS does not have its own direct access to police materials on suspects and only encounters a case when it has already been (socially) constructed by the police (McConville et al., 1991).

The CPS became a body quite unlike, for example, the French investigating magistrate charged with safeguarding the rights of the accused and with filtering out weak cases. It was still the state police, in England and Wales, under their common law powers, who determined whether or not to prosecute. Subsequent developments attempted to prompt the CPS towards greater independence and to a more proactive role as in Scotland, in other common law countries, and in Western Europe.[9] The Glidewell Report (1998) heavily criticized the CPS for not fulfilling initial expectations. A fifth of the 2,000 CPS lawyers (in an echo of the later debate about frontline policing and also in the abortive attempt to specify performance targets for both the CPS and the police) spent less than a third of their time on casework and advocacy. The CPS was to be decentralized to match police area boundaries. The report recommended that the CPS take over the prosecution of a case immediately after a defendant was charged. But little has been achieved. Ultimately, the CPS is a police-dependent body. This is not just a matter of over-identification with police goals and ideology, but also a structural problem: that while the police made the initial decisions the CPS were not decision makers, but decision reversers. While formally decisions to prosecute are now to be taken by the CPS (breaking with historical, if accidental, tradition), not police (as legislated for by the Criminal Justice Act 2003), the problem of case construction will remain, i.e. the CPS will still be assessing cases prepared by the police, usually without any prosecutor involvement.

Construction of a case for the criminal courts involves not simply the use, selection and interpretation of evidence but its *creation*. '"What happened?" is the subject of interpretation, addition, subtraction, selection, and reformulation' (McConville et al., 1991 p. 12). Case construction occurs at every part of the criminal justice process. The 'suspect' population is drawn from the Other according to police cultural criteria, increasingly added to, in serious cases, by the new breed of profilers, replacing the Victorian mystics. The police station is an environment in which the police can construct cases in 'circumstances favourable to them' (ibid. p. 36). 'Confessions' obtained in the interrogation process and framed in interview records are also constructed. Case files and paperwork are structured in way that fits the police version of events. The ways in which a case is dealt with or disposed of are influenced far more by the police's own rules rather than the Home Office or Crown Prosecution guidelines (see Box 5.5). Different criticisms have emerged. An inquiry by the National Audit Office (National Audit Office, 2011) documents the flawed nature of police administration, with four out of five prosecution cases examined suffering from defective police preparation. There were faults in most such cases, and police supervisors and CPS officials frequently 'signed-off' material that did not follow the procedural rules. The choice of charge itself is used as an 'organizing matrix round which the case is built' (ibid. p. 116). The CPS normally follows a framework constructed by the police, rather than acting as an independent agency.

Instead the CPS, unlike its counterparts in other jurisdictions, seems to have become in practice an adjunct of the state police, in assisting a conveyor model procedure of criminal justice, as typified by the riots of August 2011 (see Box 5.6). The peculiarity of the British remains. Proposals for local community prosecutors[10] will not in any way develop the system as independent from the traditional influence of the Office of Constable over the process. The Green Paper, despite all the available international models of independent prosecution systems, does not seem to recognize the juridical consensus elsewhere. Indeed, the coalition

---

Box 5.6   Framing the suspects: the 2011 riots

'Three quarters of the adults charged already had a conviction'. Isn't there just a possibility that the number of those arrested and charged was biased towards those the police and other authorities already knew so were more easy to identify from the video and verbal information already available?

(Letter, *Guardian*, 13 September 2011)

---

government appears to extend the influence of the state police in the prosecution process, with a proposal to increase police powers in relation to prosecution (see above). Despite the development of the CPS, police practice in a number of high profile cases seems to be relatively untrammelled. Once the police find someone who 'fits the frame', arrest and the search for supportive evidence follows. In 2011 a profiled suspect, Christopher Jefferies, was held in custody after a Bristol murder on the basis that he appeared to fit due to his alleged personal peculiarities; an 'obvious offender'. The CPS does not have a good record in preventing such police abuse of powers (Deans, 2012).

Policing the 'communities of the Other'

There is a cliché amongst police scholars that community policing (or in its British variant, Neighbourhood Policing) works best where it is least needed and worst where it is most needed. Affluent, homogeneous suburbs with little crime cooperate most readily with neighbourhood police officers. Early 'hotspot' analysis, fuelled by Home Watch schemes, showed that such locations reported high levels of suspects. But that was simply a function of rampant over-reporting of minor misdemeanours by 'respectables'. Rather than content himself with golf or gardening the elderly retired colonel, peering through his net curtains, had found a new function. Home Watch schemes fell into disuse as both officers and public recognized their disutility. Consequently, such levels of the reporting of misdemeanours and of suspect youth fell to something vaguely approaching reality.

Conversely, diverse lower socio-economic class locations, from dilapidated inner cities to peripheral council estates (frequently the location of the Other), were bizarrely labelled as 'communities' on the basis of geographic official shorthand. This drew upon normative assumptions rather than evidential data (Ashby, 2005), boundaries determined by police beat tradition and electoral boundaries rather than empirical self-designation (Sampson and Raudenbush, 2004). Heterogeneous in composition, deprived in life chances, they were 'redlined' by insurance practices, with little property of value. Attitudinally, they featured a structurally imbibed distrust of the police, showing by passivity rather than activity a general antipathy to agents of the state. From indices such as electoral turnout to more recently the proliferation of ASBOs, such locations are the primary location of victimization. They have the most need of police support, from minor acquisitive crime to household and street violence, drug offences, gang conflicts, and a variety of 'incivilities'. The term is loaded in police discourse like the management-speak which replaces interrogation cells with interview rooms. Social capital was lacking, the localities were unpopular as a posting for the new Neighbourhood Police officers as they had been as rookeries for the New Police, because of the social and physical milieus and because of the general hopelessness of police function.

In the riots launched from such areas in August 2011, the more politically sensitive of the locals were fully aware of state hypocrisy. Typically, David Cameron had denied being present when his Bullingdon club of 'toffs' at his university had broken windows and smashed up restaurants (Sparrow, 2011), described later as simple 'high spirits'. That double standard assumed that the Other were blind, with an assumed Nelsonian touch, to the gross inequalities in wealth between themselves and the 'toffs', in their experience of law enforcement. It also assumed that such locals were passive (respondents in such areas furnish low response rates to opinion pollsters) to the dissimilarity of legal reaction to high level fraud, legal tax avoidance (normative crime), in its various legal and quasi-legal manifestations by those primarily responsible for the financial crisis, the members of a complex political and economic elite.

Gross inequalities were evident especially in the attraction of status goods: not just from proximity but also through the new media (although it is worth recalling that the Toxteth and Brixton riots of the early 1980s did not require hand-held technology to encourage copycat disorders). Low level quality of life crime and more seriously, in terms of emergent drugs problems, knifing epidemics, and 'postcode' gangs (though the two latter appear to have been also subject to media and police driven moral panics), much of the 'youth offender' problems remained as impossible to resolve as a state policing problem as they did for the residential victims.

The new Neighbourhood Policing teams, despite much painstaking work by committed officers, better trained than their predecessors over issues of racism and diversity, proved as impotent to resolve the structural sources of social eruptions as their riot squad colleagues (dressed in clumsy post-modernist armour). Even the late RUC as the most emblematic example of police militarization and export was likewise unable to pursue nimble, streetwise, local youth. Media accounts, as in previous riots, claimed that the local Neighbourhood Police were relatively accepted – 'outside' police were portrayed as the problem. Such accounts, as much of that media coverage, are impossible to substantiate. There were few proxies for the police to mobilize: the euphemism of illegitimate gangs coloured official statements, especially via the rhetoric of the imported Bill Bratton, in raising the narrow demonology of gangsterism.[11]

Undercover policing

State police officers rarely break the law. Given the flexibility of the common law inheritance, in relatively minor cases, discretionary permissive law does not need breaking (McBarnet, 1981). It is much easier to bend legislation where statutes are unclear, vague, or where new technology emerges, leaving past legislation its wake. In such cases, there is often a public outcry. This may be followed by a limited inquiry and practice reaffirmed by new legislation. Alternatively, judicial case law determines the legitimacy of police practice. This has been most obviously the situation in the recent police innovations of crowd control through the process of 'kettling' demonstrators (including non-participants in the demonstration) (see Box 5.7). Similarly, the ubiquity of police filming non-violent demonstrators and storing their profiles has been declared legitimate.

The state police may use technology and legislation to restrict rights of peaceful protest in other ways. For example, restrictions on peaceful assembly and peaceful protest are contained in the 1986 Public Order Act, 1992 Trade Union Act, 1994 Criminal Justice Act, 1997 Protection of Harassment Act, 2003 Anti-Social Behaviour Act, and the 2005 Serious Organised Crime and Police Act. Together, they permit the police to either restrict or declare illegal any protest they wish and arrest the participants. Law is 'made' by the police and then sanctified by the courts, as in the videoing and recording of individual demonstrators.

For example, part of the pensions protest march of November 2011 was sealed off with 3-metre high steel walls (no bystander could see the placards). In a leaflet sent to 'key trusted partners' in advance of the march, the City of London Police appeared to define its role as advising the corporate banking institutions of the City against peaceful activists who sought to vocalize their protest against recent banking scandals. Strangely, the leaflet also equated the Occupy movement with the activities of al-Qaida and the Colombian narco-terrorists, FARC (Malik, 2011). Attempts by some in the Metropolitan Police to escalate their crowd control measures by the use of water cannon and plastic bullets were resisted by more sane officers (Sir Hugh Orde obviously learnt from his Northern Ireland experience).[12] Together with the expansion of undercover work into non-violent protests as

---

Box 5.7   Kettling and the spread of police powers

Police tactics of 'kettling' protesters, used extensively during the G20 protests in London three years ago, have been found to be lawful. The appeal court has overturned a previous ruling by the high court on the controversial technique deployed to contain demonstrators during the climate camp sit-in. . . . the Master of the Rolls. . . . declared that the lower court's finding was flawed and allowed the appeal by the Metropolitan police commissioner. The case concerned the G20 protests in London on 1 April 2009, during which Ian Tomlinson, a bystander, died after being struck by an officer. Police in charge of the protest ordered a Climate Camp to be kettled and then cleared, but officers were left to decide how much force they should use.

(*Guardian*, 19 January 2012)

agents provocateurs, there is a clear trend towards entrepreneurially redefining the point at which the state police regard it as their role to prevent non-violent protest.[13]

Recent revelations relating to undercover policing (its extent and nature) have pointed to the regular use of such police in the surveillance of non-violent organizations protesting within the law, as well as violent organizations protesting outside it. The two are conflated in policing of the Other. Undercover policing has a legitimate history in modern societies. Uniformed policing may be counterproductive in dealing with sophisticated criminality. It is democratically relevant to uncovering serious criminality and in violent political subversion. There is no substantive problem with such a strategy. However, there tend to be few mandatory rules governing that infiltration. In any case, such rules are rarely enforced. Officers may go 'native' (such as making female protesters pregnant, under their assumed identity). They assume the behaviour of the suspect group, and frequently act as agents provocateurs in encouraging and promoting criminal action (a tactic illegal in the USA). It is dubious practice when the group infiltrated does not represent any threat, violent or otherwise to the dominant social order. Undercover policing has a long history in the UK, most notably with the case of Sergeant Popay. The latter, a member of the early Metropolitan Police, had infiltrated the National Political Union and encouraged it to develop a more inflammatory stance in 1831. Revealed by a comrade in the union as being an agent provocateur (in political circles being a symptom of so-called 'French' policing), he was forcibly dismissed like his uniformed colleague Sergeant Dean, whose 'offence' had been to reveal his identity on the basis that such practices were illegitimate in 'English' society (Dean, curiously, was found to be 'insane' by his superiors). Over the years, such practices have been conducted against a variety of threatening and non-threatening groups, political and/or violent, especially in relation to so-called 'Irish' terrorism, unemployed workers and Communist Party affiliated groups in the 1930s and 1970s, as well as organized crime. Some of this undercover policing is rightly scorned, such as the entrapment of gay men in public toilets. But in the present era, as Gary Marx has shown (Marx, 1992), undercover policing has changed in three ways: in its coverage of an increasingly wide spectrum of perceived deviance; in its integration with private security; and the invisible line of infiltrating both violent and non-violent organizations. One manifestation is the expansion of undercover police practices as part of the rise of the new surveillance (computer dossiers, electronic location monitoring, drug and DNA testing, video and audio monitoring). The new surveillance is revolutionary; for example in transcending distance, darkness, and physical barriers, and in storing records (easily stored, retrieved, combined, analysed, and communicated). It is more intensive: probing beneath surfaces, discovering previously inaccessible information. Second, specialist private companies increasingly use undercover staff – including where they can rely on both serving and former police officers as 'experts' in the field. There is both a revolving door of personnel from the state to the corporate sector (and vice versa) and a growing symbiosis of state and corporate interests (O'Reilly and Ellison, 2006). There is a financial dividend and interest in discovering the future tactics of protesters in relation to their clients. The same undercover officer may use his or her new credibility to infiltrate avowedly law-breaking organizations such as the Animal Liberation Front, or the non-violent Animal Protection Agency, which is simply exercising its legal right to protest. The criminal and the overtly political agencies to be unveiled are often blurred. The same techniques can be used by the officers in both private and public contexts (Marx, 1992).

Undercover work (like that of police on overseas missions) has many temptations for extroverted officers: freedom from formal rules and hierarchical controls, thrill-seeking, playing the poacher rather than gamekeeper (but a poacher who cannot be penalized), and relative affluence – spending the state's money without formal accounting. It is also voyeuristic. But the downside is also true: examples are marital problems, the temptation to go too far, occasional danger, and conceiving children with female protesters (as above) as part of creating the right persona. It is a schizophrenic practice. At some stage the officer has to return to the formal rules of his/her force and re-establish a stable self (Taylor, 2002). However, recent revelations suggested that it is common to breach assumed restrictions. A unit of the covert Special Demonstration Squad (SDS) was formed in 1961, as a part of the Metropolitan Police's Special Branch. Control of it was oddly transferred to the 'hands-off' authority of the non-accountable ACPO in the 1990s. Its officers who manage – in Orwellian speak – 'covert human intelligence sources' are often expected to infiltrate non-violent groups, as well as violent ones (such as the Animal Liberation Front). Discretionary policing operates without accountability in such cases. Formally, such practices have only been regulated since the Police Act 1997 and the Regulation of Investigatory Powers Act 2000. While conducting these activities, supervision appears to have been rare. The regulation of undercover policing has recently been transferred back to the statutory authority of the Metropolitan Police. Legal and informal sanctions against officers have been few. In a recent case prosecutions of members of the anti-climate change group have been quashed due to legal scepticism regarding the role of one particular undercover officer, Mark Kennedy (Evans and Lewis, 2011a).

Kennedy had also apparently breached the Criminal Procedure and Investigations Act (1996) in withholding the fact that he had surreptitiously taped evidence, and in not declaring it to prosecution and defence. He had been transferred to the National Public Order Intelligence Unit (NPOIU) in the early 2000s. The NPOIU appeared to deposit yearly some £200,000 into his account on top of his salary of some £50,000 per annum. Money apparently was no object in sustaining an infiltrator who seems, on reflection, to have contributed little to the 'public good' in combating the varied Other. Amongst other potential crimes committed by Kennedy and his colleagues is the amorphous charge of 'malfeasance in public office', an offence that could also apply to his superiors. The German Federal Criminal Police Office has admitted that it was aware that Kennedy had committed criminal offences whilst in that country, including arson. It is also alleged that he took part in a protest in Ireland including an attack on An Garda Síochána, as well as committing further offences in Denmark. Kennedy had conducted many offences in his role as an infiltrator. Again the Metropolitan Police claimed curiously that such offences were entirely within the law. These international offences were enabled by his possession of a false driving licence and passport (see Box 5.8). Subsequently on leaving the police, Kennedy apparently resumed similar work with a private company, largely manned by former senior police officers, to continue his infiltration activities.[14]

Gary Marx (1992) points to many of the issues raised by such practices, including the promotion of crime that would not otherwise have occurred, the frequent drug use by undercover officers, the use of public money for unspecified and unquantifiable goals, and the non-prosecution of offences committed by those criminals because of the utility of the latter. (In Northern Ireland, it was the regular practice for police detectives to pass over to Special Branch petty criminals for use as informers in relation to paramilitary groups – '£10 touts' as they were referred to locally. See Ellison, 2007.)

Box 5.8   Legalizing the illegal

Britain's most senior police officer has defended the practice of undercover officers using fake identities in court, claiming there is no specific law forbidding it. He told the authority: 'There's no law that says it can't happen. The fact that someone has concealed their identity doesn't mean the crime didn't happen. In absolute terms, the criminal law does not make a crime of it. If you are dealing with more serious crimes, we have to seek all options.' He added that the Met was seeking legal advice on the issue. He said that fake identities had not been used in court in current operations. 'If it was happening in the past, it won't be happening now.' The commissioner has set up an inquiry into past deployments to establish how many times undercover police officers have been prosecuted under their fake identities. Senior police officers have been accused of authorizing the practice so police spies could build credibility with other activists and fortify their cover as a committed campaigners. The IPCC is investigating claims that Jim Boyling, an officer who infiltrated an environmental movement, lied about his identity in court. Documents suggest he concealed his true role when prosecuted alongside activists. Scotland Yard is reviewing similar allegations involving a second undercover officer, Bob Lambert, to see if they should also be investigated by the IPCC. Macdonald said: 'If the commissioner is saying that there is no law against undercover officers giving evidence under their false identities without revealing that to the court, I think that's a pretty stunning assertion . . . It seems to me that there are potentially all sorts of offences which could be committed. The very fact of saying "I am John Smith" when my name is really PC Simon Brown may not be perjury, but when you go on to recount your role in the offence, and your relationships with other people in the case, you could very easily stray into perjury. And at the very least, the senior officers who are sending these undercover PCs into court to give evidence in this way are putting them at serious risk of straying into perjury.'

(*Guardian*, 27 October 2011)

Senior officers apologized to Parliament for having previously given false information about such practices. Four different enquiries into these affairs have been opened but few, if any, seem currently to have the remit to probe and sanction the size and depth of the problem. Of course some complaints of undercover action are open to charges of paranoia. The British National Party website contends it has been infiltrated by such officers, including Mark Kennedy. Similar claims are frequently and presumably legitimately made by parties at the other end of the political spectrum, such as the Socialist Workers Party. But the main lesson is that practices that verge on the formally illegal frequently become legal as police organizations entrepreneurially exploit, with the connivance of the judiciary, vague and non-prescriptive areas of criminal and civil law.

Overview

We have argued that many studies of the state police in Britain have ignored the importance of criminal and common law. Critical legalists, historians, and sociologists (and indeed postcolonial psychology, in its situation of the mentality of the colonized) have rarely combined in their analysis of state policing. Postcolonial theory requires a conjoint endeavour. This chapter has sought to reconcile those critiques. Social science without history and critical jurisprudence explains little of the consequence of the fiscal crisis on the practice of social ordering by the British state police.

Typically, attempts to combat racism in the police have concentrated on changing police attitudes. But despite years of committed diversity training, little has changed in discriminatory practice. Failure to examine the larger structure of the criminal justice process has resulted in a myopic misunderstanding of the source of police discrimination and wrongdoing. Such practice could not have happened without the enabling facility of criminal law. The Office of Constable permitted the state police to penetrate the locations of the Other and embark on processes of criminalization without appropriate determination of duties. A vast and increasing body of criminal law operates outside the framework of due process legislation. Similarly, the Other fails to be treated without reference to their essential inequalities – in effect, to lose their legal status as equal citizens. Legal inequality compounds social and economic inequality.

Response (and police entrepreneurship) to expressed fear of crime has led the police of England and Wales to develop a commitment to respond to the infinite minutiae of social life, with traditional reactions. From ASBOs to incivilities, police officers and provincial forces are encouraged to ignore financial and violent crime, to reinforce the resourcing of the frontline policing of the Other in public space. That criminalizing focus ignores the legal mandate to use constable and constabulary discretion to ignore the major imperative of social harm. Finally, despite the development of the CPS, police officers structure and influence a key aspect of the criminal justice process in a way that would not be accepted by state police in other jurisdictions. Democratic policing requires a fundamental base in equality in law. That situation is clearly not evident in England and Wales.

6 Policing the Other

Continuity of practice from St Giles to Dale Farm

[A] postcolonial perspective in criminology [has] the potential to offer new theoretical insights, and to expand the discipline in an engaged and reflexive endeavour that is cognisant of cultural and historical difference. . . [It] demands we recognize the ongoing and enduring effects of colonialism on both the colonized and the colonizers. Colonization and the postcolonial are not historical events but continuing social, political, economic and cultural processes. The postcolonial exists as an aftermath of colonialism and it manifests itself in a range of areas from the cultures of the former imperial powers to the psyches of those that were colonized.

(Cunneen, 2011, p. 249)

Equality before the law and equal protection are seen as the defining features of a legal system built on the rule of law. A postcolonial perspective does not necessarily argue against these principles and the rights they bestow but rather demonstrates the way in which marginalized and colonized people are constrained in their capacity to enjoy these protections and rights. Part of the constraint arises from the social and economic position of marginalized groups, as well as racialization and lack of tolerance of cultural diversity. There is a palpable tension between a universal principle like equality and the recognition of cultural difference and this tension is constantly played out in law, policy and practice.

(Cunneen, 2011, p. 256)

Introduction: from the beat to the frontline via the Other

The central paradox in this text is that the British state police, in the middle of a major financial crisis, continue to act without reference to that crisis. Crisis has simply reinvigorated original practices, while accelerating policing-for-profit. Traditionally sanctified duties such as the pursuit of incivilities continue. 'The frontline must be maintained' irrespective of socio-economic and political realities. This organizational myopia is evident from several perspectives.

The primary function of this final chapter is to locate the development of British state policing within the heuristic framework of postcolonial theory. The central thesis is that one cannot adequately understand the major fault line – the failure of British policing, most evident at a time of economic crisis – without reference to

---

Box 6.1   Homogenizing the heterogeneous Other

The police got a warrant to search a whole Gypsy site. It would not happen on a council estate. People would not tolerate it. Sealing off entire sites to catch a criminal – would they seal off a council estate to do the same thing?

(Traveller quoted in Coxhead, 2007 p. 85)

---

the relations between the key state ordering agency and the Other of postcolonial theory. There is a direct continuity between the original police designation with regard to practice and to objectives, in its relationship with the social construction of a criminal or dangerous class in early nineteenth-century London. The first part of the chapter offers an alternative account of origins from those traditionally espoused. The second part uses the example of one such colonized part of the Other, the Roma (Gypsies and Travellers) to illustrate and conflate the major themes of this text.

In Chapter 5, we referred to the advent of the New Police in terms of its access to an array of summary street powers. The first part of this chapter places that material in the context of the construction of the dwellers of the rookeries, transient and resident, in their many varieties. That place also, at the time of the Queen Caroline riots of 1819–20, brimmed over with newly discharged sailors and soldiers. The end of the Napoleonic wars in 1815 had also ushered in the terminal period of Empire and of colonization.

Moral panics and constructing the Other

Within the political and social crisis of the early nineteenth century lurked a contrived moral, entrepreneurial induced panic. The foundations of the New Police were built on a deliberately engineered folly. A contrived process gave rise to one of the major problems in British policing today. Cultivated fear of the dangerous classes was central to the formation of the New Police, especially in its exaggerated potential to ally with the labouring classes. By the 1840s, the dominant view of crime was that it was a product, not of poverty, but of weakness of character in the criminals. But it was a fear that was deliberately exaggerated by key moral entrepreneurs such as Patrick Colquhoun, William Augustus Miles, and Edwin Chadwick.

In a detailed scrutiny of their collective writings, Philips (2003) demonstrates vividly how this trio, in separate statistically filed publications, deliberately exaggerated the threat from the Other (in this case, the dangerous class) in order to promote the case for a particular form of divisive policing, one essentially committed to socially order the minority Other. Irrespective of concern with specific vicarious crimes, these entrepreneurs furnished detailed, if exaggerated accounts of the claimed extent of the London and provincial underworld and its many threats. It was that threat from a notional Other that gave rise to the New Police. Colquhoun, Miles and Chadwick saw to it that the proper object of the police was to 'deal' with this class of undesirables. The dangerous class, the street people, the Other was to be the primary police target. The lineage and structure that has given rise to the current focus of the state police on public space incivilities and petty crime by the Other in the twenty-first century was established on the basis of a deliberately created moral panic. Crime per se was not a major catalyst.

To this end police duties were committed to the control and surveillance of public space, and districts were divided into beats, each of which was patrolled by an officer on foot. The beat became, in today's discourse, the 'frontline' – committed to the surveillance of known characters. 'Darkness', night beats, patrolling the unknown, was the priority. Most constables walked their beats of the suspect city streets, patrolling the known nefarious evil (Gatrell, 1990; Storch, 1975; 1976). It was a patrol commitment that was deliberately exaggerated by the moral entrepreneurs, recycling each others' flawed data (as Chadwick did with Miles' accounts of evil lodging houses), all of whom advocated a state-run police to cope with the fault of character. Crime was a function of a particular social collectivity in contested public space; an image that contributed substantially to a partisan creation of that image of crime and criminals. Many contemporaries accepted that image as fundamentally correct. The two concepts, the Other and the New Police were regarded as symbiotic, as reflected in the new print categories and doggerel of the nineteenth century that refer to the proximity of the rookery of St Giles and the Palace of Westminster:

> In St James the officers mess at the club,
> In St Giles they often have mess for the grub,
> In St James they feast on the highest of game
> In St Giles they live on foul air just the same.

The 'good', the constable's character, was counterpoised with the 'evil' of the threatening class. Hence the well-known police aphorism, spelling out the key police ordering duty: 'it is an axiom of the police that you guard St James by watching St Giles' (*Edinburgh Review*, July 1852 p. 5). Amplified by the development of initially print and later visual imagery (as in the vicarious portrait of Dickens' *The Lascar's Den*, and more soberly in Jack London's *The People of the Abyss*), it was defined by character (immoral and criminal) and by location (the public streets) rather than by action: the Other was an enabling concept to explain otherwise inarticulate challenges to social order. More latent than active, from the Victorian rookeries to the 'poor white' and ethnic minority areas of modernism, it always represents a perceived threat.

But crisis meant different things to different strata. On one hand, for the migratory poor, it was a case of economic survival. Street life was a street economy practised by the Other. Jobs might be available for the literate, but scavenging, hawking, begging, selling second-hand or stolen goods, prostitution, and sundry street practices of the poor, vividly described by the three entrepreneurs, were crimes of survival ('social crime' as the Warwick School termed it). As the records of the Old Bailey would testify (amongst other sources), crime for the most part was petty – the crimes of the poor in public space and intra-class crime. Relatively few of the upper classes were robbed by their inferiors or suffered the grievous bodily harm of household abuse. Threats at the time of the inception of the New Police were trivial, between locals, with the occasional foreign seaman as victim. For their betters, the articulate members of the old gentry and the new manufacturing class, crime was not in itself a problem. Few of them were murdered on the Radcliffe Highway or on Blackheath Common. Employers could abuse the Master and Servants Act at will and only rarely encountered their opposites, such as fences and pilfering from their commercial premises.

Petty crime was merged with the contagion of disease and a notion of moral health. The 'Other' or 'dangerous classes' were as much a moral as a physical danger. Contagion was physical (petty crime), moral (the 'lewd' behaviour of the criminal class), and unsettling (the contribution of the newly established print media). Crime, disease and immorality were part of a continuum of threat. The New Police were invented as an 'urban prophylactic' against the normative practices of the Other. Indeed, many an officer took refuge in such practices (such as alcoholic relief), given the tedious and isolated nature of their panopticon-style patrol practice.

State policing and postcolonial theory

State policing would not exist in a utopian world of social and economic equality. In the dystopian world of neoliberalism, spatial restructuring, de-industrialization, and the re-imaging of the urban landscape in particular have produced significant shifts in the form, meaning, and nature of policing. The privatization of security, revanchism, the marketing of urban power (Davis, 1990), and the related securitization of sites of consumption are understood to have driven changes in the variety and connotation of policing (Zukin, 1991). These shifts in the delivery of policing strategies aim to 'discipline the deleterious social consequences and the escalating socio-spatial contradictions' (McLeod, 2002 p. 603). The consequences of recapitalization and the construction of 'security' and order in the re-modelled urban landscape have increased spatial fracturing and the construction of micro-spaces, divided not only by social class and race but also by variant modes of policing delivery (Herbert, 2008).

Social control, that indefinable concept, implies a 'normal' (Occident) and the abnormal Other (Orient). Similar metaphors linked the emerging Occident with the strangeness of the Orient Other, as in the missionary Joseph Salter's book about the East End Lascars (Salter, 1873). The police and the Other are locked in dialectical opposition. State policing, through practice as well as by legislation, as a key social ordering device, has the primary mission of acting both within the law and sometimes outside it to deal with the Other. The latter concept is imprecise, often illusory, drawing as much upon caricature as on objective reality. Its origins lie in the mists of imperial contacts with the savage Other; an Other that had invaded the citadels of the Occident – from Gypsies, to alien ethnic groups, to foreign seamen. The Other is a generic term – like its opposite the 'noble savage' (such as the social construction of Inkatha in late South African apartheid), and the 'martial races' (Sikhs and Gurkas who served in British colonial exploits – see Rand, 2006). The threatening heathen Other is linked to the same mythology of 'here be dragons' in pre-Enlightenment society. It was later used to embrace all those apparently disparate groupings that existed beyond the known cartographic world.

Historically, the Other has come to embrace both external and internal groups from Travellers to alien ethnic rioters. It is an umbrella term, in which individuality and heterogeneity are submerged in a homogeneous mass defined by its opposite. Western European civilization, the rule of law and of evolved morality has come in turn to embrace myriad groups, later defined and measured by the imported early police sciences. Measured uncivilized character was juxtaposed with the rationality displayed by the inhabitants of post-Enlightenment society. Initially, it encompassed a notion of a different species – one that could only with great difficulty be civilized by the tutelage of the Enlightened West: with the growth of Empire and a muscular Christianity, and new forms of character recognition under early positivism, of the pseudosciences of anthropometry, ethnology, and, inter alia, the Salvation Army's home-grown 'science' of 'curocriminology'.[1] The emergent positivism of the mid-nineteenth century furnished practical policing tools of classifying the Other. The concept was refined later in the century by Galton's social Darwinism, as a lower species on the lowest rung of the human race: a social formation that needed social ordering and tutelage in order to bring it within the understanding of the new Occidental civilization. The left-behind could be rescued by the new panopticon ordering mechanisms of the nineteenth century, by police scientists, by church missionaries, and by the New Police. In the same way that early colonial administrators learnt to 'know the country', over time the New Police learnt to 'know the Other'. The concept came to embrace myriad groups: externally, black savages and barbarians who threatened the missionary social order of Empire; and internally the colourful images of the criminal classes and dangerous classes, the Victorian mob, the migrant peasantry of early industrialization, and specific ethnic groups such as the Irish, and those uncivilized people that crossed the Occident–Orient divide, such as the seafaring Lascars of London's Dockland.

The Other was composed of locals, immigrants from Empire, and especially Irish and Scottish (as indeed was the first Metropolitan Police). Migrants brought not just different languages and cultures, they were assumed to be conduits for an alien contagion, from crime and immorality to disease. Pressures on accommodation, on basic services such as sanitation, on thoroughfares and the workhouse (to name just a few) were immense. Overseas experience was common and crossed social classes. Typically, James and John Stuart Mill, like Thomas Malthus, worked in the East India Company's offices. Politicians like Peel had served their time in the nearest colony, Ireland. Earlier, Colquhoun in particular, as administrator of London's Dockland, had been familiar with the external Other such as the Lascar seamen who dominated the East India trade (together with ayahs (nannies), the household prize for overseas service) (see Nijhar, 2009). Among the respectable public, the discourse of the dangerous class was rapidly captured in a popular discourse about the Other; a phenomenon that could be responded to by the new beat policing and surveillance of that public space. Terms such as 'thug' (from Hindi) and 'hooligan' (supposedly derived from Patrick Hoolihan, a notorious Irish bouncer in London) were adopted into normative discourses as characterizations of the Other, as were 'street Arabs', 'ruffians' or 'roughs'. They represented the mainstream of popular discourse rather than a recounting of the socially excluded, and came to represent actions categorized as 'un-English' or 'un-British'.

Policing public space

Despite Peel's foundational principles, historical evidence (see above) suggests that public space and its occupants were (and are) the primary focus of state policing. The New Police in its particular beat form would not have been constructed without the caricature of the Other. Nor would the latter have been sustained as a concept without the symbolism of control of public space by the Blue Locusts (Storch, 1975). The Other appeared to threaten the established normative order more by its cultural values rather than actual practices. The New Police would not have been sustained beyond the pre-modern format without the continuity of the concept. In symbolic uniform and stature, the New Police

> were a bureaucratic instrument for the ordering of the promiscuity of the urban mob by cleansing the disorderly, the disreputable, and street hawkers from the main streets and central thoroughfares of the capital. Police beat practices formalized the idea that streets were rule-governed places . . . to expel the presence of the Other (Pile et al., 1999 p. 116).

State policing today would have taken a different form but for the creation of the Other. Colonialism and the early policing sciences developed a range of 'packages', accessible later for postcolonial and so-called transitional societies, which would improve the lot of such inferiors, to give them some of the wisdom of the West. The same model was applied internally, to the enemy within. For some (e.g. Wilson and Herrnstein, 1998), the latter were incorrigible by virtue of their biology, as in the notion of the underclass. For, others, the children residing on a sink estate or Gypsy encampment could be nourished and improved with a panopticon of control from policing to education. Fundamentally, they became the primary policing target, especially in a crisis: when the gap between poverty and affluence became too great, symbolically between sink estate and affluent shopping mall, the Other was resurrected. In more prosperous times, it could be segregated by the policing of the beat system of demarcation as the primary social ordering device. But in times of continuing fiscal crisis, despite the early intervention, wisdom and models of neighbourhood police officers, it might break out and rock the boat of civility. The 'mob' was reborn in all its feral fury. History has repeated itself: the traditional policing of the Other has been resurrected with the new technologies of the twenty-first century compared to the brute force of the baton.

The Other as active

The Other – the metaphorical Orient – was traditionally perceived as passive, as in Said's earlier work on postcolonial theory. It was the recipient of the label and structure of subordination imposed on it. The dangerous class was the dumb receptor of rules imposed by the New Police. But in a development of Said's work (Bhabha, 1994a; 1994b) the view of the Other as passive and subordinate has been discarded in favour of an active agent, one capable not only of challenging the label imposed on it but also of combating the discourse and actions of the Occident. Both epistemologically and politically, therefore, the Other is central to understanding social ordering by the state police institution in Britain, disrupting that ordering process, and claiming its own legitimacy.

From the Macclesfield weavers in the Royal Commission of 1839 to the miners' strike of the 1980s, a discourse of the Other has been used to indict and stigmatize striking employees. And, of course, most recently, it has been used in official discourse in respect of the riots that took place in a number of cities across the UK in August 2011. During the premiership of Margaret Thatcher the striking miners were labelled as the 'the enemy within'. In return, the miners were to perceive the state police as 'Thatcher's private army' (Milne, 2004). The industrial Other claimed a counter-image and legitimacy. Today, the 'underclass' comprising potentially 'radicalized' Muslims, youths of African/Caribbean descent, and lower-class whites (crudely characterized as 'chavs') are perceived to pose a threat (Jones, 2011). Variants of the terms used today have been used before, for example, to stigmatize migrant communities. In turn, such groups (young black males, for instance) claim legitimacy for their struggle against what they perceive as police oppression – specifically with regard to the claim of racist reliance on police stop-and-search powers.

The battleground for the internally colonized – the local Other – is, as it has always been, the metaphorical public space (known to the colonizer as 'the beat', or in more recent discourse, 'the frontline'). The latter is simply the contemporary version of the line of sanitation drawn between Peel's New Police and the dangerous classes. New discourses of policing have emerged, new techniques and strategies developed through metaphorical wars against various nouns – 'terrorism', 'drugs', 'poverty'. The historically sanctified area of dispute remains the same. The process continues. Public space as a theatre of war between the Occident and the Orient is depicted regularly in cameos ranging from enabling summary street powers, the Tottenham riots, and occasional forays into territories of dispute such as Traveller 'encampments'. State policing is defined primarily in terms of what it practises, confronting the roughs, the uncouth, the uncivilized, ethnic minorities, the underclass youth, on behalf of the respectables. In the example below, Travellers play the part of the Other, the state police play the role of the Occidental guardian of the standards of the suburban civilized respectables, and the public space territory is the encampment claimed by both Travellers and by respectables.

Policing the Other: the Gavver[2] and the Travellers

In times of economic crisis, as the gap between rich and poor widens dramatically, groups such as Travellers suffer most and are also more likely to be in conflict with ordering institutions. In that resistance, they furnish a legitimation for what might be regarded as aberrant behaviour by the state's social ordering system. In the 'fight-back', they are caricatured as reinforcing the deviant features through which they have previously been assessed. Travellers were traditionally dehumanized. They were regarded as a collective by the Occident, without individual rights and conceptions of self. Perceived character and status marked their identity (as indeed does the Occident from the perspective of the Other). Until 1976, in Britain, they were simply characterized as a group by their 'nomadism'.

Criteria for being part of the Other are vague. But they included the following propositions. First, the term 'Gypsies' (now laden with racist overtones), confuses and conflates a heterogeneous grouping under a generic label – from Irish Travellers to Eastern European itinerant Roma (Richardson, 2007). Second, the Other exists, in part, because of continuing confrontation with the social ordering instrument of the majority. In that conflict, the Other is not just passive but maintains a continuing if sporadic and combative sense of self through that conflict. Schism, opposition, and inequality in power are the major defining features of its existence. Its members are 'known' to the wider society partly through that conflict in which the social ordering agency attempts to determine the rules governing the relationship, the criminal and civil law. In return, the Other constructs its own image of the Occident as oppressive and illegitimate. The Other is regarded as marginal by the dominant hegemony, and as inferior in many ways – from crime to morality to maintenance of uncivilized norms and values. As marginalized members of the Other, Gypsies and Travellers have the worst life chances of any group in Britain: infant mortality is three times that of the general population, educational attainment the lowest, and life expectancy below average. Life expectancy of Traveller women is 12 years less than that of settled women, and that of men 10 years below. Only some 30 per cent live to more than 60 years and are consequently considered to be 'elderly' by their compatriots. Medically, they suffer from high levels of depression and anxiety, leading to occasional suicide (Cemlyn et al., 2009). Abuse of drugs and alcohol is common (Richardson, 2007). In resisting the 'settled' values, the Other demonstrates to its opponents that it is indeed a species lower on the ladder of progress. Its members are frequently excluded by default, from the electoral rights of the 'citizen' to experience of equitable justice.

Historically, they were dealt with under an array of permissive legislation by the state's policing agency. The British state's response to contemporary Travellers shows a movement from legislation directed at the Gypsies in the early modern period to non-specific (summary) statutes of the nineteenth and early twentieth centuries. In England and Wales they were treated under the brutal sixteenth-century vagrancy laws, and were specifically included in the 1597 Vagrants Act. The Vagrancy Acts of 1744 and 1821 formed the later legal framework of summary justice of a week's incarceration in a house of correction, corporal punishment, or removal to a place of 'settlement' (such as by transportation, initially to Calais and later to Australia). With the evolution of the Poor Law in 1834, novel pass laws were applied by the New Police (as originally designated for hawkers) and vagrancy legislation continued to have its impact. Because vagrancy was not a felony, control was unilateral without recourse to the legal process. Gypsies inhabited the rookeries of St Giles and Whitechapel during the formation of the New Police and suffered like others from the moral entrepreneurship of its advocates. Henry Mayhew was typical of the moral entrepreneurial commentators on Gypsies. Vagrancy, roguery and vagabondary were associated with the 'wandering tribes', as he was to term Gypsies, who were seen as an affront to civilized sedentary values:

> Of the thousand millions of human beings that are said to constitute the population of the entire globe, there are – socially, morally, and perhaps even physically considered – but two distinct and broadly marked races, viz., the wanderers and the settlers – the vagabond and the citizen – the nomadic and the civilized tribes . . . The nomadic or vagrant class have all an universal type, whether they be the Bushmen of Africa or the 'tramps' of our own country.
>
> (Mayhew, 1865 vol. 3, p. 349)

Today, criminalization under such summary legislation is easy. Travellers continue to be non-citizens, lacking rights and access to legal process in the eyes of state police (despite several local initiatives). Young male Travellers become 'youth at risk' as they rarely attend secondary school and spend much time in public space where petty crime may be frequent and illegal drugs accessible, attracting beat policing. Consequently, they are over-represented in the administration of ASBOs and other summary justice procedures, in young offender institutions, and in the adult penal system (Cemlyn et al., 2009). At the same time, Travellers rarely feel able to report crimes against themselves to the police, experiencing a high rate of surveillance coinciding with under-protection. Justice operates only one way, against Travellers. In the case of the murder of 15-year-old Irish Traveller Johnny Delaney in Liverpool in 2003, the court did not find that it was a racially aggravated offence despite the evidence of a number of witnesses about the racist comments shouted during the fatal attack. The then chair of the Commission for Racial Equality (CRE) commented that 'it is extremely hard to see how this particular killing wasn't motivated in some way by racial prejudice' (cited in Cemlyn et al., 2009 p. 147). In relation to less serious but nonetheless hurtful offences, Travellers rarely report racially-based offences against them (James, 2007).

In a circular process, supported by the Occidental majority both in the UK and other parts of the West, Gypsies and Travellers are stereotyped into belonging to criminal communities (James and Richardson, 2006; Richardson, 2007). This is

---

Box 6.2 Travellers as the Other

... the paradoxical view held by the police service of Gypsies and Travellers as the 'enemy' of and yet 'stranger' to them. A police officer commented 'In our work we are not going to come into contact with law abiding Travellers' ... police officers are still happy to talk about pikeys and Gippos.

(Coxhead, 2007 p. 65)

Travellers are lawless criminal people. The Government has issued a decree to local Councils to provide more caravan pitches for gypsies. Their argument seems to be that people have a 'right' to be gypsies and that if councils provide more authorized sites there will be less of a problem with gypsies occupying land illegally. This is a policy of appeasement of lawlessness. If people want to spend their lives travelling around in caravans then they must operate within the law. They should also rely on finding people willing to accommodate them – not expect special favours from the state. A local council consulted residents on proposals for a new caravan site for Travellers – then dismissed 3,100 of the 3,500 complaints as racist ... It is not racist to state that gypsy camps frequently cause an increase in crime and mess. It is a statement of fact.

(*Mail Online*, 6 January 2009)

---

expressed through public and media allegations of rises in crime when Travellers enter a neighbourhood, despite evidence to the contrary, both locally and nationally (see Box 6.2). Despite that labelling, the evidence suggests, counter-intuitively, that they are not disproportionately represented in activities other than in petty, public space, nuisance activities, as acknowledged by the police themselves (see Richardson, 2007).

The research shows that the police work with multiple public and private agencies to control the movement and settlement of Gypsies and Travellers, but the engagement of these groups in community policing initiatives is limited (Coxhead, 2007). The police primarily engage with them through enforcement practice. Gypsies and Travellers are shown here to respond to their experiences of policing in a number of ways that attempt to place them beyond the gaze of formal agencies (James, 2007). Despite having no higher recorded crime levels than other communities, the suspicion with which Travellers are regarded means they are likely to be reported by the public or targeted unfairly by the police. A rare study undertaken in Kent in 1994, reported that 'the Gypsy Traveller issue ... arouses extreme prejudice and hostility' within the police service (Pizani-Williams, 1998 p. 16). A former police officer described how this was carried through into active harassment, leading to a response that could be criminalized: '[he] described how officers were encouraged, if a Traveller was stopped and questioned and no offence appeared to have been committed, to verbally harass them to provoke a Section 4 assault' (Pizani-Williams, 1998, p. 23). (Under section 4 of the Public Order Act 1986, a constable may arrest a person without a warrant if '(a) he engages in offensive conduct which [a] constable warns him to stop, and (b) he engages in further offensive conduct immediately or shortly after the warning'.) Some years later, Dawson (2000 p. 9) found that it was very common for unfounded allegations to be made against Travellers, and described massive police operations against encampments, as in the Dale Farm episode (below). Blanket raids on groups of Travellers are frequently reported (Coxhead, 2005; 2007; Greenfields and Home, 2006), attracting a high level of publicity, while the subsequent lack of charges is hidden in the corner of a newspaper (Pizani-Williams, 1998). The latter also found that the police obtained search warrants for entire sites rather than particular habitations. She refers to 'intensive and provocative policing which frequently leads to confrontation' (Pizani-Williams, 1998 p. 25). Nearly a decade after Pizani-Williams' study, Power (2004 p. 80) reported similar findings from a police interview in his study of Irish Travellers' experiences: 'Society almost condones you to do whatever with a transient group. Whatever you do that gets rid of them, it's OK by us.' One measure of the experience of police harassment is the use of stop-and-search powers, which is an issue for many ethnic minority communities (Equality and Human Rights Commission, 2010). In Pizani-Williams' (1998) sample of Gypsy Travellers, 15 out of 21 said they had been stopped or searched more than five times in the last year. Power (2004) also found a disproportionate experience of stop and search in his interviews with Irish Travellers. Derbyshire Gypsy Liaison Group conducted their own survey of a sample of Travellers (Dawson, 2006). Out of 525 questionnaires that were distributed, 370 were completed and returned. All those who responded had been stopped and searched in the last few months, while a third had been stopped more than once on a single day. Coxhead (2007), a former police officer, discussed the discriminatory attitudes in the police towards Gypsies and Travellers and referred to this as 'the last bastion of racism'. A culture of prejudice exists within the police in detail, at management as well as frontline level. The pervasive and aggressively proactive nature of this prejudice is summed up in the words of one officer: 'prejudice towards Travellers in the police is not only accepted, it's expected' (Coxhead, 2007 p. 47). It was claimed that police trainers were complicit in this view of the travelling Other (Power, 2004 p. 83). Such attitudes of the police towards Travellers are not just confined to the UK. In his study of the (dire) relationship between An Garda Síochána and the Traveller community in the Republic of Ireland, Aogán Mulcahy suggests that:

> Police relations with them [Travellers] are deeply fraught: Police misconduct towards Travellers – involving derogatory language, harassment, provocation, and other forms of questionable and/or illegal behaviour is both commonplace and expected.
>
> (Mulcahy, 2012 p. 4)

Mulcahy notes that impact of diversity and equality legislation in the Republic of Ireland has meant that members of the police have been officially discouraged from using the term 'Knacker' to refer to members of the Travelling community. However, during an interview with one of his Garda respondents, Mulcahy highlights the racist humour that is a feature of the police occupational culture: 'One Garda officer noted that official discouragement of the term "Knackers" had led some officers to substitute it with "stills", on the basis that the Travellers are "still Knackers"' (p. 9).

Of course, the state police are only one part of the larger complex of surveillance and control. Control of space for dwellings is the keystone of their Otherness. Typically, 90 per cent of planning applications by Gypsies and Travellers are rejected, compared with 25 per cent of domestic ones. Police eviction powers had been vastly increased under the previous Conservative government (Cemlyn et al., 2009). For instance, the Criminal Justice and Public Order Act (1994) accorded the police wide powers enabling police officers to direct Travellers to leave land if they are held to have damaged property (which might include urinating in a hedge or leaving footprints on the grass), and to have their vehicles removed and crushed at the Travellers' expense (Monbiot, 1995). The Equality and Human Rights Commission (EHRC) chair, Trevor Phillips, observed that for this group Britain 'is still like the American deep south for black people in the 1950s' (cited in Crawley, 2004). Cowan and Lomax (2003), in criticizing the dangers of localism in criminal justice decision-making, documented how decisions about whether to evict Travellers from unauthorized encampments depended on whether the occupants were perceived to be conforming to normative notions of acceptable behaviour (Cowan and Lomax, 2003 p. 287).

Travellers are 'policed' in the widest sense of the word. They are subject to increased surveillance in society because of their status as 'Other' or 'deviant'. The discourse in the media, by the public and politicians, serves to socially construct the Other as dangerous and contagious in public space. In this analysis, welfare is linked with divisive practices and, therefore, exclusion. Richardson (2007) discusses how surveillance is not just about controlling groups seen to be deviant; it is also about labelling those groups in the first place. This involves gathering intelligence about them and interpreting that intelligence in a way that portrays them as 'Other'. More direct forms of surveillance were also described by James and Richardson (2006) in relation to an inter-agency model of site management where the encampments were monitored by CCTV cameras (see Box 6.3).

Caricaturing of the Other is normal in the tabloid press. The police are involved in a war against the lawless Other. Hyperbole is normal (see Box 6.4). For example, a recent story in the *Daily Mail* accused a group of Travellers in Bedfordshire of running a modern-day slave ring by allegedly forcing migrant workers to sleep in horse boxes and dog kennels (*Mail Online*, 12 September 2011). The same newspaper described the 'rescue' of the migrant workers from the Traveller settlement in triumphalist terms: 'Two hundred police officers including marksmen and dog handlers, raced on to the site supported by a police helicopter and human trafficking experts at around 5.30am'. The workers were kept 'in a shocking echo

---

Box 6.3   The Other resists

The gang used axes to smash five windows – causing thousands of pounds worth of damage to the only police helicopter in the county. The vandalism followed weeks of aerial surveillance on a travellers' site where stolen cars and goods are believed to be being kept . . . As the helicopter is the only one owned by Surrey Police neighbouring forces are having to provide air cover during police operations in the county. Detectives were apparently ready to raid the gipsies' site on the back of evidence filmed from the air, according to *The Sun* newspaper. A Surrey Police spokesman said the identity of the vandals was 'unknown'. He said: 'The incident is part of an ongoing investigation and security measures are being reviewed as part of this. We are working with a maintenance contractor to ensure the aircraft is back on line as soon as possible.'

(*Daily Telegraph*, 14 May 2009 – see the similar
Liverpool reference in Chapter 3)

---

of wartime concentration camps', and the police 'arrested four men and a pregnant woman'. In addition, media reports, typically based on conjecture rather than evidence, also suggest that Travellers are becoming involved in 'distraction burglary', whereby a member of the public, often an older person, is kept talking while burglary takes place.

Police regulation is a frequent trigger for engagement with criminal justice. Harassment frequently relates to vehicle monitoring at festivals (Coxhead, 2007). Minor discretionary motoring charges furnish the opportunity for escalation, leading to rapid criminalization and often overnight incarceration (Power, 2004). Bail conditions are imposed that are hard to meet, leading to further remands in custody. Travellers are assumed to be more likely to skip bail, and therefore face higher probability of custody in the first place. The introduction of ASBOs (see Chapter 5) under the Crime and Disorder Act 1998 had a particular impact on Gypsy and Traveller families. Often used for civil law minor behavioural incivilities, a breach is a criminal offence and means potential future custody. Different cultural behaviour patterns of Traveller families, particularly on crowded housing estates, are likely to lead to negative neighbour reports and subsequent ASBOs. Objections have included visits from extended families, children being out of school, noise, and the behaviour of young people and their relatives and friends (Greenfields and Home, 2006).

Unauthorized sites are particularly vulnerable to theft or harassment (James, 2007). But informal barriers obstruct reporting and redress. Experiences with the state police, whose main role has been to control and limit their lifestyle, do not encourage Traveller victims to place their trust in a serious police response to their victimization (Greenfields and Home, 2006; James 2007). Different studies

---

Box 6.4   Traveller 'invasion' as moral panic

Five thousand Gypsies descended on . . . the tiny village of Woodham Ferrers . . . The picturesque village – which has a population of just 414 – is the venue for the Gypsy church's 2011 Light and Life Festival, . . . the Pentecostal Christian group, which is made up of Romany and Irish travellers, promised to leave by tomorrow and clear up after themselves. But villagers are furious about the invasion . . . Margaret Wicking, who has lived in Woodham Ferrers for 48 years, said: 'It's upset me terribly. My house backs on to the field and they are using my garden for a toilet . . . ' Katie Jarrett, 24, of nearby South Woodham Ferrers, said: 'It's been an absolute nightmare. Pubs have closed because of the trouble, and the beauty salons have closed.' But Andrew Richardson, of the 120-acre Birkett Hall Livery Stables and Farm, defended his decision to allow the festival to come to Essex. 'This isn't just a commercial venture. Gypsies are Europe's last persecuted minority', said Andrew, 58. 'We are doing our bit to help them. There is fear and bigotry among the villagers, but these Gypsies are peaceful. I am not saying they are whiter than white, but any crime is in the sphere of the police . . .' Gypsy minister Robert Finney. . . . said 'At a big event like this, people expect the worst, from past history with Gypsies. They think we will never leave. But we will be gone by Friday evening, and there will be no rubbish left behind. We are just here to convert non-believers.' Chief Supt Steve Robinson said: 'We have a chief superintendent, an inspector, three sergeants and 21 PCs. . . . experienced at policing the Gypsies . . .' Arthur Roberts, a member of the security team at the festival, said: 'We police ourselves. We've got it under control.' Traveller Douglas Jones, who has been 'saved' for 25 years, said: 'Local people are scared of us, but they have nothing to worry about. They should all come and see what we're about – I will guarantee their safety and enjoyment.'

(*Essex Chronicle*, 28 July 2011)

---

consistently note that many Gypsies and Travellers adopt a resigned approach towards state police encounters, seeing them as an intrinsic part of their cultural experience, not expecting assistance from the authorities. Meek (2007 p. 141) reported a young Traveller's experience of police harassment before his prison sentence: 'There was a bit of harassment before I came in. Just after Christmas we was raided four times like. Nothing you can do about that I suppose.' Police failure to follow up reports of victimization is assumed to be a natural hazard and it is considered a waste of time to report such events.

According to Power (2004 p. 258), the systematic lack of recognition of their ethnicity leads to Irish Travellers being constructed as a criminal community. Power's interviews indicated that official reports could contain coded messages implying untrustworthiness to magistrates, who could also be expected to be prejudiced. Power concluded that 'given that attitude to the young [Irish Traveller] people – it's obvious that they are going to accumulate really hefty criminal records within a very short space of time' (Power, 2004 p. 260). Accelerated criminalization can occur at all stages. Pizani-Williams (1998) found that 52 per cent of Gypsies and Travellers had never been cautioned for a prior offence before they were prosecuted. Fast-tracking into custody is common. The 2011 Census will furnish the first official recognition of Travellers as a recognized ethnic group. The state history of the social ordering process, in which the Occident seeks to incorporate the Orient at a lower level of the Great Chain of Being, continues. The *Westmorland Gazette* reported in October 1871: 'This migratory tribe was largely represented [at Brough Hill fair], there being scores of camps along the fair hill, and as many children rolling about in the straw, or playing about outside, as would almost populate a young colony'. The same paper reported, in March 2010: 'The detail of a policing strategy to combat crime and anti-social behaviour by Appleby Horse Fair travellers has been revealed at a packed public meeting in Sedbergh' (cited in Woolnough, 2011) Some things change. Others do not. The state policing of the Other through discretionary legal powers continues as the key practice.

Joining the dots: the Other at Dale Farm

This text has used the vehicle of the financial crisis to explain a conundrum: the extent to which the British style of policing is partisan in its commitment to focus on particular types of crime, committed by particular types of people, in particular contexts. In an age of austerity, the financial crisis means cutting peripheral assets. In doing so, the key features – priorities, functions, and procedures – of the institution are exposed. The essence of British policing is laid bare when it is forced to demonstrate its priorities. Meanwhile, the marginal group, the Other, is suffering most: it is squeezed by the Occident. Other parties are involved. Privatization is evident as the market economy seizes the opportunity to convert state policing into policing-for-profit. Moral entrepreneurs reappear, leading the wolf-pack of the tabloid press in demonizing the Other. Marginal deviance is exaggerated and the Other caricatured. Flexible legislation, civil and criminal, is a key weapon for the state police and other agencies of social ordering. But despite the inevitability of the contest, the Other is active, not passive, in its defence.

These are the key themes of this text. The drama, the metaphor of Dale Farm (discussed below), displays the central components of postcolonial theory in demonstrating how the police institution fulfils its traditional and perceived mandate, in defining (and defending) the Occident against the Orient.

The actors – from Orient to Occident

Until recently, Dale Farm was largely unknown to the outside world. A smallholding in the county of Essex, for many years it had been a small legal Traveller encampment, increasingly surrounded by suburbs of white residents, who retained the residual memory of the state police as the symbolic unifying emblem of normative social order. Over the years, as the marginal Travellers were excluded from other arenas of public space across the country, in the context of pressure over land, residential space, and more general resources, its population expanded. Other Travellers arrived, given the lack of action by local parish pump councils to fulfil legal obligations for new encampments, making Dale Farm the largest Traveller site in the UK.

Over several years, pressure on the residents increased. Legal contestation absorbed considerable energy and resources on both sides over the years. The suburban residents of the town of Basildon – alarmed by the likely effects on their property valuations – campaigned to be protected from the Traveller Other, with their assumed contagious practices. The dangerous class was back; its perceived deviance fanned by moral entrepreneurial media (see Box 6.5). Public space was contested fiercely, as the Occident, in the form of a conservative, property-holding council, fulfilled its obligations to the law-abiding citizens of the normal world. Vociferous 'normal' residents contributed their own view.

Pressure from the larger fiscal crisis was being felt by the Essex Police, the local constabulary. Criminal statistics were fiddled to meet performance targets. The former chief superintendent, Mike Thwaites, noted that increasingly the summary justice of cautions and ASBOs was being used to ensure that 'crimes reported' were resolved without being dealt with through due process of law. Extra-legal practices were encouraged by institutionalized avoidance of failures in the 'clear-up rate'. He stressed that community sentences, cautions and restorative justice could be appropriate in certain circumstances (Smith, 2012). Failures of state policing would

---

Box 6.5   The voice of the Occident

The resident is outraged the gypsy traveller community is receiving inordinate media coverage, whilst the local residents' plight has been reduced to no more than a side issue. It is clear the residents have a strong case to rebut most of the arguments put forward by the travellers and have an even stronger argument to highlight how they have suffered over the years at the hands of the gypsy community. At 'Whistle Blowers' we are non-partisan but it does appear the resident, who contacted us, has made out a case for a more even handed approach by the media. One argument put forward by the resident, who spoke to us, is that the authorities are intimidated by the travellers and will not confront or investigate them. If you are a resident of Crays Hill or have been adversely affected by members of the traveller community, we would like to hear from you. Likewise if you are one of the travellers, we would like to hear from you, too. If you are a police officer, council worker, postman, tax inspector, utility worker or have a job, where you are in contact with the travellers, please contact us.

(Whistle Blowers Press Agency, 30 September 2011)

not appear in the official records of criminality. Image management was important to ensure faith in the English Bobby. Backroom functions of the county police were being privatized with a £32 million deal for crime management systems to be awarded to Northgate Information Solutions (Best, 2010).

A private social ordering agency – Constant and Company Investigators and Baliffs Ltd – described as the country's primary specialist in evicting Travellers – conducted the secondary work of eviction. Their contract with the council was for some £2.2 million. The irony was that the core of the bailiff group appeared to constitute temporarily recruited minority ethnic workers – the Orient used by the Occident to boot out the Orient – who received nominal salaries and minimal legal training. Other parties of the larger Foucauldian 'gaze' contributed, from council planning officers to highly partisan media.

The Other was more heterogeneous than depicted. The majority were Travellers of different backgrounds. Some had legal rights to be present, others not, adding to the complexity not perceived by the Occident. Some were involved in resistance, others not. They were supported by a small numbers of external activists, in turn variously caricatured by the media. Police have charged sixteen people with offences linked to the clearance of the UK's largest Travellers' site. More than thirty supporters are reported to have refused the discretionary police cautions.

In the event, the eviction process was short, efficient, and relatively peaceful, with the assistance of appropriate technology, from Tasers to a 'cherry-picker'.[3] The final scenes in the decade-long saga marked a victory for the council after it had spent £22 million of taxpayers' cash clearing the former scrapyard in Basildon. The police had prepared under cover of darkness and marched over nearby countryside to arrive at the back of the site just before 7.30 a.m. Bulldozers were used to smash down fences. Police hacked through shabby fences to get into the site. Riot-trained officers entered Dale Farm, appropriately equipped with the accoutrements of the new riot gear, at dawn, and quickly advanced, establishing a position which allowed them to begin removing the main scaffold gate. Small-scale sporadic violence was reported on both sides. But within a relatively short period, caravans were being towed off the site. Neighbouring farms and supermarkets contributed to the social ordering process, by blocking access to avoid an alternative resting place for the Travellers.

The saga continues, however. An estimated eighty families were evicted from the 6-acre site after the decade-long planning conflict. Within weeks, at least ten families had moved back onto roads inside the site. There are an estimated fifty caravans parked illegally in the area, both on the roadside and on the legal site, taking it above its thirty-four-plot authorized capacity (BBC News, 12 January 2012). Basildon Council won a Pyrrhic victory on behalf of its 'citizen' constituents, at extraordinary cost: a process in which state policing priorities were clearly focused while other state policing activities relatively discarded.

Little Noddy and PC Plod

There are too many caricatures in the relation between the institution of the state police (representing the Occident) and the Travellers (symbolizing the Orient), without this text adding to them. This has not been an account of quaint Little Noddy being stopped and searched before being charged with an incivility, on the high street of Toytown, by a brutal, insensitive PC Plod. If only social ordering in modern and Victorian societies were so easy to understand. But in a deeply divided society, enhanced by the austerity of the continuing legacy of a neoliberal global market economy, social and economic inequality expands. Typically, in Britain over the last decade, chief executives' pay has risen to nine times that of a median earner. Some chief executives (as at British Gas and Barclays) are paid over one thousand times the national median wage. The share of national income accruing to the top 0.1 per cent rose from 1.3 per cent in 1979 to 6.5 per cent in 2007 (Monbiot, 2012). Pressures on marginal groups have increased correspondingly. It would be surprising if the state police institution in its key practice did not reflect that inequality. As we said before (in part), the rich get richer as the Other receives an ASBO.

State policing is partisan, as it was in St Giles in 1829 and it is at Dale Farm in 2012. Modernization of traditional Peelite styles, rather than structural reform, ensures that British policing continues and enhances the old summary justice practice against marginal elements of society. Policing-for-profit increases, and irrespective of any notional financial savings, results in a system of policing devoid of accountability and responsibility. Democratic local policing in the shape of the elected police and crime commissioners is likely to increase the tyranny of the majority over the minority. Occidental pressures will outweigh contestation by the Orient – again Dale Farm represents the nature of such postcolonial 'democratic' innovations. Police cuts have reinforced partisan policing against the Other, with consequent reaction. The fetish of the 'English Bobby', increasingly being consigned to elderly Reithian texts by academics, nevertheless remains a popular default ideology. Cost of state policing bears no relation to equity in social provision. Individual police officers may have attitudinally changed in reaction to the demographics of ethnicity, of sexuality and of gender. But structurally, inequity is obfuscated through reliance on opaque data, especially as produced through a populist (if largely imaginary) localism as provincial forces practise different ways of enumerating procedures, while structurally continuing within the moral parameters and priorities of 1829. The residual 'golden' memory of a harmonious social ordering agency declines in the face of external and international critique, and changes in population diversity. The Dale Farm experience furnishes an apt metaphor for social ordering in an age of austerity.

State, local and central policing in the UK, with the key practice of policing the Other, was not founded, as we have said, in 1829. It was part of a continuing process, exacerbated by a manufactured moral panic in the early part of the nineteenth century. With the impact of modernism, some things have changed, and there are some positive elements. State policing is no longer as attitudinally partisan. But changes in attitudes do not equate with changes in structure. The pattern of policing the Other as the primary focus continues. Terminology has changed. The frontline has replaced the beat. Where technology and police science have developed from their nineteenth-century antiquity – from gas-lamps to DNA – they have simply reinforced institutional goals cast in concrete.

The future is clear for the major ordering system of the UK. As the fiscal crisis deepens, the Other will suffer the primary consequences. It will fight back but the structural odds are against it. The state police will eventually become formally unified, with notional localism discarded under expedient pressures. Foucauldian loci of political power will become more discursive. Policing-for-profit will be subtly expanded. Some things change. History repeats itself, first as tragedy and second as . . .

Epilogue
Treading the thin blue line

At the time of this book going to press, events involving the state police in England and Wales have been moving fast. Part 2 of the Winsor review of police and civilian staff remuneration is being revealed. The Leveson Inquiry has displayed the dysfunctionality of senior command practice. LGC Forensics has bungled a major rape enquiry: scores of convictions may have to be reviewed (Dodd and Malik, 2012). Schismatic revelations have reinforced our analysis. The conflict between internal lobbies has been re-opened with the major proposals for expanded policing-for-profit, from conducting foot patrols to making major contributions to investigative functions. ACPO is pushing hard for the privatization of many previously sacrosanct duties, with major commitments from the West Midlands and Surrey police forces to transfer duties to the private security sector, allowing the latter to profit further from the public purse (the proposed contracts are worth £1.5 billion over 7 years[1]) without serious public accountability, under a variety of legitimations (Travis and Williams, 2012). Meanwhile the Lincolnshire Police has contracted the security services firm G4S to build and 'staff' the first private police station in the country (Travis, 2012c). There is a precedent here since the force had already outsourced over half of its 900 civilian staff to G4S (Kelly, 2012). It is not just key elements of state policing that have been outsourced: G4S has been awarded a £300 million contract to provide 'services' to the courts in England and Wales, is involved in training magistrates for their 'customer journey', and is contracted to run two key prisons (Kelly, 2012).

Much of this has been promoted as good, old-fashioned common sense under the guise of 'modernization'. But as Harris (2012) points out, 'this debate is also about accountability, transparency and the most fundamental elements of democracy – not to mention the question of who the police are there to serve and what they are there to do'. Serious questions remain not only about the legal relation of the police to the policed in this scenario, but to the role of the state in the provision of security and core public services generally (see Loader and Walker, 2007). The Police Federation has vainly sought to stem the tide (using the threat to the emblematic Office of Constable as its key weapon), rightly perceiving policing-for-profit as a threat to its members' jobs. The thin end of the wedge of 'one man and his dog' profit-based social ordering (Brogden and Nijhar, 2005) has been replaced by pressure from the multinational corporate sector of neoliberal economics. Further, as predicted, civilian 'backroom staff' are being discarded and replaced by higher paid, untrained, but unsackable sworn officers, thus undermining any efficiencies that might have been made in the first place. All that has happened is that the mountain of police bureaucracy has been passed from civilian staff to the police and will have implications for the so-called 'frontline'. The problems of limited police shelf life have also increased, with one-seventh of all police costs being now spent on their pensions (*Telegraph*, 2012).

Revelations of corruption continue in various guises. At one end of the scale, the commonly accepted view that corruption was one reason for the failure of the Metropolitan Police to promptly arrest those suspected of the murder of Stephen Lawrence and the stonewalling of the subsequent investigation, has been given new lease of life with the release of previously confidential Metropolitan Police files.[2] These indicate that a key officer in the initial murder hunt was long suspected by senior anti-corruption officers in the Metropolitan Police of being at the centre of a ring of 'bent detectives . . . operating as a professional organised crime syndicate' (Metropolitan Police intelligence report, cited in Gillard and Flynn, 2012). At the other end of the scale, the Leveson Inquiry[3] had disclosed more riveting details of the intertwining of corporate media and state policing interests.

Two of the key command-level officers, Andy Hayman and John Yates,[4] involved in the murkier aspects of the phone-hacking affair, resigned with the latter taking up a lucrative advisory post in order to export the 'British Bobby' to an authoritarian regime in the Middle East (following the example of the previous chief of HMIC, Sir Ronnie Flanagan). Failure in the domestic policing context is apparently no barrier to success or advancement elsewhere. Again serious questions arise about the 'policing for export' activities of these officers. While they are ostensibly dressed up in the garb of democratization and capacity building, we remain sceptical about their modus operandi (and efficacy) and concur with Sheptycki (2007) when he argues that the overseas activities of senior officers are often antithetical to the development of a state policing that has a commitment to social equality and democracy at its core. The export of British policing contributes to the globalization of the conflict between the Occident and the Orient. In the authoritarian Gulf States, British policing seeks to commodify its expertise (and sell its related crowd control techniques[5]) in the social ordering of the Other. Sir Ronnie Flanagan and his colleagues (the former has specific expertise of controlling the Other in Northern Ireland) will find symmetry with local elites seeking to renovate the control of their own, local, Other.[6] Bahrain is an ideal location for such divisive state policing.

There has been some progress. The English Defence League has now been stigmatized as an extremist group, with several arrests. Scotland is moving ahead with plans to centralize its current eight forces into one national unit. Whether centralization will deliver the savings and efficiencies suggested is debatable, but on balance the move seems rather more palatable than the widespread privatization and outsourcing of policing services and chunks of the state infrastructure planned for south of the border.[7] In England, major problems remain over a number of other policing issues; the coalition government had not expected that the new police and crime commissioners – as with city mayors – might furnish the Labour Party with a new power bloc. In any case, police and crime commissioners represent a cynical attempt at political populism: where is the 'localism' in a commissioner representing some 3 million people (say in the Greater Manchester area) from heterogeneous backgrounds?

Certain former senior officers, such as Sir Ian Blair, have reinforced our own argument on the absurdity of attempting to distinguish between the police 'frontline' and 'back-office' functions (Blair, 2012). Blair also rightly criticizes the obsession with sworn officer numbers in relation to crime resolution. He, however, spoils his own critique by simultaneously advancing the policing-for-profit agenda which will still, apparently, be 'within a public service ethos' as long as the numbers subsequently employed are still balanced by the availability of superior sworn officers and by the latter's discharge of key directive functions! He is naive in perceiving the expansion of PCSOs and private security personnel within the 'extended policing family' as one solution.[8] Does private profit equate with the public good? As a normally perceptive professional, he almost entirely ignores the key political, and, especially, legal, questions relating to policing-for-profit. Ironically, the Office of Constable is as much a problem for potential private corporations encroaching on state policing territory as it is for those who seek to legitimize current state practices through that symbol. However, Sir Ian Blair is hardly a neutral observer. He has an undoubted interest in the policing-for-profit agenda and heads the corporate security consultancy firm 'BlueLight Global Solutions' that provides a range of services to law enforcement organizations and national governments in relation to policing and national security matters.[9] Again, the revolving door from the state to the corporate sector is clearly in evidence: BlueLight Global Solutions also includes on its staff four retired senior British police officers including Bob Quick, former head of counter-terrorism for the UK police (and a key player in the phone-hacking enquiry) and Bill Hughes, former director-general of SOCA. Surprisingly, there are few checks on what employment senior officers are permitted to take upon retirement or what advisory posts they are allowed to pursue. In the murky and labyrinthine world of private security there are potential risks that senior officers may capitalize on their knowledge of privileged material obtained as a state official (e.g. around sensitive national security and intelligence matters) and market this within the corporate sector, where it becomes just another commodity to be bought and sold. In the knowledge economy of twenty-first-century policing everything is up for grabs.

James Sheptycki (Sheptycki, 2010) has proposed a metaphor based on the nautical myth of the Raft of the Medusa to illustrate how contemporary Western (state) policing is drifting off into neoliberalism and authoritarianism. Certainly, the reforms outlined in current government proposals reflect a narrow concern with neoliberal outsourcing and the privatization of policing and related criminal justice functions. It is a process that, as Klein (2007) forecast, occurs not by full-frontal assault, but by nibbling at the edges. Policing in England and Wales is unique in succumbing to the depth of this neoliberal assault. If these developments proceed in line with their anticipated governmental outcomes – and it has to be said the complicity of some senior police officials – then the next decade will fundamentally transform the landscape of British state policing. In our view not necessarily for the better.

Endnote

'Turning over the pebble' (Chapter 1) has helped reveal fissures of major proportion in the state police of Great Britain and in the wider polity. In particular, privatization of the state policing agency continues apace. Under the 'spin' of the failed austerity drive of neo-liberal economics, in the UK such practices have reached levels unparalled in Western Europe. Illustratively, at the core, the opportunism of the giants of criminal justice policing-for-profit (and wider criminal justice and health service function) has been temporarily stalled in the examples of (in particular) the West Midlands and Surrey Police Services (in assuming major state police and criminal justice functions, including influencing policy), due to local and national resistance (from certain laudable senior police officers to trade unionists), and more widely by the excellence of the Leveson Enquiry. The chosen few of globalized corporations, including G4S, Serco, and Halliburton (some with more dubious international histories than others), have been temporarily obstructed due to international and national opposition. Their 'spin doctor' claims of savings in the police budget are readily, typically, exposed by evidence of the dubious labour practices required of their foot-soldiers. The Independent Police Complaints Commission fights a losing battle to make private operatives accountable and transparent, as do other oversight bodies in the wider criminal justice system and the NHS.

Second, policing the Other through summary powers continues through the replacement of ASBOs with the Criminal Behaviour Order (CBO). Of the more than 20,000 ASBOs issued in England and Wales during the decade to 2010, 57 per cent were breached, 42 per cent more than once. Over half of the breaches were fast-tracked into custody (and presumed subsequent criminal careers). The replacement CBO is old wine in new bottles. Like ASBOs, CBOs crudely continue to create under civil law a criminal offence. Due process is ignored for the majority of the Other. Standard of proof is lower and the test of anti-social behaviour broader. Third, the controversy over the legitimate Winsor Report Part 2 is yet to reach a crescendo. The latter proposed major radical reforms in British policing – breaching the totemic rights of the Office of Constable in making police officers liable under the normative provision of labour law; reducing inflated police pay and perks in certain instances while increasing it for specialist tasks; instituting higher academic qualities for recruits (and fast-track promotion for the more skilled) and proposing mid-level recruitment of certain professionals; and raising ages of police retirement. We agree with the majority of these proposals for reforming a system first instituted in 1920. The meetings of the Police Negotiation Body will be interesting to observe over the next few months with a divided ACPO (whose private status is untouched, with many such officers looking forward to new commercial opportunities resulting from the privatization process) and ferocious opposition from the Police Federation. The brand, Corporate Britain, is on the way, through subterfuge and by vested neo-liberal interests, independently of democratic process and public interest. Watch this space.

Mike Brogden   Graham Ellison
Melin Cadnant, Llandegfan   Queens University, Belfast
                   4th June 2012

Notes

1 Introduction: turning over the pebble

1 See Chapter 2.
2 See Chapter 2.
3 There is, however, a more recent claim by HMIC of police infiltration of far-right groups – see Chapter 5.
4 See 'Policing Improvement Agency: A Botched Execution', *Guardian*, editorial, 1 September 2011. Available: www.guardian.co.uk/commentisfree/2011/sep/01/police-improvement-agency-botched-editorial
5 For the most thoughtful and recent contribution to the debate on the police role, see Robert Reiner (2012).
6 *Police*, BBC Television, 1982.
7 See Chapter 5.
8 See Chapter 2.
9 For critiques of Broken Windows and Zero Tolerance policing see Young (1999).
10 As in the 1993 White Paper on police reform, the 1993 Sheehy Report on pay and career structures, and the 1994 Police and Magistrates' Court Act.
11 Young (2011 p. 15), for example, cites a study by Weisburd and Piquero (2008) that looked at reported variance levels (usually delineated as R-squared) in all multivariate studies published in *Criminology* between 1968 and 2005. In multivariate analyses R-squared is an indicator of the predictive power of a model, so for example, a variance level of .90 (though this would never be achieved in practice) would suggest that there is a 90 per cent likelihood that what is being observed is not occuring by chance and is indicative of some causal relationship between the variables. However, the average R-squared in *all* the studies reported in *Criminology* was .40 – meaning that there is only a 40 per cent likelihood that the model is explaining what is ostensibly being observed. In some studies the reported R-squared was .1 – which to all intents contains no explanatory potential at all.
12 Ibid.
13 See Chapter 5.
14 See Chapter 5.
15 See Chapter 5.
16 Oddly mirrored in the apartheid policing of South Africa and its commitment to 'functional policing'.
17 See Chapter 6.
18 Pre-social Darwinism and the 1840 import of the concept of the 'criminal classes'.
19 As earlier in Storch, 1976.
20 Terms not in common discourse until the 1840s.
21 See Emsley (2009) on Robert Roberts and the latter's experience of policing a Salford slum.

22 See Chapter 5.
23 See Chapter 2.
24 Ibid.
25 See Chapter 6.
26 The Winsor Report 2011/2 was commissioned by the coalition government to report primarily on police remuneration and conditions.
27 See Chapter 2.
28 For example, more than three-quarters of PSNI staff on civilian contracts are former RUC officers who have been re-hired as intelligence and security analysts. The severance legislation enacted following the ICP expressly forbids the re-hiring of former RUC officers to the PSNI, but a loophole does not apply to their being re-hired as 'civilians'. See Vincent Kearney, 'Ex-RUC in "sensitive" policing jobs', BBC News, 17 January 2012. Available: www.bbc.co.uk/news/uk-northern-ireland-16600069
29 See Chapters 2 and 3.
30 See Chapter 5.
31 R v. Metropolitan Police Commissioner, ex parte Blackburn [1968] 2 QB 118. Mr Blackburn sought to compel the police to enforce the law against illegal gaming in London because it was impacting on his legitimate business activities. Lord Denning ruled that it was up to the police to exercise their discretion in such matters as when or if they enforce the law.
32 Despite our reservations in Chapter 5 on police 'making law'.
33 Cannabis was again reclassified to B in 2008.
34 The peculiar 'Office of Constable' in England, Wales and Northern Ireland is rooted for instance in the Norman Conquest of 1066. According to the Police Federation (n.d.) the term 'constable first appeared on the scene after the Norman conquest, and towards the end of the 12th century acquired the local significance it has held ever since'.
35 See 'Reflections on Colonial and Postcolonial Policing in the (Former) Portuguese Empire', Fourth GERN (Post)colonial Policing Workshop, 14–15 April 2011. Available: www.open.ac.uk/Arts/copp/4th-GERN-programme-Feb2011.pdf

2 The state of the police of the state

1 The Royal Commission on the Police in a 1960 interim report, and its 1962 final report; the *Committee of Inquiry on the Police* in 1978 (Edmund-Davies Committee); and the *Inquiry into Police Responsibilities and Rewards* (Sheehy, 1993).
2 It is notoriously difficult to put a figure on the police reform process in Northern Ireland. However, the corporate financial services firm Deloitte has estimated that it has cost the UK government £100 million annually since 1999, meaning that the reforms will have cost – at a conservative estimate – £1.3 billion by the end of 2012. This figure is over and above the £1 billion annual spend on policing and justice in Northern Ireland. Already the ICP voluntary and severance scheme for RUC/PSNI officers has topped £500 million. See Deloitte (2007).
3 The former RUC overstated female membership by including part-time officers!
4 See Oaksey Report (Findings) (Oaksey, 1949).
5 Some provincial forces appear not to use the system.
6 *The Telegraph*, Thursday 16 April 2009. Available: www.telegraph.co.uk/news/uknews/law-and-order/5164982/Royal_Protection_Officer_conned_colleagues_at_Buckingham_Palace.html
7 See *Daily Post*, 21 October 2010. Available: www.dailypost.co.uk/news/north-wales-news/2010/10/21/bonus-payout-to-top-north-wales-cops-55578-27515105/
8 BBC News, 26 September 2011. Available: www.bbc.co.uk/news/uk-england-tyne-15063645
9 *The Telegraph*, Wednesday 8 February 2011. Available: www.telegraph.co.uk/news/politics/8367333/Bonuses-go-in-bonfire-of-police-perks.html

10 *The Mirror*, 8 November 2011. Available: www.mirror.co.uk/news/uk-news/chief-constables-given-130000-in-bonuses-90168

11 'Huddersfield University Libya Police Training Criticised' BBC News, 6 March 2011. Available: www.bbc.co.uk/news/uk-england-bradford-west-yorkshire-12659549

12 Centrex provided training and development to police forces in the UK and enforcement agencies throughout the world until it was abolished in March 2007.

13 *Mail Online*, 18 December 2007. Available: www.dailymail.co.uk/news/article-503212/Anger-highest-paid-police-chief-260-000-despite-retiring-6-months-ago.html

14 *The Mirror*, 15 November 2011. Available: www.mirror.co.uk/news/uk-news/inquiry-into-alleged-corruption-and-fraud-at-cleveland-91535

15 Normally advertised by the OSCE.

16 See Chapter 4.

17 Although to be fair many other public servants, such as academics and politicians, enjoy the same extracurricular and untaxed benefits.

18 All data from Home Office Police Pensions and Retirement Policy. Available: www.homeoffice.gov.uk/police/police-pensions/

19 Chaired by Professor John Goodman of Manchester School of Management.

20 Although we should point out that the British armed forces also permit gay and lesbian officers to serve openly and also to parade in uniform in Gay Pride parades.

21 There have been many well-meant attempts to reform the iniquitous stop-and-search powers over the last 30 years – most recently by the Metropolitan Police and by the worthy online contributions by *Police Oracle*. All to date have failed. That fault lies in a misconstruction of the problem. Such partisanship and discrimination is a fault of traditional policing structure, not that of individual police officers. Racist police may exist – but no more than in any other public service organization. There is no point pouring endless resources into changing police attitudes when the organization in which they operate actually gears them to use such discriminatory tactics in the policing of the Other.

22 *Police Complaints: statistics for England and Wales 2009/10.*

23 Quoted in *The Briefing*, Series 2, edition 1, May 2011, The Police Foundation.

24 Virgo and Drury were members of the so-called 'Dirty Squad' that policed London's sex industry. The Dirty Squad was a law unto itself. It was to transpire that both officers had been receiving bribes from the owner of a number of strip clubs (see Travis, 2000).

25 Challenor was charged with a litany of corruption offences but the charges were subsequently dismissed on mental health grounds. Challenor had a reputation for racism, brutality and general corruption. He shared the Sergeants' Office with two future chief constables, Maurice Buck and Kenneth Oxford. 'Doing a Challenor' became slang in the Metropolitan Police for avoiding disciplinary punishment by taking medical leave (see Taylor, 1988).

26 The *Guardian* has provided full coverage and documentation in relation to the 'phone-hacking' scandal on its website: www.guardian.co.uk/media/phone-hacking

27 Cited in HMIC Press Release, 024/2011. Available: www.hmic.gov.uk/news/press/releases-2011/0242011-corruption-not-endemic-police/

28 The IPCC also deals with complaints against personnel in the Serious Organised Crime Agency, the UK Border Agency and Her Majesty's Revenue and Customs.

29 Alan Campbell, cited in *Labournorth*. Available: www.labournorth.com/tories-are-going-soft-on-crime-says-home-secretary-as-crime-in-n

30 See UK Home Office, 'Street Level Crime Maps'. Available: www.homeoffice.gov.uk/police/street-level-crime-maps/

31 Twenty years ago, attempts to determine local police establishments always included a caveat to the effect that irrespective of population, local mileage and so on, determinations be subject to local command knowledge. More detailed and complex formulae have since appeared. www.statistics.gov.uk/hub/crime-justice/police/police-personnel-and-resources

32 Previously Berry headed the Police Federation of England and Wales, an entity that is not exactly known for its love of paperwork and form filling. She later became the 'Independent Reducing Bureaucracy in Policing Advocate' (sic!) tasked with implementing some of the reforms in Sir Ronnie Flanagan's review of policing.

33 See, amongst many other examples, the account of undercover policing in Chapter 5.

34 Curiously, Northumbria Police justified their unorthdox acquistion of the Taser in this way by citing the 1998 Human Rights Act. The Select Committee noted, however, 'that we are not persuaded by this argument' (Home Affairs Committee, 2011, Introduction, Part 1, paragraph 2).

35 See Charter Systems website. Available: www.charter-systems.co.uk/

36 See http://wideshut.co.uk./privately-run-security-to-do-police-work-in-britain/

37 See www.securityoracle.com/news/detail.html?id=16987

38 See G4S UK, 'G4S to revolutionise custody suite provision' 15 October 2010. Available: www.g4s.uk.com/en-gb/Media%20Centre/News/2010/10/15/G4S%20launches%20revolutionary%20outsourced%20custody%20suite%20solution/

39 Cited in Ben Leapman, 'Growth in Private Police Forces' *London Evening Standard*. Available: www.thisislondon.co.uk/news/article-19063721-growth-in-private-police-forces.do

40 'Private Security Boss Fined for Impersonating a Police Officer', *Mail Online*, 23 October 2009. Available: www.dailymail.co.uk/news/article-1222289/Private-security-boss-fined-for.html

3 Smoke and mirrors: the cuts in policing and the technological fix

1 This was a result of the transition from apartheid to a democratic state.

2 Reduced from 12,000 full-time officers in the RUC to 7,000 in the PSNI under the Good Friday Agreement. The latter also included a major change in the recruitment of Catholic officers.

3 See *The Telegraph*, 'Christmas for Criminals if 25 per cent Police Cuts Go Ahead'. Available: www.telegraph.co.uk/news/uknews/crime/7994772/Christmas-for-criminals-if-25-per-cent-police-cuts-go-ahead.html

4 See *The Telegraph* 'Labour Attacks "Ludicrous" Plans to Forcibly Retire Police Officers', 9 February 2012. Available: www.telegraph.co.uk/news/uknews/law-and-order/8514826/Labour-attacks-ludicrous-plans-to-forcibly-retire-police-officers.html

5 As a sign of how bad things were likely to become, one chief Constable included in his list the withdrawal of cold water dispensers from police stations!

6 Contrarily, and despite promises otherwise, police officers are already being transferred to conduct back-office jobs for which they have no specific training and for which they are overpaid as compared with their new civilian colleagues.

7 *Demanding Times: The Front-line and Police Visibility* (HMIC, 2011b).

8 Steve Allen in a written submission to the parliamentary inquiry into the closure of the FSS. Available: www.publications.parliament.uk/pa/cm201011/cmselect/cmsctech/writev/forensic/m63.htm

9 Centre for Crime and Justice Studies at King's College London, 2006.

10 The Cloud provides the capability for many users, irrespective of where they are located, to share and edit documents in real time via the internet. Hand-held mobile devices such as smart phones and touch pads are ideally suited to cloud computing technologies.

11 See University of Liverpool Research Intelligence Issue 27. Available: www.liv.ac.uk/researchintelligence/issue27/blastresistantbins.html

12 Much of the older Chicago School's approach to criminology was partly based on this assumption.

13 Of course, the term hotspots may have a more positive meaning – as in certain European cities (Frankfurt, Hamburg, Amsterdam among others), where the term may be used to

designate safe areas for sex-workers, while in Amsterdam one might easily conclude that part of the centre of the city is a 'drugs hotspot' given the legal availability of cannabis there. Ultimately 'hotspots' are subjective, not objective entitites. As more sociologically sophisticated analyses attest (e.g. Sampson and Raudenbush, 2004), perceptions of disorder are social contructions and 'imbued with social meanings that go well beyond what essentialist theories imply' (p. 319).

4 Commodifying state policing: the export of the 'UK Police plc' brand

1 See UK Government Stabilisation Unit, 'Policing Roles'. Available: www.stabilis ationunit.gov.uk/how-to-get-involved/multilateral-deployments/police-roles.html (accessed 24 January 2012).
2 For example, as we discuss below, during the August 2011 riots the PSNI was asked to deploy officers and armoured Land Rovers to London.
3 This reference to the UK Police plc brand was made by Assistant Chief Constable Colin Firth, when he was seconded to the FCO. See www.iraqinquiry.org.uk/media/46534/ smith-statement.pdf (accessed 27 September 2011).
4 One need only look at some of the online discussion fora aimed at British police personnel who want to participate in overseas missions (www.britishexpats.com; www. policespecials.com; www.ukpoliceonline.com; www.police-forum.com) to get a sense that it is officers in the PSNI or who have firearms or counter-terrorism experience who appear to be considered for such missions with greater frequency and regularity.
5 Statement on John Anthony Signs website. Available: www.johnanthonysigns.com/sec-tors_public-metropolitan_police.php
6 We would like to acknowledge the assistance of Conor O'Reilly, who provided information in relation to UK police training missions in Iraq and Afghanistan. Some of the ideas in the latter part of this chapter are developed from Ellison and O'Reilly, 2008a, b.
7 We are using RUC/PSNI to refer (a) to those officers who were originally in the RUC but following the ICP reform programme are now employed in the PSNI, and (b) to those officers who availed themselves of the ICP severance and left either organization to work in the private security sector.
8 See Soufan Group website. Available: http://soufangroup.com/about/
9 It is not just Northern Irish police and military personnel that are taking positions overseas. Prison officers from HMP Maze and HMP Maghaberry have been head-hunted to become wardens in in Israel, Iraq and Somalia (Amnesty International, 2007 p. 23).
10 In many ways it continues to do so. There are approximately 2,500 unsolved murders in Northern Ireland stemming from the conflict and recently the Historical Enquiries Team (HET) has passed a number of cold cases to the Police Ombudsman in Northern Ireland, who is investigating whether the original murder investigations may have been compromised by some RUC officers in order to protect informants.
11 And we are not factoring in military and intelligence agency personnel here.
12 In line with our argument in Chapter 3, one of the main beneficiaries of the fiscal crisis has been the private/corporate security sector. This is as true of the international context also. However, it is not just police that migrate to the corporate security sector; Major General Graham Binns, who commanded British troops in Southern Iraq, is now chief executive of Aegis Defence Services, which supplies private security personnel to Iraq on behalf of the British FCO (see Lane, 2010).
13 This was the case in Turkey, for example. British, Italian, Spanish and French policing agencies competed for market share in a project to reform Turkey's civilian oversight of the internal security sector.
14 Derived from Ellison and O'Reilly (2008a).

5 Policing the Other through law

1 Police Federation for England and Wales, 'The Office of Constable: The Bedrock of Modern Day British Policing', n.d. Available: www.polfed.org/OC_Final.pdf

2 See Chapter 2.

3 The local Vigilance Committee demanded via the Liverpool Watch Committee that the City Police clamp down on prostitution in the district of Kensington. Nott Bower argued that any such process would simply spread prostitution throughout the city. The case was not, as Jefferson and Grimshaw (1984) claim, the beginning of the end of constabulary independence.

4 For detail, see C. A. Williams (2003) at www.historyandpolicy.org/papers/policy-paper-16.html

5 The judicial system in England and Wales furnishes a tariff system in sentencing – but this a trimming and not central to legal practice.

6 For a crucial heuristic discussion of the typical application of summary justice, applied by untrained magistrates, to the working class Other in the mid-nineteenth century, see Hay and Craven (eds), 2004.

7 In a media statement in the aftermath of the riots, the prime minister, David Cameron, stated that anyone involved in the riots, however peripherally, should automatically face a prison term. The Courts Service subsequently issued 'instructions' to magistrates to disregard sentencing guidelines and jail every riot defendant. See the *Guardian*, 'Riots Sentencing: A Sinister Attempt to Upend the Judicial Process', 18 August 2011. Available: www.guardian.co.uk/commentisfree/2011/aug/18/riots-sentencing-courts

8 See Chapter 3.

9 Glidewell Report, 1998 and Auld Report, 2001.

10 See Home Office (2009).

11 Gangs are a common folk-devil. Rarely are they associated with low level crime but occupy a folk devil status in police culture, a term easily – if totally incorrectly – conveyed to the media. Few such 'gangs' were discovered in the August 2011 riots. The importation of the American police advisor Bill Bratton to advise on a resolution to the riots, carrying with him certain assumptions about 'gang culture', is simply inappropriate to the UK context and misses the contexts of the riots.

12 Like the authors of this text.

13 As noted earlier, the voracity with which police officers used CCTV to catch the August 2011 rioters was matched only by similar functionary commitment in the Poll Tax riots. An interesting use of discretionary powers by senior officers when compared with the banking and phone-hacking sagas.

14 See http://nopolicespies.org.uk/wp-content/uploads/2011/02/Background-briefing-Feb-11.pdf

6 Policing the Other: continuity of practice from St Giles to Dale Farm

1 In the nineteenth century the British state delineated a number of 'notified' and 'denotified' tribes in India. Notified tribes, whose nomadic existence was at odds with the colonial administration's emphasis on settled commodity production, were classed as 'criminal' under the Criminal Tribes Act (1871). Some of these nomadic tribes were resettled in gated compounds, shackled, brutally beaten, and forced to perform hard labour. It was believed that this 'curocriminology' would ultimately bring redemption and a desistance from crime and the propensity to offend (Nijhar, 2009).

2 A Travellers' term for the state police.

3 Sometimes referred to as a 'bat cat' – a device used to pull protestors from trees or other inaccessible places.

Epilogue: treading the thin blue line

1 The contract may rise to £3.5 billion, depending on how many other forces join the proposed scheme.
2 See the detailed account in the *Independent*, 6 March 2012 (Gillard and Flynn, 2012). Curiously, the material also reveals yet again the way officers facing potentially serious charges could retire early on health grounds and in this case relocate to Spain. One senior officer, John Yates, had dismissed the particular case with the memorable distinction between 'grass-eaters and meat-eaters'. Was he himself a 'grass-eater', a 'meat-eater' or more probably merely a 'champagne-drinker' in his relationship with the so-called 'Chipping Norton' political and media coterie in curtailing the phone-hacking inquiry?
3 The Leveson Inquiry was established in 2011 by the prime minister under the Inquiries Act to investigate the culture and ethics of the British press as well as the relationship between News International and senior officers in the Metropolitan Police. See Chapter 1.
4 There is much yet to be revealed over the role played by senior Metropolitan Police officers in the phone-hacking episode. But transparency is occurring only by pioneering journalism, not by legal imperatives.
5 *Guardian*, 16 March 2011.
6 See Dalrymple, 2006, for the social history of such relationships between elites.
7 Although G4S has already entered into discussions with two Scottish forces, so centralization may merely be the organizational pretext for the eventual outsourcing and privatization of police services on a scale not previously witnessed (Kelly, 2012).
8 It is debatable what effect PCSOs have, and they are just as likely to alarm the public by their presence as reassure them (see Johnston, 2007). Furthermore, Johnston (2007) remarks that whatever cost and efficiency savings have been gained by hiring PCSOs have been undermined by the amount of time and resources spent by sergeants and inspectors dealing with disciplinary and the day-to-day administrative tasks associated with their employment in the first place.
9 See BlueLight Global Solutions: www.bluelightglobalsolutions.com/

Bibliography

Aas, Katja F. (2007) *Globalisation and Crime*, London: Sage.

ACAS (2012) *Decision of the Police Arbitration Tribunal*, January. Available: www.polfed. org/FULL_AWARD-formatted_and_final_100112.pdf

ACPO (Association of Chief Police Officers) (1997) *Memorandum and Articles of Association*, Available: www.acpo.police.uk/documents/ArticlesofAssociation.pdf (accessed 22 January 2012).

Agozino, B., Bowling, B., St. Bernard, G. and Ward, E. (2009) 'Guns, crime and social order in the West Indies', *Criminology and Criminal Justice* 9(3): 287–305.

Amnesty International (2007) *Northern Ireland: Arming the World – the Manufacture, Trade and Transfer of Military, Security and Police Equipment and Services in Northern Ireland*, Amnesty International UK. Available: www.amnesty.org.uk/uploads/documents/doc_17903.pdf

Anderson, D. M. and Killingray, D. (1992) 'An orderly retreat? Policing and the end of empire', in D. M. Anderson and D. Killingray (eds), *Policing and Decolonization*, Manchester: Manchester University Press, 1–21.

Ashraf, M. A. (2007) 'The lessons of policing in Iraq: a personal perspective' *Policing: A Journal of Policy and Practice* 1(1): 102–10.

Ashby, David I. (2005) 'Policing neighbourhoods: axploring the geographiews of crime, policing and performance assessment', *Policing and Society* 15(4): 435–69.

Audit Commission (2010) *Sustaining Value for Money in the Police Service: Community Safety*. Audit Commission. July. Available: www.audit-commission.gov.uk/national studies/communitysafety/policevfm/Pages/default.aspx#downloads

Auld Report (2001) *Criminal Courts Review*. Available: www.justice.gov.uk/lawcommission/docs/lc324_High_Courts_Jurisdiction_report.pdf

Balbus, Isaac D. (1977) 'Commodity form and legal form: an essay on the relative autonomy of the law', *Law and Society Review* 11(3): 571–88.

Baldwin, Robert and Kinsey, Richard (1982) *Police Powers and Politics*, London: Quartet Books.

Bayley, C. A. (1993) 'Knowing the country: Empire and information in India', *Modern Asian Studies* 27(1): 3–43.

Bayley, David H. (1996) *Police for the Future*, Oxford: Oxford University Press.

— (2008) 'Post-conflict police reform: is Northern Ireland a model?', *Policing: A Journal of Policy and Practice* 2(2): 233–40.

Bayley, David and Perito, Robert (2011) *Police Corruption: What Past Scandals Teach About Current Challenges*, United States Institute for Peace, Special Report 294, November. Available: www.usip.org/files/resources/SR%20294.pdf

BBC News (2008) 'Chief speaks out on police racism', 5 October. Available: http://news.bbc.co.uk/1/hi/uk/7651605.stm

— (2009) 'Private "police" provoke concern', 14 November. Available: http://news.bbc.co.uk/1/hi/uk/8359948.stm

— (2010a) 'North Wales Police jobs warning ahead of cuts', 23 July. Available: www.bbc.co.uk/news/uk-wales-north-west-wales-10743070

— (2010b) 'Probation officers condemn cuts and threaten strikes', 7 October. Available: www.bbc.co.uk/news/uk-11486747

— (2010c) 'One in 10 police on sick leave or restricted duties', 4 December. Available: www.bbc.co.uk/news/uk-11917656

— (2010d) 'Coalition reveals list of 142 court closures', 14 December. Available: www.bbc.co.uk/news/uk-politics-11993436

— (2011a) 'Police dog bites costs forces thousands in compensation', 12 March. Available: www.bbc.co.uk/news/uk-12713723

— (2011b) 'Police service hated by government officers told', 17 May. Available: www.bbc.co.uk/news/uk-13425351

— (2011c) 'PSNI offer Land Rover help over London riots', 9 August. Available: www.bbc.co.uk/news/uk-northern-ireland-14468005

— (2011d) 'Thames Valley Police made no hunting prosecutions last year', 16 September. Available: www.bbc.co.uk/news/uk-england-14947650

— (2011e) 'Calls for stronger oversight as police avoid scrutiny', 31 October. Available: http://news.bbc.co.uk/panorama/hi/front_page/newsid_9624000/9624787.st

— (2012a) 'South Wales police officers gave Sean Wall, 17, cider', 16 January. Available: http://www.bbc.co.uk/wales-16460642

— (2012b) 'Metropolitan Police's speaking clock calls cost £35,000', 18 January. Available: http://www.bbc.co.uk/news/uk-england-london-16616790

Belfast Telegraph (2011) 'Security guards given police powers', 21 March. Available: www.belfasttelegraph.co.uk/news/local-national/uk/security-guards-given-police-powers-15120726.html

Berry, Jan (2009) *Reducing Bureaucracy in Policing*, full report. UK Home Office. Available: www.policesupers.com/uploads/news/reducing-bureaucracy-policing.pdf

Best, David and Eves, Kate (2004) *Following Fatal Pursuit: An Investigation of Serious Road Traffic Incidents (RTIs) Involving the Police, 2001–2002*, Police Complaints Authority. Available: http://webarchive.nationalarchives.gov.uk/20100908152737/ipcc.gov.uk/fatalpursuit2.pdf

Best, Jo (2010) 'Essex police awards £32m crime management deal', *Guardian*, 20 January. Available: www.guardian.co.uk/government-computing-network/2012/jan/20/essex-police-crime-management

Bhabha, Homi K. (1994a) *The Location of Culture*, London: Routledge.

— (1994b) 'Remembering Fanon: self, psyche and the colonial condition', in *Colonial Discourse and Post-colonial Theory: A Reader*, eds R. J. Patrick Williams and Laura Chrisman, New York: Columbia University Press.

Bittner, Egon (1994) 'Florence Nightingale in pursuit of Willy Sutton: a theory of the police', in H. Jacob (ed.), *The Potential for Reform of Criminal Justice*, Beverley Hills, CA: Sage.

Blair, Ian (2012) 'The police: the chance to modernise', *Guardian*, 4 March.

Blunkett, David (2009) *A People's Police Force; Police Accountability in the Modern Era*. Rt Hon David Blunkett MP. July. Accessed at: davidblunkett.typepad.com/files/a-peoples-police-force.pdf

Bowcott, Owen (2012) 'Kettling protestors is lawful appeal court rules', 19 January. Available: http://www.guardian.co.uk/uk/2012/jan/19/kettling-protestors-lawful-appeal-court

Bowcott, Owen and Dodd, Vikram (2011) 'Metropolitan Police drop action against the *Guardian*', 20 September. Available: http://www.guardian.co.uk/media/2011/sep/20/metropolitan-police-drop-action-guardian

Bowling, Ben (1999) 'The rise and fall of New York murder: zero tolerance or crack's decline?', *British Journal of Criminology* 39(4): 531–54.

Box, Steven (1987) *Recession, Crime and Punishment*, Basingstoke: Macmillan.

Boxell, James (2009) 'Unease as security group takes police roles', *Financial Times*, December 15. Available: www.ft.com/cms/s/0/c63abc5c-e917-11de-a756-00144feab49a.html#axzz1lts17N2Q

Boyd, Edward, Geoghegan, R. and Gibb, Blair (2011) *Cost of the Cops: Manpower and Deployment in Policing*. Policy Exchange. Available: www.policyexchange.org.uk/publications/item/cost-of-the-cops-manpower-and-deployment-in-policing?category_id=24

Bradford, B., Jackson, J. and Stanko, E. (2009) 'Contact and confidence: revisiting the impact of public encounters with the police', *Policing and Society* 19: 20–46.

Brasnett, Laura, Evans-Sinclair, Mahlon and Gottschalk, Eva (2010) *Understanding Overtime in the Police Service*, Home Office Productivity Unit, February. Available: http://library.npia.police.uk/docs/homeoffice/police-overtime.pdf

Brodeur, Jean-Paul (2005) 'Trotsky in blue: permanent policing reform', *Australian and New Zealand Journal of Criminology* 38(2): 254–67.

Brogden, Mike (1977) 'A police authority – the denial of conflict', *Sociological Review* 25(2): 325–49.

— (1982) *The Police: Autonomy and Consent*, London and New York: Academic Press.

— (1987a) 'The emergence of the police – the colonial dimension', *British Journal of Criminology* 27(4): 4–14.

— (1987b) 'An act to colonise the internal lands of the island: Empire and the origins of the professional police', *International Journal of the Sociology of Law* 15: 179–208.

— (1991) *On the Mersey Beat: Policing Liverpool Between the Wars*, Oxford: Oxford University Press.

— (1999) 'Community policing as cherry pie', in R. I. Mawby (ed.), *Policing Across the World. Issues for the Twenty-first Century*, London: UCL Press.

— (2000) 'Burning churches and victim surveys: the myth of Northern Ireland as low crime society', *Irish Journal of Sociology* 10: 27–48.

Brogden, Mike and Nijhar, Preet (1998) 'Corruption and the South African Police', *Crime, Law and Social Change* 30(1): 89–106. DOI: 10.1023/A:1008377601108.

— (2005) *Community Policing: National and International Models and Approaches*, Cullompton: Willan Publishing.

Brogden, Mike and Nijhar, Saranjit K. (2004) *Abuse of Adult Males in Intimate Partner Relationships in Northern Ireland*, Office of the First and Deputy First Minster, Northern Ireland Assembly. March. Available: www.ofmdfmni.gov.uk/index/equality/equalityresearch/research-publications/publication-az.htm

Brogden, Mike and Shearing, Clifford (1993) *Policing for a New South Africa*, London: Routledge.

Brogden, Mike, Jefferson, Tony and Walklate, Sandra (1988) *Introducing Policework*, London: HarperCollins.

Button, Mark (2002) 'Specialised police units', ch. 5 of *Private Policing*, Cullompton: Willan Publishing.

Cain, Maureen (1979) 'Trends in the sociology of police work', *International Journal of the Sociology of Law* 7(2): 143–67.

— (2000) 'Orientalism, Occidentalism and the sociology of crime', *British Journal of Criminology* 40(2): 239–60.

Canter, D. (2000) 'Offender profiling and criminal differentiation', *Journal of Legal and Criminological Psychology* 5(1): 23–46.

Cashmore, Ellis (2002) 'Behind the window dressing: ethnic minority police perspectives on cultural diversity', *Journal of Ethnic and Migration Studies* 28(2): 327–41.

Cemlyn, Sarah, Greenfields, Margaret, Burnett, Sally, Matthews, Zoe and Whitwell, Chris (2009) *Inequalities Experienced by Gypsy and Traveller Communities: A Review*, Equality and Human Rights Commission. Research Report 12. Available: www.equalityhumanrights.com/uploaded_files/research/12inequalities_experienced_by_gypsy_and_traveller_communities_a_review.pdf

Chainey, Spencer and Thompson, Lisa (eds) (2008) *Crime Mapping Case Studies: Practice and Research*, Oxford: Wiley-Blackwell.

Chambliss, William (1964) 'A sociological analysis of the law of vagrancy', *Social Problems* 12(1): 67–77.

Chan, Janet (1996) 'Changing police culture', *British Journal of Criminology* 36(1): 109–34.

Churcher, Sharon and Verkaik, Robert (2011) 'Cameron's U.S. supercop advisor quit over inquiry into free holidays from billionaire tycoon', *Mail Online*, 21 August. Available: www.dailymail.co.uk/news/article-2028388/Bill-Bratton-Camerons-US-Supercop-advisor-quit-inquiry-free-holidays-billionaire-tycoon.html (accessed 7 February 2012).

Clarke, Ronald. V. and Mayhew, Pat (1988) 'The British Gas suicide story and its criminological implications', *Crime and Justice* 10: 79–116.

Cohen, Stanley (1985) *Visions of Social Control*, New York: Wiley-Blackwell.

Committee of Inquiry on the Police (Edmund-Davies Committee) (1978) Available: http://discovery.nationalarchives.gov.uk/SearchUI/Details.mvc/Collection/?iAID=3033

Copson, G. and Holloway, K. (1997) 'Offender profiling', Paper presented to the annual conference of the Division of Criminological and Legal Psychology. British Psychological Society (October).

Cowan, Dave and Lomax, Delia (2003) 'Policing unauthorized camping', *Journal of Law and Society* 30(June): 283–308.

Cowie, I. (2010) 'Arresting the cost of police pensions', *Daily Telegraph*, 6 July. Available: http://blogs.telegraph.co.uk/finance/ianmcowie/100006804/arresting-cost-of-police-pensions-and-five-steps-to-boost-yours/

Coxhead, John (2005) *'Moving Forward'. How the Gypsy and Traveller Communities Can Be More Engaged to Improve Policing Performance*, London: Home Office.

— (2007) *The Last Bastion of Racism? Gypsies, Travellers and Policing*, Stoke-on-Trent: Trentham Books.

Crawford, Adam (1997) *The Local Governance of Crime: Appeals to Community and Partnerships*, Oxford: Clarendon Press.

— (2006a) 'Networked governance and the post-regulatory state? Steering, rowing and anchoring the provision of policing and security', *Theoretical Criminology* 10(4): 449–79.

— (2006b) 'Policing and security as "club goods": the new enclosures?' In J. Wood and B. Dupont (eds), *Democracy, Society and the Governance of Security*, Cambridge: Cambridge University Press, 111–38.

Crawford, Adam and Lister, Stuart (2004) *The Extended Policing Family: Visible Patrols in Residential Areas*, Joseph Rowntree Foundation / Centre for Criminal Justice Studies, University of Leeds.

Crawley, Heaven (2004) 'Britain as the Deep South', *Guardian*, 20 January. Available: www.guardian.co.uk/politics/2004/jan/20/immigrationpolicy.race

Crooks, Jill (2011) 'Register lists the gifts given to police', *Gazette and Herald*, 1 October. Available: www.gazetteandherald.co.uk/news/9274260.Bobbies_get_a_bit_of_bubbly/

Cunneen, Chris (2011) 'Postcolonial perspectives for criminology', in Mary Bosworth and Carolyn Hoyle (eds), *What is Criminology?* Oxford: Oxford University Press, ch. 17.

Daily Mail (2009) 'Scotland Yard chief quits with £80,000 pension . . . to take up £120,000 job with quango', 20 January. Available: http://www.dailymail.co.uk/news/article-1123704/Scotland-Yard-chief-quits-80-000-pension-120-000-job-quango.html

— (2010) 'Nearly 10% of police are off sick or on limited duty but thousands still receive full pay', 4 December. Available: www.dailymail.co.uk/news/article-1335612/Nearly-10-police-sick-limited-duty-thousands-receive-pay.html

— (2011) 'Disgraced police chief who tried to help a relative join his force gets £200,000 payout', 1 November. Available: http://www.dailymail.co.uk/news/article-2056010/Disgraced-police-chief-tried-help-relative-join-force-gets-200-000-pay-out.html

Dalrymple, William (2006) *The Last Mughal: The Fall of a Dynasty*, London: Bloomsbury.

Davies, Caroline (2010) 'Deaths in police custody since 1998: 333; officers convicted: none', *Guardian*, 3 December. Available: www.guardian.co.uk/uk/2010/dec/03/deaths-police-custody-officers-convicted (accessed 7 February 2012).

Davis, Mike (1990) *City of Quartz: Excavating the Future in Los Angeles*, London: Verso. New edn 2001, Berkeley, CA: Odonian Press.

— (2002) *Late Victorian Holocausts*, London: Verso.

Davis, Rowenna (2010) 'Private security the police can't provide', *Guardian*, 28 July. Available: www.guardian.co.uk/society/2010/jul/28/private-security-companies-police-housing-estates

Dawson, Robert (2000) *Crime and Prejudice: Traditional Travellers*, Matlock: Robert Dawson.

— (2006) *Police Stop and Search of Travellers: A National Survey*, Matlock: Derbyshire Gypsy Liaison Group.

Deans, Jason (2012) 'Christopher Jefferies calls for inquiry into police leaks to newspapers', *Guardian*, 25 January. Available: www.guardian.co.uk/media/2012/jan/25/christopher-jefferies-police-leaks

Deloitte (2007) *Research into the Financial Cost of the Northern Ireland Divide*, London: Deloitte MCS Limited, April.

Desborough Committee of Inquiry and Report into the Police Service (1919) London: HMSO.

Dixon, David (1997) *Law in Policing: Legal Regulation and Police Practices*, Oxford: Clarendon Press.

— (1999) 'Beyond zero tolerance', Australian Institute of Criminology. Available: www.aic.gov.au/criminal_justice_system/policing/~/media/conferences/outlook99/dixon.ashx

Dodd, Vikram (2011) 'Former Met police detectives cleared as retrial collapses', *Guardian*, 19 October. Available: http://www.guardian.co.uk/uk/2011/oct/19/met-police-detectives-cleared-retrial

Dodd, Vikram and Malik, Shiv (2012) 'Forensics blunder "may endanger convictions"', *Guardian*, 8 March.

Dubber, Markus Dirk (2005) *The Police Power: Patriarchy and the Foundations of American Government*, New York: Columbia University Press.

Edinburgh Review (1852) Volume XCVL: July–October.

Edwards, Richard (2010) 'Suspended officers cost taxpayer £53 million in past five years', *The Telegraph*, 8 February. Available: www.telegraph.co.uk/news/uknews/law-and-order/7352404/Suspended-police-officers-cost-taxpayer-53-million-in-past-five-years.html

Ellison, Graham (2007) 'A Blueprint for democratic policing anywhere in the world? Police reform, political transition, and conflict resolution in Northern Ireland', *Police Quarterly* 10(3): 243–69.

Ellison, Graham and O'Rawe, Mary (2010) 'Security governance in transition: the compartmentalizing, crowding out and corralling of policing and security in Northern Ireland', *Theoretical Criminology* 14(1): 31–57.

Ellison, Graham and O'Reilly, Conor (2008a) 'From Empire to Iraq and the War on Terror: the transplantation and commodification of the (Northern) Irish policing experience', *Police Quarterly* 11(4): 395–426.

—— (2008b) 'Ulster's policing goes global: the police reform process in Northern Ireland and the creation of a global brand', *Crime, Law and Social Change* 50(4–5): 331–51.

Ellison, Graham and Pino, Nathan (2012) *Globalization, Police Reform and Development: Doing it the Western Way*, Basingstoke: Palgrave Macmillan.

Emsley, Clive (1991) *The English Police: A Political and Social History*, London and New York: Longman.

—— (1996) 'Albion's fatal attractions: reflections upon the history of crime in England', in C. Emsley and L. A. Knafla (eds), *Crime History and Histories of Crime: Studies in the Historiography of Crime and Criminal Justice in Modern History*, Westport, CT: Greenwood Press.

—— (2009) *The Great British Bobby: A History of British Policing from 1829 to the Present*, London: Quercus Publishing.

—— (2012) 'Marketing the brand: exporting British police models 1829–1950', *Policing: A Journal of Policy and Practice*, DOI: 10.1093/police/par061. 6 January, pp. 1–12.

Equality and Human Rights Commission (2010) *Stop and Think: A Critical Review of the Use of Stop and Search Powers in England and Wales*. Available:www.equalityhumanrights.com/uploaded_files/raceinbritain/ehrc_stop_and_search_report.pdf

Essex Chronicle (2011) '5,000 Gypsies move in on village of 414', 28 July. Available: http://www.thisistotalessex.co.uk/search/search.html?searchPhrase=gypsies&where=&searchType=

Evans, Martin (2011) 'Phone hacking: Sir Hugh Orde concerned scandal has damaged public confidence in the police', *Telegraph*, 19 July. Available: www.telegraph.co.uk/news/uknews/phone-hacking/8646834/Phone-hacking-Sir-Hugh-Orde-concerned-scandal-has-damaged-public-confidence-in-police.html

Evans, Rob and Lewis, Paul (2011a) 'Undercover police officer unlawfully spied on climate activists, judges rule', *Guardian*, 20 July. Available: www.guardian.co.uk/environment/2011/jul/20/police-spy-on-climate-activists-unlawful

—— (2011b) 'Progressive academic Bob Lambert is former police spy', *Guardian*, 16 October. Available: www.guardian.co.uk/uk/2011/oct/16/academic-bob-lambert-former-police-spy

—— (2011c) 'Met chief says officer' use of fake identities in court was not illegal', 27 October. Available: http://www.guardian.co.uk/uk/2011/oct/27/met-police-activists-fake-identities

— (2011d) 'Former lovers of undercover officers sue police over deceit', *Guardian*, 16 December. Available: www.guardian.co.uk/uk/2011/dec/16/lovers-undercover-officers-sue-police

Fallon, Amy (2011) 'Police officers escaping punishment by resigning', *Guardian*, 31 October. Available: www.guardian.co.uk/uk/2011/oct/31/police-officers-escaping-punishment-resigning-panorama

Filkin, E. (2012) *The Ethical Issues Arising from the Relationship Between the Police and Media*, January. London: Metropolitan Police.

Fiske, J. (1990) *Introduction to Communication Studies*, London: Routledge.

Flanagan, Ronnie (2006) *An Assessment of the UK's Contribution to Security Sector Reform (Policing) in Iraq*, Declassified document to Chilcot Inquiry. Available:www.iraqinquiry.org.uk/media/46210/060131-Flanagan-HMIC-Assessment-UK-contribution-security-sector-reform.pdf

— (2007) *The Review of Policing: Interim Report*. London: Home Office. Available: www.polfed.org/Review_of_Policing_Interim_Report.pdf

— (2008) *The Review of Policing: Final Report*, London: Home Office. Available: www.polfed.org/Review_of_Policing_Final_Report.pdf

France, Anatole (1894) *Le Lys Rouge* (The Red Lily), ch. 7.

Gardner, Stephen and Standaert, Mike (n.d.) 'Estonia and Belarus: branding the Old Bloc', *Brandchannel*, Available: www.brandchannel.com/features_effect.asp?pf_id=146 (accessed 24 January 2012).

Gash, Tom (2011) 'Police staff and poor areas lose out in police funding shake-up', Available: http://tomgash.com/?p=94

Gatrell, V. A. C. (1990) 'Crime, authority and the policeman-state', in F. M. L. Thompson (ed.), *The Cambridge Social History of Britain, 1750–1950, Vol. 3: Social Agencies and Institutions*, Cambridge: Cambridge University Press, 243–310.

Gentleman, Amelia (2011) 'Police force's colour-coded redundancy letters give staff the blues', *Guardian*, 11 January. Available: www.guardian.co.uk/uk/2011/jan/11/police-force-colour-coded-redundancy

Ghandi, Leela (1998) *Postcolonial Theory: A Critical Introduction*, New York: Columbia University Press.

Gill, Peter (1987) 'Clearing up crime: "the big con"', *Journal of Law and Society* 14(2): 254–65.

Gillard, Michael and Flynn, Laurie (2012) 'The copper, the Lawrence killer's father, and secret police files that expose a "corrupt relationship"', *Independent*, Tuesday 6 March.

Glidewell Report (1998) '*The Review of the Crown Prosecution Service*. Summary of the main report with the conclusions and recommendations', Cm. 3972. Available: www.archive.official-documents.co.uk/document/cm39/3972/3972.htm

Goldsmith, Andrew (2010) 'Policing's new visibility', *Theoretical Criminology* 50(5): 914–34.

Goldsmith, Andrew and Sheptycki, James (eds) (2007) *Crafting Transnational Policing: Police Capacity Building and Global Police Reform*, Oxford: Hart.

Goldson, Barry (2002) 'New Labour, social justice and children: political calculation and the deserving-undeserving schism', *British Journal of Social Work* 32(6): 683–95.

— (2005) 'Youth policy: bullying the New Labour way', *Socialist Review*, October. Available: www.socialistreview.org.uk/article.php?articlenumber=9543

Grabosky, Peter (1998) 'Crime and technology in the global village', paper presented at the conference on 'Internet Crime', Melbourne, 16–17 February. Australian Institute of

Criminology. Available: www.aic.gov.au/crime_types/cybercrime/~/media/conferences/internet/grabosky.ashx

Gramsci, Antonio (1971) *Selections from the Prison Notebooks*, London: Lawrence and Wishart.

Greenfields, Margaret and Home, Robert (2006) 'Assessing Gypsies' and Travellers' needs: partnership working and "The Cambridge Project"', *Romani Studies* 16(2): 105–31. Available: http://liverpool.metapress.com/content/22834t6344t5mj15/

Greenwood, Chris (2011a) 'Travellers who kept, beat and starved slaves were organised crime ring running the family business', *Mail Online*, 12 September. Available: http://www.dailymail.co.uk/news/article-2036153/Bedfordshire-slavery-ring-Travellers-organised-crime-ring-running-family-business.html

—— (2011b) 'Hundreds of police officers resigning on the quiet despite admitting serious offences', *Mail Online*, 31 October. Available: http://www.dailymail.co.uk/news/article-2055682/Hundreds-police-officers-resigning-quiet-despite-admitting-offences.html

Griffiths, Chloe (2010) 'Merseyside police officer from Southport found guilty of being part of plot to sell cannabis seized in drug raids', *Liverpool Echo*, 23 January. Available: www.liverpoolecho.co.uk/liverpool-news/local-news/2010/01/23/merseyside-police-officer-from-southport-found-guilty-of-being-part-of-plot-to-sell-cannabis-seized-in-drug-raids-100252-25665723/

The *Guardian* Letters (2011) 'A social deficit behind the riots', 13 September. Available http://www.guardian.co.uk/2011/sep13/social-deficit-behind-riots

The *Guardian* (2012) 'Police forces confess 944 officers have a criminal record' 2 January. Available: http://www.guardian.co.uk/uk/2012/jan/02/police-944-officers-criminal-record

Hall, Macer (2002) 'Police hire private firm for crime scene duty', *Telegraph*, 3 March. Available: www.telegraph.co.uk/news/uknews/1386602/Police-hire-private-firm-for-crime-scene-duty.html

Hall, Stuart, Critcher, Chas, Jefferson, Tony, Clarke, John and Roberts, B. (1978) *Policing the Crisis: Mugging, the State and Law and Order*, New York: Holmes and Meier.

Hanman, Natalie (2010) 'CPS cuts will put justice for the vulnerable at risk, says Law Society', *Guardian*, 15 July. Available: www.guardian.co.uk/law/2010/jul/15/crown-prosecution-service-law-society-cuts

Harris, John (2012) 'New police privatisation was recast as common sense', *Guardian*, 5 March.

Hay, Douglas and Craven, Paul (eds) (2004) *Masters, Servants and Magistrates in Britain and the Empire, 1562–1955*, Chapel Hill: University of North Carolina Press.

Health and Safety Executive (HSE) (2007) *Managing Sickness Absence in the Police Service*, Institute for Employment Studies. Available: www.hse.gov.uk/research/rrpdf/rr582.pdf

Henderson, Maryta (2010) 'Thousands of "sicknote" police still on full pay', 4 December.

Herbert, Joanna (2008) *Negotiating Boundaries in the City: Migration, Ethnicity and Gender in Britain*, Aldershot: Ashgate.

Hills, A. (2009) 'The possibility of transnational policing', *Policing and Society* 19(3): 300–17.

Hillyard, Paddy and Tombs, Steve (2007) 'From "crime" to social harm', *Crime, Law and Social Change*, 48: 9–25.

HMIC (2010a) *Learning Lessons: An Overview of the First Ten Joint Inspections*. HMIC and the Audit Commission. Available: www.hmic.gov.uk/media/learning-lessons-20100314.pdf

— (2010b) *Anti-Social Behaviour Inspection Findings*. Available: www.hmic.gov.uk/media/anti-social-behaviour-inspection-findings-20100923.pdf

— (2011a) *Without Fear or Favour: A Review of Police Relationships*. December. Available: www.hmic.gov.uk/media/a-review-of-police-relationships-20111213.pdf

— (2011b) *Demanding Times: The Front-line and Police Visibility*. Available: www.hmic.gov.uk

HMSO (1995) Posen Report, Review of Police Core and Ancillary Tasks.

Hobsbawm, E. J. (1952) 'Economic movements and some social movements since 1880', *The Economic History Review* 5: 1–25. DOI: 10.1111/j.1468-0289.1952.tb01448.

Home Affairs Committee (2011) *Police Use of Tasers*, Fifth Report. Available: www.publications.parliament.uk/pa/cm201011/cmselect/cmhaff/646/64602.htm

Home Office (2001) *Policing a New Century: A Blueprint for Reform*, cm 5326. London: Home Office.

— (2004) *Overseas Deployment Manual for Police Officers*, London: Home Office.

— (2008a) *Green Paper: From the Neighbourhood to the National: Policing Our Communities Together*, London: Home Office. Available: http://files.homeoffice.gov.uk

— (2008b) *Review of Police Injury Benefits: Government Proposals*, London: Home Office. Available: www.nypolfed.org.uk/assets/uploads/PDFs/injurybenefits.pdf

Home Office (2009) *Green Paper: Engaging Communities in Criminal Justice*, London: Home Office. Available: www.official-documents.gov.uk/document/cm75/7583/7583.pdf

House of Commons Science and Technology Committee (2011) *The Forensic Science Service*, Seventh Report of Session 2010–12, Volume 1. 22nd June. Available: www.publications.parliament.uk/pa/cm201012/cmselect/cmsctech/855/855.pdf

Hoyle, Carolyn and Noguera, Stephen (2008) 'Supporting young offenders through restorative justice: parents as (in)appropriate adults', *British Journal of Community Justice* 6(3): 67–85.

Hughes, Gordon (2002) 'Crime and disorder reduction partnerships', in Gordon Hughes, Eugene McLaughlin and John Muncie (eds), *Crime Prevention and Community Safety: New Directions*, London and Thousand Oaks, CA: Sage Publications.

Hughes, Mark (2009) 'Police pay – the great overtime bonanza', *Independent*, 17 August. Available: www.independent.co.uk/news/uk/home-news/police-pay-ndash-the-great-overtime-bonanza-1773086.html

— (2011) 'We don't know what the "frontline" is, Home Office admits', *Telegraph*, 15 March. Available: www.telegraph.co.uk/news/8383846/We-dont-know-what-the-frontline-is-Home-Office-admits.html

ICP (Independent Commission on Policing) (1999) *A New Beginning: Policing in Northern Ireland*, Belfast: Northern Ireland Office. Available: http://cain.ulst.ac.uk/issues/police/patten/patten99.pdf

Ignatieff, Michael (1996) 'Ideology as history: a look at the way some of the English police historians look at the police', in Robert Reiner (ed.), *Policing. Volume 1. Cops, Crime and Control: Analysing the Police Function*, Aldershot: Ashgate.

The Independent (2012) 'Rate of deaths in custody is higher than officials admit', 31 January. Available: http://www.independent.co.uk/news/uk/crime/rate-of-deaths-in-custody-is-higher-than-officials-admit-6297270.html

Independent Police Complaints Commission (IPCC) (2011a) *Corruption in the Police Service in England and Wales*. First Report. IPCC. Available: www.official-documents.gov.uk/document/other/9780108510991/9780108510991.pdf

— (2011b) *Deaths in Custody Report*. Available: www.ipcc.gov.uk/en/Pages/deathscustodystudy.aspx

— (2011c) *Police Complaints: Statistics for England and Wales 2009/10*, February.

James, Richard (2012) 'Ian Hislop rejects calls for statutory regulation of the press', *Metro*, 17 January. Available: www.metro.co.uk/news/887633-leveson-inquiry-ian-hislop-rejects-calls-for-statutory-regulation-of-the-press

James, Zoe (2007) 'Policing marginal spaces: controlling Gypsies and Travellers', *Criminology and Criminal Justice* 7(4): 367–89.

James, Zoe and Richardson, J. (2006) 'Controlling accommodation: policing Gypsies and Travellers', in A. Dearling, T. Newburn and P. Somerville (eds), *Supporting Safer Communities: Housing, Crime and Neighbourhoods*, Coventry: Chartered Institute of Housing, Policy and Practice Series.

Jefferson, Tony and Grimshaw, Roger (1984) *Controlling The Constable: Police Accountability in England and Wales*, London: Frederick Muller/The Cobden Trust.

Johnson, Wesley and Morgan, Tom (2011) 'All domestic murders to be reviewed', *Independent*, 13 April. Available: www.independent.co.uk/news/uk/crime/all-domestic-murders-to-be-reviewed-2267096.html

Johnston, Les and Shearing, Clifford. D. (2003) *Governing Security: Explorations in Policing and Justice*, London: Routledge.

Johnston, Philip (2007) 'Thatcher kept the police onside', *Daily Telegraph*, 7 December. Available: http://blogs.telegraph.co.uk/news/philipjohnston/3674891/Thatcher_kept_the_police_onside/

Jones, Owen (2011) *Chavs: The Demonization of the Working Class*, London: Verso.

Jones, Stephen (1985) 'The Police and Criminal Evidence Act 1984', *The Modern Law Review* 48(6): 679–93.

Jones, Trevor and Newburn, Tim (2006) *Policy Transfer and Criminal Justice*, Milton Keynes: Open University Press.

Jones, Trevor and Van Sluis, Arnie (2009) 'National standards, local delivery: police reform in England and Wales', *German Policy Studies* 5(2): 117–44.

Kelly, Mel (2012) 'Police, magistrates and prisons by G4S? Is this what the British people want?' *Open Democracy*. Available: www.opendemocracy.net/ourkingdom/mel-kelly/police-magistrates-and-prisons-by-g4s-is-this-what-british-people-want

Kempa, M. (2010) 'Academic engagement of international policing assistance: putting Foucauldian geneology to practical use 1', *Canadian Journal of Criminology and Criminal Justice* 52(3): 271–83.

Klein, N. (2007) *The Shock Doctrine*, New York: Metropolitan Books.

Kleinig, J. (1996) *The Ethics of Policing*, New York: Cambridge University Press.

Kocsis, Richard. N. (2006) *Criminal Profiling: Principles and Practice*, Totowa, NJ: Humana Press.

Körlin, Jenny, Alexanderson, Kristina and Svedberg, Pia (2009) 'Sickness absence among women and men in the police: a systematic literature review', *Scandinavian Journal of Public Health* 37(3): 310–19.

Laja, Sade (2011) 'Metropolitan Police tenders for custody system', *Guardian*, 27 May. Available: www.guardian.co.uk/government-computing-network/2011/may/27/metropolitan-police-authority-tender-custody-system

Lakhani, Nina (2011a) 'Alarm at private police operating beyond the law: outsourced officers beyond reach of watchdog', *Independent*, 24 October. Available: www.independent.co.uk/news/uk/home-news/alarm-at-private-police-operating-beyond-the-law-2375094.html

— (2011b) 'CSI chief condemns forensic cuts', *Independent*, 9 January. Available: www.independent.co.uk/news/uk/crime/csi-chief-condemns-forensic-cuts-2179744.html

Lane, Edwin (2010) 'The rise of the UK's private security companies', BBC News, 2 November. Available: www.bbc.co.uk/news/business-11521579

Lavender, Jane (2004) 'Allowing top cop in £5m trial collapse to retire ruled unlawful', 8 December. Available: http://menmedia.co.uk/stockportexpress/news/s/322294_allowing_top_cop_in_5m_trial_collapse_to_retire_ruled_unlawful

Laville, Sandra (2009) 'Former royal protection officer guilty of £3m scam', *Guardian*, 17 July. Available: www.guardian.co.uk/uk/2009/jul/17/royal-protection-officer-fraud-guilty

— (2012) 'Cardiff Three corruption case fiasco', *Guardian*, 27 January. Available: www.guardian.co.uk/uk/crime-and-justice-blog/2012/jan/27/police-corruption-case-fiasco

Lawless, Christopher J. (2011) 'Policing markets: The contested shaping of neo-liberal forensic science', *British Journal of Criminology* 51(04): 671–89.

Lea, John (1992) 'Left realism: a framework for the analysis of crime', in Jock Young and Roger Matthews (eds), *Rethinking Criminology: The Realist Debate*, London: Sage.

— (2004) 'Courts and prosecution in nineteenth century Britain'. Available: www.bunker8.pwp.blueyonder.co.uk/history/36807.htm

— (2006) 'The prosecution of crime', Available: www.bunker8.pwp.blueyonder.co.uk/cjs/26904.htm

Lea, John and Young, Jock (1993) *What Is To Be Done About Law and Order*, revised edn, London: Pluto Press.

Leach, Ben (2009) 'Gypsies trash £5m police helicopter', *The Telegraph*, 14 May. Available: http://www.telegraph.co.uk/news/uknews/5322574/Gypsies-trash-5million-police-helicopter.html

Lewis, Paul (2010) 'CCTV aimed at Muslim areas in Birmingham to be dismantled', *Guardian*, 25 October. Available: www.guardian.co.uk/uk/2010/oct/25/birmingham-cctv-muslim-areas-surveillance

— (2011) 'Ian Tomlinson death: IPCC rules Met officer "reckless" in conduct', *Guardian*, 9 May. Available: www.guardian.co.uk/uk/2011/may/09/ian-tomlinson-death

Loader, Ian (1997) 'Policing and symbolic power: questions of the social', *British Journal of Sociology* 48(1): 1–18.

— (1999) 'Consumer culture and the commodification of policing and security', *Sociology* 33(2): 373–92.

Loader, Ian and Mulcahy, Aogán (2001) 'The power of legitimate naming', *British Journal of Criminology* 41(2): 252–65.

— (2003) *Policing and the Condition of England: Memory, Politics and Culture*, Oxford: Oxford University Press.

Loader, Ian and Walker, Neil (2007) *Civilizing Security*, Cambridge: Cambridge University Press.

Local Government Chronicle (2012) 'Inside out – redesigning the truncheon', 2 February. Available: www.lgcplus.com/opinion/inside-out-redesigning-the-truncheon/5040628. article

Lord Denning's Report (1963) 25 September. Cmnd 2152. London: HMSO.

Loveday, B. (2006) *Size Isn't Everything: Restructuring Policing in England and Wales*, London: Policy Exchange.

Lustgarten, L. (1986) *The Governance of Police*, London: Sweet and Maxwell.

Macpherson, Sir William (1999) *Report of the Inquiry into the Death of Stephen Lawrence*. Cm 4262-I. London: HMSO.

Maguire, Mike (2002) 'Regulating the police station: the case of the Police and Criminal Evidence Act 1984', in M. McConville and G. Wilson (eds), *Handbook of Criminal Procedure*, Oxford: Oxford University Press.

Malik, Shiv (2011) 'Occupy London's anger over police "terrorism" document', *Guardian*, 5 December. Available: www.guardian.co.uk/uk/2011/dec/05/occupy-london-police-terrorism-document

Mann, Steve, Nolan, Jason and Wellman, Barry (2003) 'Sousveillance: inventing and using wearable computing devices for data collection in surveillance environments', *Surveillance and Society* 1(3): 331–55.

Manning, Peter K. (1992) *Organisational Communication*, Berlin and New York: Aldine de Gruyter.

— (2010) *Democratic Policing in a Changing World*, London: Paradigm Publishers.

Marenin, Otwin (2007) 'Implementing police reforms: the role of the transnational policy community', in Andrew Goldsmith and James W. Sheptycki (eds), *Crafting Transnational Policing: Police Capacity-Building and Global Policing Reform*, Oxford: Hart Publishing, 177–203.

Marx, Gary (1992) 'Some reflections on undercover: recent developments and enduring issues', *Crime, Law and Social Change* 18(1–2): 193–217.

Matthews, Roger (1988) *Informal Justice*, London: Sage.

May, Tiggey, Duffy, Martin, Warburton, Hamish and Hough, Mike (2007) *Policing Cannabis as a Class C drug: An Arresting Change?* Joseph Rowntree Foundation. Available: www.jrf.org.uk/system/files/1961-policing-cannabis-classc.pdf

Mayhew, Henry (1865) (reprint) *London Labour and the London Poor: The Condition and Earnings of Those That Will Work, Cannot Work, and Will Not Work*, 4 vols, London: Charles Griffin and Company.

McAdam, Noel (2008) 'Foreign post for Sir Ronnie Flanagan', *Belfast Telegraph*, 17 October. Available: www.belfasttelegraph.co.uk/news/local-national/foreign-post-for-sir-ronnie-flanagan-14006978.html

McBarnet, Doreen (1981) *Conviction*, London: Macmillan.

McConville, Mike, Sanders, Andrew and Leng, Roger (1991) *The Case for the Prosecution*, London: Routledge.

McLaughlin, Eugene (2005) 'Forcing the issue: New Labour, New Localism and the democratic renewal of police accountability', *Howard Journal of Criminal Justice* 44(5): 473–89.

— (2007) *The New Policing*, London: Sage.

McLeod, Gordon (2002) 'From urban entrepreneurialism to a "revanchist city"? on the spatial injustices of Glasgow's renaissance', *Antipode* 34(3): 602–24.

Meek, Rosie (2007) 'The experiences of a young Gypsy-Traveller in the transition from custody to community: an interpretative phenomenological analysis', *Legal and Criminological Psychology* 12(1): 133–47.

Meikle, James (2012) 'Olympics counter-terrorism training offered to London burger vendors', *Guardian*, Thursday 19 January. Available: www.guardian.co.uk/uk/2012/jan/19/london-olympic-street-vendors-counter-terrorism (accessed 22 January 2012).

Meltzer, Tom (2011) 'A farewell to ASBOs', *Guardian*, 4 January.

Metropolitan Police (2007a) *Detections and Case Disposal Policy*, Criminal Justice Strategic Directorate, London Metropolitan Police. Available: www.met.police.uk/foi/pdfs/policies/detections_and_case_disposal_policy.pdf

— (2007b) *Crime Screening and Secondary Investigation within the Metropolitan Police Service*. Territorial Policing Crime Operations Strategic Committee, October. Available: www.met.police.uk/foi/pdfs/policies/crime_screening_policy.pdf

Mills, Helen, Silvestri, Arianna and Grimshaw, Roger (2010) *Police Expenditure 1999–2009*. Centre for Crime and Justice Studies/The Hadley Trust. June. Available: www.crimeandjustice.org.uk/opus1779/Police_expenditure_1999-2009.pdf

Milne, Seumas (2004) *The Enemy Within: Thatcher's Secret War Against The Miners*, London: Verso.

Monbiot, George (1995) 'Britain's Cultural Cleansing', *Guardian*, 15 May. Available: www.monbiot.com/1995/05/15/britains-cultural-cleansing/

— (2012) 'Only a maximum wage can end the great pay robbery', *Guardian*, 23 January. Available: www.guardian.co.uk/commentisfree/2012/jan/23/george-monbiot-executive-pay-robbery

Morgan, R. and Newburn, T. (1997) *The Future of Policing*, Oxford: Clarendon Press.

Morton, James (1994) *Bent Coppers: A Survey of Police Corruption*, London: Time Warner Paperbacks.

Mosley, Layna (2007) 'The political economy of globalisation', in David Held and Anthony McGrew (eds), *Globalisation Theory: Approaches and Controversies*, Malden, MA: Polity Press, 106–25.

Mulcahy, Aogán (2006) *Policing Northern Ireland: Conflict, Legitimacy and Reform*, Cullompton: Willan Publishing.

— (2012) 'Alright in their own place': policing and the spatial regulation of Irish Travellers', *Criminology and Criminal Justice*, 9 January. DOI: 10.1177/1748895811431849.

National Audit Office (2011) *Crown Prosecution Service: The Introduction of the Streamlined Process*. 2nd November. Available: www.nao.org.uk/publications/1012/cps_streamlined_process.aspx

National DNA Database (2009) *Annual Report*. National Policing Improvement Agency (NIPA) Available: www.npia.police.uk/en/docs/NDNAD07-09-LR.pdf

Neocleous, Mark (2000) *The Fabrication of Social Order: A Critical Theory of Police Power*, London: Pluto.

Newburn, Tim (1999) *Understanding and Preventing Police Corruption: Lessons from the Literature*. Home Office. Police Research Series, Paper 110. Available: www.popcenter.org/problems/street_prostitution/PDFs/Newburn_1999.pdf

— (2011) 'Reading the riots: the riots and policing's sacred cow', *Guardian*, 6 December. Available: www.guardian.co.uk/commentisfree/2011/dec/06/policing-sacred-cow-reading-riots

Newburn, Tim, Jones, Trevor and Smith, David (1994) *Democracy and Policing*, London: Policy Studies Institute.

News Letter (2011) 'College could train FBI staff', 20 December. Available: http://www.newsletter.co.uk/news/local/college-could-train-fbi-staff-1-3374385

Nijhar, Preeti (2009) *Law and Imperialism: Criminality and Constitution in Colonial India and Victorian England*, London: Pickering and Chatto.

Nuffield Trust (2011) *NHS Reforms: Survey of Public Opinion*. 9 March. Available: www.nuffieldtrust.org.uk/talks/slideshows/nhs-reforms-survey-public-opinion (accessed 23 January 2012).

Oaksey, Lord (1949) *Police Conditions of Service* (Oaksey Report), London: Home Office. HC Deb 23 1949 vol 466 cc434–35. Available: http://hansard.millbanksystems.com/commons/1949/jun/23/oaksey-report-findings

Oldham, Jeanette (2011) *West Midlands Police Counter-Terrorism Unit Hires Private Contractors to Cover for Cuts in Staffing*. 4 September. Available: www.birminghammail.net/news/top-stories/2011/09/04/west-midlands-police-counter-terrorism-unit-hires-private-contractors-to-cover-for-cuts-in-staffing-97319-29362007/#ixzz1ltqjWN4W

O'Leary, Brendan (2000) 'Protecting human rights and securing peace in Northern Ireland: the vital role of police reform', *Hearing Before the Commission on Security and*

Co-Operation in Europe (CSCE), 106th Congress, Second Session, 22 September. Washington, DC: CSCE.

O'Reilly, Conor (2010) 'The transnational security consultancy industry: a case of state-corporate symbiosis', *Theoretical Criminology* 14(2): 183–210.

— (2011), 'From kidnaps to contagious diseases': elite rescue and the strategic expansion of the transnational security consultancy industry', *International Political Sociology* 5(2): 178–97.

O'Reilly, Conor and Ellison, Graham (2006) '"Eye spy, private high": reconceptualising high policing theory', *British Journal of Criminology* 46(4): 641–60.

Packwood, Angela (2002) 'Evidence based policy: rhetoric and reality', *Social Policy and Society* 1(3): 267–72.

Palmer, Stanley (1988) *Police and Protest in England and Ireland*, Cambridge: Cambridge University Press.

Pashukanis, E. B. (2007) [1924] *General Theory of Law and Marxism*, New Jersey: Transaction Publishers.

Pease, Ken (2010) 'Prison, community sentencing and crime', *Civitas*, August. Available: www.civitas.org.uk/crime/CommunitySentencingAug2010.pdf

Petrow, Stefan (1994) *Policing Morals: The Metropolitan Police and the Home Office 1870–1914*, Oxford: Clarendon Press.

Phibbs, Harry (2009) 'It is not racist to state that gypsy camps frequently cause an increase in crime and mess – it is a statement of fact', *Mail Online*, 6 January. Available: http://www.dailymail.co.uk/debate/article-1105510/It-racist-state-gypsy-camps-frequently-cause-increase-crime-mess-statement-fact.html

Philips, David (2003) 'Three "moral entrepreneurs" and the creation of a "criminal class" in England, 1790–1840', *Crime, History and Society* 7(2): 79–107.

Philips, David and Storch, Robert D. (1999) *Policing Provincial England 1829–1856: The Politics of Reform*, Leicester: Leicester University Press.

Pile, Steve, Mooney, Gerry and Brook, Chris (1999) *Unruly Cities?: Order/Disorder?* London: Routledge.

Pino, Nathan and Wiatrowski, Michael D. (eds) (2006) *Democratic Policing in Transitional and Developing Countries*, Aldershot: Ashgate.

Pizani-Williams, Linda (1998) *Gypsies and Travellers in the Criminal Justice System: The Forgotten Minority?* Cambridge Cropwood Occasional Papers. University of Cambridge Institute of Criminology.

Police Federation (n.d.) *The Office of Constable: The Bedrock of Modern Day British Policing*. Available: www.polfed.org/OC_Final.pdf

Police Oracle (2012) 'Police compensation tops £12 million', 27 January. Available: http://www.policeoracle.com/news/Police-Compensation-Tops-12-Million-44117.html

PolicyExpert (2011) 'One in three alleged crimes never investigated by the police', 3 August. Available: www.policyexpert.co.uk/news/home-insurance/one-in-three-alleged-crimes-never-investigated-by-police/5088/

Port, Sir Colin (2011) 'ACPO International', Newsletter, December. Available: www.stabilisationunit.gov.uk/attachments/article/586/ACPO%20Inetrnational%20Affairs%20Newsletter%20-%20December%202011.pdf

Power, Colm (2004) *Room to Roam: England's Irish Travellers*, London: Brent Irish Advisory Service.

Punch, Maurice (2009) *Police Corruption: Deviance Accountability and Reform in Policing*, Cullompton: Willan.

Rand, Gavin (2006) '"Martial races" and "imperial subjects": violence and governance in colonial India, 1857–1914', *European Review of History* 13(1): 1–20.

Reiner, R. (1978) *The Blue Coated Worker: A Sociological Study of Police Unionism*, Cambridge: Cambridge University Press.

— (1992) 'Policing a post-modern society', *Modern Law Review* 55(6): 761–81.

— (2007) 'Watching the watchers: theory and research in policing studies', in Mike Maguire, Rodney Morgan and Robert Reiner (eds), *The Oxford Handbook of Criminology*, Oxford: Oxford University Press.

— (2010a) 'Citizenship, crime, criminalization: marshalling a social democratic perspective', *New Criminal Law Review* 13(2): 241–61.

— (2010b) *The Politics of the Police*, Oxford: Oxford University Press.

— (2011) 'Fewer police does not mean Christmas for criminals', *Guardian*, 10 March. Available: www.guardian.co.uk/commentisfree/2011/mar/10/police-crime-disorder-cuts

— (2012) *In Praise of Fire Brigade Policing: Contra Common Sense Conceptions of the Police Role*, London: Howard League for Penal Reform.

Richardson, Joanna (2007) 'Policing gypsies and travellers', in J. Ryan and M. Hayes (eds), *Otherness: Aspects of Irish Postcolonial Identity*, Cambridge: Cambridge Scholars Press.

Roberts, M. J. D. (1988) 'Public and private in early nineteenth-century London: the Vagrant Act of 1822 and its enforcement', *Social History* 13(3): 273–94.

Royal Commission on the Police (1960) *Interim Report*. Cmnd 1222. London: HMSO.

— (1962) *Final Report*. Cmnd 1728. London: HMSO.

Said, Edward. (1979) *Orientalism*, London: Vintage.

Salter, Joseph (1873) *The Asiatic in England: Sketches of Sixteen Years among Orientals*, London: Seeley, Jackson and Halliday.

Sampson, Robert J. and Raudenbush, Stephen, W. (2004) 'Seeing disorder: neighbourhood stigma and the social construction of "broken windows"', *Social Psychology Quarterly* 67(4): 319–42.

Savage, Stephen (2007) *Police Reform: Forces for Change*, Oxford: Oxford University Press.

Scarman, Lord (1982) *The Brixton Disorders 10–12 April 1981: Report of an Inquiry by Lord Scarman*, London: HMSO.

Schneider, Anne. L. (1981) 'Methodological problems in victim surveys and their research implications for research in victimology', *Journal of Criminal Law and Criminology* 72(2): 818–28.

Scott, Paul (2008) 'Colwyn Bay and Rhos-on-Sea knife search draws a blank', *North Wales Weekly News*, 15 August. Available: www.northwalesweeklynews.co.uk/conwy-county-news/where-i-live/bay-of-colwyn-news/2008/08/15/colwyn-bay-and-rhos-on-sea-knife-search-draws-a-blank-55243-21541076/

Shearing, Clifford (1992) 'The relation between public and private policing', *Crime and Justice* 15: 399–434.

— (2001) 'A nodal conception of governance: thoughts on a policing commission', *Policing and Society* 11(3–4): 259–72.

Shearing, Clifford and Stenning, P. C. (1987) 'Say "cheese!": the Disney order that is not so Mickey Mouse', in C. D. Shearing and P. C. Stenning (eds), *Private Policing*, Thousand Oaks, CA: Sage.

Shearing, Clifford and Wood, Jennifer (2006) *Imagining Security*, Cullompton: Willan.

Sheehy, Sir Patrick (1993) *Inquiry into Police Responsibility and Rewards*. CM 2280.1. London: HMSO.

Sheptycki, J. (2007) 'The constabulary ethic and the transnational condition', in *Crafting Transnational Policing: Police Capacity Building and Global Policing Reform*, Oxford: Hart, 32–71.

— (2010) 'The Raft of the Medusa; further contributions towards a constabulary ethic', in *Cahiers Politie Studies*, Special Issue: Policing in Europe, no. 16: 39–56.

Sherman, Lawrence W. (1992) *Policing Domestic Violence: Experiments and Dilemmas*, New York: Free Press.

— (1995) 'Hot spots of crime and criminal careers of places', in John E. Eck and David Weisburd (eds), *Crime and Place. Crime Prevention Studies*, vol. 1. Monsey, NY: Criminal Justice Press, 35–52.

— (1998) *Evidence Based Policing*, Washington, DC: Police Foundation. Available: www.policefoundation.org/pdf/Sherman.pdf

— (2001) 'Reducing gun violence: what works, what doesn't, what's promising', in *Perspectives on Crime and Justice: The 1999–2000 Lecture Series*, vol. IV, March. Washington, DC: National Institute of Justice, 69–96.

— (n.d.) 'The cost-effectiveness of evidence-based policing', Expertgruppen för studier i Offentlig Ekonomi, Sweden. Available: www.eso.expertgrupp.se/Uploads/Documents/Sherman.pdf

Shields, Rachel (2010) 'Fourfold increase in police officers with second jobs', *Independent*, 13 June. Available: www.independent.co.uk/news/uk/home-news/fourfold-increase-in-police-officers-with-second-jobs-1999204.html

Siddle, John (2011) 'Merseyside police officers received £4.5m in bonuses last year', *Liverpool Echo*, 15 April. Available: www.liverpoolecho.co.uk/liverpool-news/local-news/2011/04/15/merseyside-police-officers-received-4-5m-in-bonuses-last-year-100252-28524836/

Sinclair, Georgina (2006) *At the End of the Line: Colonial Policing and the Imperial Endgame*, Manchester: Manchester University Press.

— (2012) 'Exporting the UK Police brand: The RUC-PSNI and the international policing agenda', *Policing: A Journal of Policy and Practice*. Advance access: http://dx.doi.org/doi:10.1093/police/par062

Skogan, Wesley G. (2005) 'Citizen satisfaction with police encounters', *Police Quarterly* 8(3): 298–321.

Skolnick, Jerome (2005) 'A sketch of the policeman's "working personality"', in Tim Newburn (ed.) *Policing: Key Readings*, Cullompton: Willan Publishing, 264–79.

Sky News (2011a) 'Police chief "spied on" while in Cayman Islands', 8 October. Available: http://news.sky.com/story/890104/police-chief-spied-on-while-in-cayman-isles

— (2011b) 'Three more held after "RoboCop" hit and run', 30 November. Available: http://news.sky.com/home/uk-news/article/16120619

Smith, Laura (2012) 'Cautions for criminals "to boost clear up rates"', *Southend Standard*, 5 January. Available: www.southendstandard.co.uk/news/9451793.Cautions_for_criminals-_to_boost_clear_up_rates-/

Smith, M. J. and Tilley, N. (eds) (2005) *Crime Science and New Approaches to Preventing and Detecting Crime*, Cullompton: Willan.

Sotiropoulos, Alexis (2008) *Making Time: Freeing Up Front Line Policing*. The Serco Institute. Available: www.serco.com/Images/making_time2a%20(Single%20pages)_tcm3-29348.pdf

Sparrow, Andrew (2011) 'Bullingdon Club antics were nothing like the riots, says Cameron', *Guardian*, 2 September. Available: www.guardian.co.uk/politics/2011/sep/02/bullingdon-club-david-cameron-riots

Squires, Peter (ed.) (2008a) *ASBO Nation: The Criminalisation of Nuisance*, Bristol: Policy Press.

— (2008b) 'Anti-social behaviour policy: driving fast, running on empty?' *Crime Stoppers*, June. Available: www.crimestoppers-uk.org/media-centre/guest-writers/crimestoppers-guest-articles/anti-social-behaviour-policy-driving-fast-running-on-empty-by-professor-peter-squires

Stallion, Martin and Wall, David (2011) *The British Police: Forces and Chief Officers, 1829–2012*, London: Police History Society.

Storch, Robert (1975) 'A plague of blue locusts: police reform and popular resistance', *International Review of Social History* 20: 61–90.

— (1976) 'The policeman as domestic missionary; urban discipline and popular culture in Northern England 1850–80', *Journal of Social History* 9(4): 481–509.

Summerfield, Derek (2011) 'Metropolitan Police Blues: protracted sickness absence, ill health retirement, and the occupational psychiatrist', *British Medical Journal* 342: d2127.

Swanson, Glen. W. (1972) 'The Ottoman police', *Journal of Contemporary History* 7(1–2): 243–60.

Taylor, Ian (1999) *Crime in Context: A Critical Criminology of Market Societies*, Cambridge: Polity Press.

Taylor, Jerome (2011) 'How Britain taught Arab police forces all they know', *Independent*, 19 February. Available: www.independent.co.uk/news/world/politics/how-britain-taught-arab-police-forces-all-they-know-2219270.html (Accessed 23 January 2012).

Taylor, Peter (2002) 'Inside job', *Guardian*, 23 October. Available: www.guardian.co.uk/uk/2002/oct/23/ukcrime.immigrationpolicy

Taylor, Richard K. (1988) *Against the Bomb: The British Peace Movement 1958–1965*, Oxford: Oxford University Press.

Thatcher, Margaret (1979) 'House of Commons', Debate on Address, 15 May. Available: www.margaretthatcher.org/document/104083

The Telegraph (2012) 'Police pensions "unaffordable" as taxpayer contributions near £2bn', 7 March. Available: www.telegraph.co.uk/finance/personalfinance/pensions/9110995/police-pensions-unaffordable-as-taxpayer-contributions-near-2bn.html

Thompson, E. P. (1963) *The Making of the English Working Class*, London: Victor Gollancz.

Tonge, R., Coombs, H. and Batcheler, M. (n.d.) 'Police and performance related pay: an exploratory study of rewarding individual performance in the police service', *Journal of Finance and Management in Public Service* 8(1). Available: www.cipfa.org.uk/thejournal/download/jour_vol8_no1_b.pdf

Transparency International (2011) *Corruption in the UK Part Two: Assessment of Key Sectors*, London: Transparency International UK.

Travis, Alan (2000) *Bound and Gagged: A Secret History of Obscenity in Britain*, London: Profile Books.

— (2011a) 'Police warn of "morale meltdown" if pay is cut as promised', *Guardian*, 2 March. Available: www.guardian.co.uk/uk/2011/mar/02/police-anger-pay-cuts-theresa-may

— (2011b) 'Car crime fall key to historic low in crime rate', *Guardian*, 16 June. Available: www.guardian.co.uk/uk/2011/jun/16/car-crime-fall-historic-low

— (2012b) 'Police pay deal gets closer as arbitrator supports government proposals', *Guardian*, 9 January. Available: www.guardian.co.uk/uk/2012/jan/09/police-pay-deal-closer-arbitrator.

— (2012a) 'Police pay deal: Theresa May accepts £150m-a-year compromise', *Guardian*, 30 January. Available: www.guardian.co.uk/uk/2012/jan/30/police-pay-deal-theresa-may

— (2012c) 'Private security firm G4S to run Lincolnshire police station', *Guardian*, 22 February.

Travis, Alan and Williams, Zoe (2012) 'Revealed: government plans for police privatisation', *Guardian*, 2 March.

Tripathi, Deepak (2011) 'When war came home', *Journal of Foreign Relations*, 14 August. Available: www.jofr.org/2011/08/14/when-war-came-home/#.TzGEoeM5JdQ (accessed 7 February 2012)

Van Ham, Peter (2001) 'The rise of the brand state: The postmodern politics of image and reputation', *Foreign Affairs*, 10 October.

Vollaard, Ben. A. (2006) *Police Effectiveness: Measurement and Incentives*, Santa Monica, CA: RAND. Available: www.rand.org/pubs/rgs_dissertations/2006/RAND_RGSD200.pdf

Vollmer, August (1930) 'The scientific policeman', *The American Journal of Police Science* 1(1): 8–12.

Von Hirsch, Andrew and Simester, A. P. (2006) *Incivilities: Regulating Offensive Behaviour: Constitutive and Mediative Principles*, Oxford and Portland, OR: Hart Publishing.

Waddington, P. A. J. (1999) *Policing Citizens: Authority and Rights*, London: UCL Press.

Wales Online (2012) 'IPCC investigates Cardiff police chase after Kyle Griffiths death', 2 February. Available: http://www.walesonline.co.uk/news/2012/02/02/investigation-launched-intro-police-pursuit-which-preceded-road-death-91466-30254116

Weinberger, Barbara (1995) *The Best Police in the World: An Oral History of English Policing*, Aldershot: Scolar Press.

Weisburd, D. and Eck, J. E. (2004) 'What can police do to reduce crime, disorder, and fear?' *Annals of the American Academy of Political and Social Science* 593(1): 42–65. DOI: 10.1177/0002716203262548.

Weisburd, David, Wyckoff, Laura. A., Ready, Justin, Eck, John E., Hinkle, Josh and Gajewski, Frank (2010) *The Police Foundation Displacement and Diffusion Study*, Police Foundation Report, September. Available: www.policefoundation.org/pdf/DisplacementDiffusionPFReport.pdf

Whistle Blowers Press Agency (2011) 30 September. Available: https://www.whistleblowers.uk.com/news/159/62/Dale-Farm---Crays-Hill-Essex/d, Jigsaw.php

White, A. (2011) 'Who has the power to police Britain? The politics of private security', Paper presented at the conference on 'Perspectives on Power'. Available: www.qub.ac.uk/sites/QUEST/FileStore/Issue4PerspectiviesonPowerPapers/Filetoupload,71740,en.pdf-2011-11-09

Whitehead, Tom (2010) 'Police earn £100 overtime for answering phone', *Telegraph*, 3 February. Available: www.telegraph.co.uk/news/uknews/law-and-order/7139525/Police-earn-100-overtime-for-answering-phone.html

Whitelaw, Ben (2011) 'Cleveland police authority extends Steria deal', *Guardian*, 29 June. Available: www.guardian.co.uk/government-computing-network/2011/jun/29/cleveland-police-authority-steria-outsourcing-contract-extension

White Paper: Police Reform (1993) *The Government's Proposals for the Police Service in England and Wales*. Cm 2281. London: HMSO.

Whyte, Dave (2003) 'Lethal regulation: state-corporate crime and the United Kingdom government's new mercenaries', *Journal of Law and Society* 30(4): 575–600.

Williams, Chris A. (2003) *Britain's Police Forces: Forever Removed from Democratic Control?* Available: http://history and policy.org/papers/policy-paper-16.htmlmorgan

Williams, Randal (2003) 'A state of permanent exception: the birth of modern policing in colonial capitalism', *Interventions* 5(3): 322–44.

Wilson, James Q. and Herrnstein, Richard, J. (1998) *Crime and Human Nature: The Definitive Study of the Causes of Crime*, New York: Simon and Schuster.

Winsor, Tom (2011) *Independent Review of Police Officer and Staff Remuneration and Conditions*. Cm 8024. London: The Stationery Office.

Woolnough, Guy (2011) 'My big fat gypsy wedding: do you think the media presents travellers fairly?' Sociology & Criminology Blogspot, Keele University. Available: http://socandcrimatkeele.blogspot.co.uk/2011/04/my-big-fat-gypsy-wedding-do-you-think.html

Wright, Oliver and Morris, Nigel (2011) 'Cuts put prisons at serious risk of riots say officers', *Independent*, 28 December. Available: www.independent.co.uk/news/uk/crime/cuts-put-prisons-at-serious-risk-of-riots-say-officers-6282179.html

Young, Jock (1999) *The Exclusive Society: Social Exclusion, Crime and Difference in Late Modernity*, London: Sage.

— (2007) *The Vertigo of Late Modernity*, London: Sage.

— (2011) *The Criminological Imagination*, Cambridge: Polity Press.

Zukin, Sharon (1991) *Landscapes of Power: From Detroit to Disneyworld*, Berkeley: University of California Press.

Index

Routledge
Paperbacks Direct

Bringing you the cream of our hardback publishing at paperback prices

This exciting new initiative makes the best of our hardback publishing available in paperback format for authors and individual customers.

Routledge Paperbacks Direct is an ever-evolving programme with new titles being added regularly.

To take a look at the titles available, visit our website.

www.routledgepaperbacksdirect.com